Museums and Galleries of London

of London

Abigail Willis

Museums and Galleries of London

Written by Abigail Willis
Cover photograph: The Great Court © British Museum
Edited by Andrew Kershman
Book design by Susi Koch and Lesley Gilmour
Illustrations by Lesley Gilmour

All rights reserved. No part of this publication may be reproduced, stored in a retrieval system or transmitted in any form or by any means electronic, mechanical, photocopying, recording or otherwise without the prior consent of the publishers and copyright owners.
Every effort has been made to ensure the accuracy of this book; however, due to the nature of the subject the publishers cannot accept responsibility for any errors which occur, or their consequences.

4th edition published in 2009 by
Metro Publications Ltd
PO Box 6336
London
N1 6PY

Printed and bound in India

© 2009 Abigail Willis
British Library Cataloguing in Publication Data.
A catalogue record for this book is available from the British Library.

ISBN 978-1-902910-31-4

To Alex, with love

Acknowledgements

This book would not have been possible without the help and support of many people. I would particularly like to thank Toot Bunnag and Ingrid Grubben, for their unfailing hospitality and a succession of delicious and sustaining meals at The Bangkok Restaurant in South Kensington. My thanks also to Nicholas Anderson for treating me to some old style London clubland meals and for accompanying me on a memorable trip to Hogarth's House. June Warrington kindly provided accommodation, research materials and information on all sorts of obscure museums, as well as much needed encouragement; Sascha Foulkes kindly gave me the run of her flat for a week and my father in law Richard Ballinger also generously helped out with accommodation. I am of course indebted to the numerous museum staff who assisted me with my research enquiries – without their kind co-operation this book would not have been possible. British life would grind to a halt without its army of volunteers and the museum sector is no exception and I would like to pay tribute to the dedication of all those whose unpaid work helps to keep our museums open. My thanks too to Andrew, Susi and Lesley at Metro for their continued support for this publication and their help in preparing this new edition. Finally, I would like thank my husband Alex for his forbearance as museum mania once again took over our household, necessitating regular research trips to London, and for his love and encouragement.

About the author

Abigail Willis is a freelance writer and art researcher. Her passion for London's museums and galleries was ignited when she arrived in the capital as a fresh-faced history of art graduate, working at the Courtauld Institute. A member of the Critics Circle, she has also been, at various times, a provenance researcher, cataloguer and curator. She lives in Somerset with her husband Alex Ballinger, and a strong-willed terrier called Louis.

Contents

How To Use This Book

museum/gallery name

address &
contact details

chapter

website

nearest transport

opening times

admission price

shop

wheelchair access

review

location

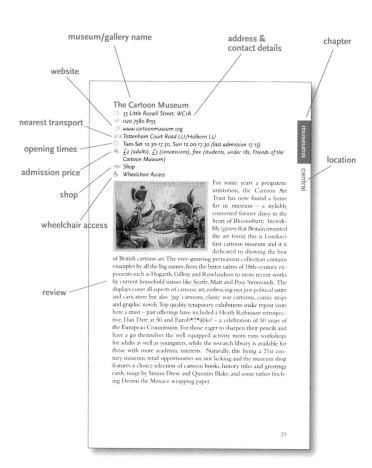

The Cartoon Museum
35 Little Russell Street, WC1A
020 7580 8155
www.cartoonmuseum.org
Tottenham Court Road LU/Holborn LU
Tues-Sat 10.30-17.30, Sun 12.00-17.30 (last admission 17.15)
£4 (adults), £3 (concessions), free (students, under 18s, Friends of the
Cartoon Museum)
Shop
Wheelchair Access

For some years a peripatetic
institution, the Cartoon Art
Trust has now found a home
for its museum – a stylishly
converted former dairy in the
heart of Bloomsbury. Incredibly (given that Britain invented
the art form) this is London's
first cartoon museum and it is
dedicated to showing the best
of British cartoon art. The ever-growing permanent collection contains
examples by all the big names, from the bitter satires of 18th-century exponents such as Hogarth, Gillray and Rowlandson to more recent works
by current household names like Searle, Matt and Posy Simmonds. The
displays cover all aspects of cartoon art, embracing not just political satire
and caricature but also 'gag' cartoons, classic war cartoons, comic strips
and graphic novels. Top quality temporary exhibitions make repeat visits
here a must – past offerings have included a Heath Robinson retrospective, Dan Dare at 50 and Eurob★!!★@ks! – a celebration of 50 years of
the European Commission. For those eager to sharpen their pencils and
have a go themselves the well equipped activity room runs workshops
for adults as well as youngsters, while the research library is available for
those with more academic interests. Naturally, this being a 21st century museum, retail opportunities are not lacking and the museum shop
features a choice selection of cartoon books, history titles and greetings
cards, mugs by Simon Drew and Quentin Blake, and some rather fetching Dennis the Menace wrapping paper.

Introduction

Revisiting London's museums and galleries for the 4th edition of this guide has been as enjoyable as ever. Ten years on from the first edition, London's museum scene remains vigorous and offers exhilarating terrain for urban explorers. Although there have been a few regrettable closures since the 3rd edition – the Theatre Museum and the Livesay Museum being two notable losses – the overall picture of London's museums is healthy with more people than ever before visiting museums. In 2006 seven out of Britain's top ten free tourist attractions were London museums, with Tate Modern just being pipped to the No. 1 position by Blackpool Pleasure Beach. What's more, new, independent museums such as the wonderful Museum of Brands, Packaging and Advertising, have also been springing up. Increased visitor figures seem to have upped the stakes and museums now routinely offer a whole raft of exciting extra activities from film and music events, to lectures workshops and tours. The big development push that accompanied the new Millennium, combined with the advent of the National Heritage Lottery Fund has not abated now that we are in the 'noughties' and at museums like the National Maritime Museum and Tate Modern the 2012 Olympics are a new catalyst for ambitious expansion projects.

Choice is the mantra of the modern world, and London's museums are no exception. Whether you're interested in dinosaurs or dentistry, fossils or firefighting, sewage or sewing machines, the chances are there's a London museum devoted to the subject – for proof, just turn to the subject index at the back of this book. From blockbusting nationals to homely local heritage centres, London museums also perfectly reflect the diverse history and character of London. Intensively visiting museums, as I do when researching this book, I'm always struck at the intricate web of connections that bind London's history, particularly its personalities – antiquarian Elias Ashmole for example is buried in the churchyard of St Mary at Lambeth (now the Garden Museum) but as a noted freemason, his likeness lives on in his portrait at the Freemasonry Museum. Similarly William Hogarth, the British painter and printmaker, crops up in several museums – the Foundling Museum, the Sir John Soane Museum and St Bart's Hospital Museum amongst others – while his house in Chiswick is also open to the public. Exploring London through its museums is a fascinating way to identify these hidden historical connections between people and places – as well as being highly useful for pub quizzes.

London is home to some of the great museums of the world but it is also rich in smaller, specialist outfits and local museums. These are often a great visit in their own right but at peak times can also be a worthwhile alternative to overcrowded big museums – for example, if you're interested in Ancient Egypt but can't face the hordes at the British Museum, why not try the Petrie Museum nearby? Or perhaps you're keen on science and technology but want to avoid armies of hyperactive school kids at the Science Museum – check out the Kew Bridge Steam Museum, the Michael Faraday Museum or the gory, glass cased specimens of the Hunterian Museum. If you're in London during May, look out for special events and activities staged as part of Museums and Galleries Month. This cultural extravaganza takes place every year and sees hundreds of museums and galleries across the UK hosting a range of activities from film shows to hands-on activities, music and artists' workshops (www.mgn.org.uk). Later in the year, in October, The Big Draw is another event which galvanises the sector with fun, drawing-related activities being organised by venues across the country (www.campaignfordrawing.org).

With more museums and galleries than ever to enjoy, the aim of this guide is to help you get the most out of London's remarkable cultural resources. The book is divided into four sections: Museums (including historic houses), Galleries (public art venues), Commercial Art Galleries (a cross-section of 'selling' galleries), and an Appendix which includes a selection of art fairs, exhibition and heritage venues, archives and libraries as well as some useful addresses. Entries are arranged by area with maps to help you find your way around and easily combine visits, and we've included both a subject and an alphabetical index.

A few tips before you embark on your voyage of discovery. As I've learned the hard way, it's always worth ringing the museum before you set out. There's nothing more frustrating than traipsing across town (or across the country) to find the place closed for renovation or to discover the exhibit you've specifically come to see is away on tour. Temporary room closures (particularly in the big museums or ones undergoing development work), staff shortages, acts of God and public holidays are all liable to affect opening times, so ring first. It's also well worth consulting the museum's website; as well as giving details of opening hours and disabled access they will also let you know about current exhibitions and special events, so you can plan your visit with military precision and really make the most of your time. To help you really cram in the culture, many of the larger museums now stay open late at least one night a week, and these are well worth checking out – there's often a bar, live music and a buzzy atmosphere, as well as the usual exhibits.

Although entrance to the nationals is free, museum and gallery going can be expensive with increasingly hefty entrance charges being applied to many special exhibitions. If you're planning regular trips to these, one way to get your money's worth is to become a 'Friend' or 'Member' of the institution in question. Perks typically include unlimited free access to paying exhibitions, special viewings, a glossy magazine and use of a special 'friends room'. Museums can be hungry work too and although in-house cafés are much better than they used to be, they tend to be pricey. Packed lunches are a practical solution, particularly for families, and lots of institutions provide pleasant picnic areas. Alternatively, if you've got the museum equivalent of cabin fever, jump ship and check out the local caffs – they're often better value and more interesting.

Museums can be hard on the feet too – London doesn't seem to be getting any smaller and this guide includes museums at several extremes of the Underground network from the Museum of Nostalgia in Upminster to the Windmill Museum in Wimbledon and all points in between. So leave your high heels at home but don't forget to bring this guide and above all, enjoy London's museums – they are among the best in the world.

Abigail Willis
November 2008

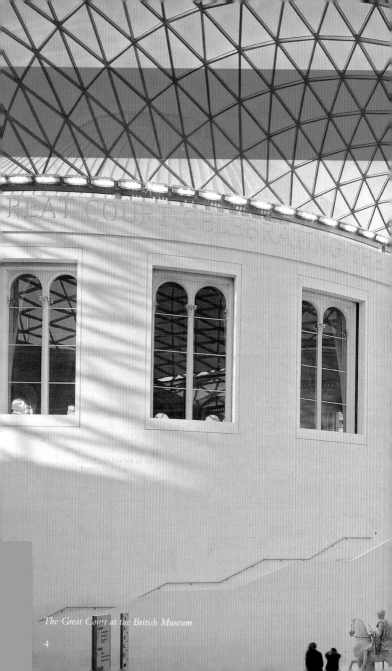

GREAT COURT CELEBRATING

American Friends of the
British Museum

The Great Court at the British Museum

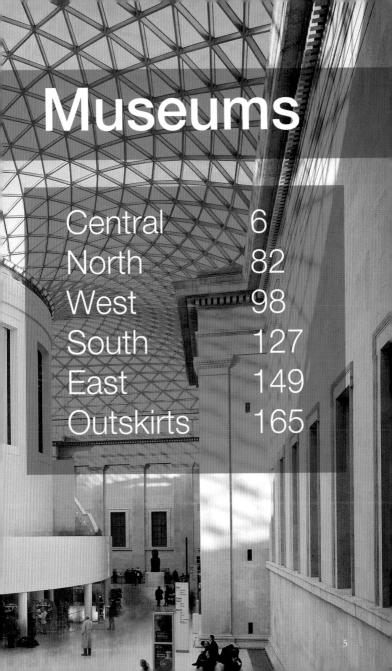

Museums

Central

All Hallows by the Tower Undercroft

- 🏛 *Byward Street, EC3*
- ☎ *020 7481 2928*
- ✎ *www.allhallowsbythetower.org.uk*
- 🚌 *Tower Hill LU*
- 🕐 *Mon-Sat 10.00-17.00*
- 💷 *Admission free (donation appreciated)*
  Optional audio guide; brass rubbing centre
- 🏬 *Shop*

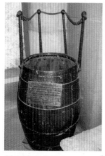

Shackleton's crows nest

This tranquil church is worlds away from the teeming tourist trap that is Tower Hill. The audio tour of the undercroft museum provides a useful commentary on the exhibits, which range from archaeological finds and church plate to a tessellated Roman floor and rare Anglo-Saxon stone crosses. Founded in AD675, All Hallows is one of London's most historic churches: Samuel Pepys watched the Great Fire from its tower and William Penn, the founder of Pennsylvania, was baptised here (the beautifully carved font cover by Grinling Gibbons can be seen in the church itself). On a more nautical note, tucked away in the undercroft is the barrel-shaped crow's nest used by Sir Ernest Shackleton on his last Antarctic expedition.

Anaesthesia Heritage Centre

- 🏛 *21 Portland Place, W1B*
- ☎ *020 7631 8811/8806*
- ✎ *www.aagbi.org*
- 🚌 *Oxford Circus LU, Regent's Park LU, Great Portland Street LU*
- 🕐 *Mon-Fri 09.30-17.00*
- 💷 *Admission free (appointment recommended)*
- ♿ *Wheelchair access*

A one room display relating to anaesthesia, pain relief and resuscitation. Early objects include the primitive hand bellows and pipes used to literally pump comatose patients back to life. Treasures in the 2000-object collection include an original 19th century John Snow chloroform inhaler from the early days of anaesthesia and the ECG machine used during George VI's final lung operation at Buckingham Palace.

Apsley House, The Wellington Museum

🖃 *Hyde Park Corner, W1*
☎ *020 7499 5676*
✐ *www.english-heritage.org.uk*
🚇 *Hyde Park Corner LU*
☺ *Wed-Sun 11.00-17.00 (Nov-Mar 11.00-16.00)*
💰 *£5.50 (adults), £4.40 (concessions), £2.80 (children)*
🛍 *Shop*
♿ *Limited access for visitors with disabilities*

Home of the 1st Duke of Wellington, Apsley House, No. 1 London, must be the swankiest address in town. Its plush interiors are dressed to impress, gleaming with gilt and gold to reflect their owner's status as the hero of Waterloo. Many medals and orders can be admired in the basement gallery, along with a changing display of the (often vicious) satirical cartoons the Duke inspired. His military successes brought material gain, and the house positively groans under the weight of lavish gifts from grateful heads of state. Commemorative porcelain and silver dinner services crowd the cabinets of the Plate and China Room while the staircase is dominated by Canova's deeply kitsch nude statue of Napoleon (apparently even the Emperor himself was embarrassed by the outsized sculpture and banished it to the Louvre).

Many of the paintings on show came from the Spanish Royal Collection, among them Velasquez's justly famous *Waterseller of Seville*. Elsewhere in the vast Waterloo Gallery earthy Dutch and Flemish genre scenes, like Jan Steen's bawdy *Egg Dance* rub shoulders with devotional subjects like van Dyck's *Saint Rosalie* and Correggio's *Agony in the Garden* – a strange mix which makes for interesting viewing. Paintings of Wellington's comrades in arms hang in the ultra masculine environment of the Striped Drawing Room and include Lawrence's stirring portrait of him, looking every inch the Iron Duke.

The Bank of England Museum

Threadneedle Street, EC2R (entrance in Bartholomew Lane)

020 7601 5545

www.bankofengland.co.uk

Bank LU

Mon-Fri 10.00-17.00

Admission free (audio tour wands may be hired for £1)

Shop

Disabled access (please telephone in advance)

What better place to get a handle on monetary matters than at the Old Lady of Threadneedle Street herself? The museum tells the story of the bank from its foundation as a private enterprise in 1694 and, like many an old institution, its history is a flamboyant one – on some occasions the gatekeeper wears full 17th-century livery, and up until 1971 the bank had its own military guard.

Displays trace the development of banking practice from goldsmiths' receipt notes through to electronic dealing, and include a full-sized reconstruction of Sir John Soane's 18th-century banking hall, one of the earliest surviving cheques (dated 8th December 1660) and a million pound note. Gold bullion and one of the millions of quill pens that the Bank's clerks in the 19th century got through every year can be found in the 1930's-style Rotunda. The Banknote Gallery displays some fine examples of the paper money-maker's art, including the master drawings for various notes, as well as following the chequered history of the £1 note from 1797 to 1988. Historically the 'quid' was a popular subject for forgery and visitors can see for themselves the tools of the trade used by forgers such as Charles Hibbert (hanged in 1819 for this treasonable offence).

A new, permanent display celebrating the career of Kenneth Grahame, the author of Wind in the Willows, opened in October 2008. Exhibits throw light on Grahame's 30 year tenure at the Bank which included being shot at by an unhinged intruder and the author's resignation under mysterious circumstances.

Interactive computers are a feature of the contemporary banking displays and offer proactive participation to help visitors get to grips with modern issues such as inflation, interest rates and the Euro. If you're feeling flush after a go on the foreign exchange game, treat yourself to a gold proof sovereign in the museum shop or drown your losses with a chocolate bullion bar.

The Banqueting House

⊞ *Whitehall, SW1*

☎ *020 7930 4179 (booking)*
020 7839 8919 (general information)

✐ *www.hrp.org.uk*

🚇 *Charing Cross Rail/LU, Embankment LU, Westminster LU*

🕐 *Mon-Sat 10.00-17.00 (sometimes closes at short notice for government functions)*

💰 *£4.50 (adults), £3.50 (senior citizen/students), £2.25 (under 16s); DVD and Audio Tours are included in admission fee*

🛍 *Shop*

♿ *Wheelchair access (telephone in advance)*

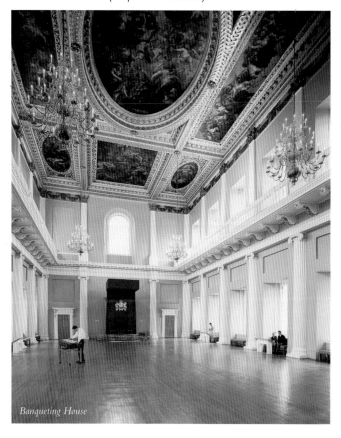

Banqueting House

Designed by Inigo Jones, the Banqueting House is an architecturally distinguished building, its beautiful Renaissance proportions having been calculated in accordance with the Roman ideal of perfection. Inside, its ceiling is graced with some typically fleshy paintings by Rubens, commissioned by King Charles I to glorify the divine nature of monarchy. Ironic, then, that the Banqueting House's place in history is assured as the venue for the execution of said king in 1649. In a nice piece of historical symmetry the Banqueting House was also where his son, Charles II, was offered the throne back in 1660.

British Dental Association Museum

⬚ *64 Wimpole Street, W1*
☎ *020 7563 4549*
✐ *www.bda.org/museum*
🚌 *Oxford Circus LU, Bond Street LU*
🕐 *Tues & Thurs 13.00-16.00 (other times by appointment)*
💷 *Admission free*
✎ *Shop*
♿ *Wheelchair Access*

Probably not one to visit en-route to your dentist, this one room museum shows a carefully edited selection of dental artefacts from the BDA's vast collection. Displays concentrate on dentistry in the 19th century with scary-looking extraction implements, a clockwork drill, early toothbrushes and a red plush hydraulic dentist's chair from the 1890s – complete with spittoon. Technical developments in dentures, fillings and orthodontics are also charted and the displays also find time to recount the story of the nation's dental health and the surprisingly new concept of 'teeth for life'. Visitors can also watch vintage footage of dentists at work and admire 'Harry' the dissectible papier maché anatomical model. The small sales point keeps its sense of humour intact with 'molar' golf tees at 3 for a £1 and postcards of 18th-century dental cartoons.

British Museum

- 🏛 *Great Russell Street, WC1*
- ☎ *020 7323 8000 / 020 7323 8181 (Box Office)*
  020 7323 8299 (disabled access and facilities)
- 🖊 *www.britishmuseum.org*
- 🚇 *Holborn LU, Russell Square LU, Tottenham Court Road LU*
- 🕐 *Daily 10.00-17.30 (late views of selected galleries Thurs-Fri until 20.30);*
  Great Court opening hours Sun-Wed 9.00-18.00, Thurs-Sat 9.00-23.00
- 🎟 *Admission free (a charge may be made for temporary exhibitions)*
- 🛍 *Shops, Bookshop*
- ☕ *Cafés & Restaurant*
- ♿ *Disabled access*

The ultimate perch for culture vultures. Established by an act of Parliament in 1753 and occupying a majestic $13^1/_2$ acre site in Bloomsbury, the BM is for many the quintessential London museum. With some $6^1/_2$ million artefacts and 90-odd galleries contained behind its Greek-temple-on-steroids façade, the BM is far too big a beast to do justice to in this review – or indeed in a single foot-slogging visit. Both should rather be regarded as an appetizer to a multi-course banquet; like most big museums, the BM is better suited to regular visits. The main entrance hall, although now magnificently redecorated and liberated from its old clutter, still bears the brunt of the BM's annual influx of 4.8 million or so visitors. If you're planning to visit galleries on the north side of the building (eg. Prints and Drawings, Oriental Collections, Egypt and Africa) you may prefer to try the often less crowded Montague Place entrance, just off Gower Street.

Once inside, where to start? The Great Court is the obvious place. Transformed by a soaring roof of glass and steel, the BM's once open central courtyard is the largest covered public square in Europe. The circle in the heart of this light-filled square is the Reading Room, once a haunt for pen pushers as various as Karl Marx, Oscar Wilde and Virginia Woolf, but currently used as an exhibition space.

At this early stage of your visit it might be worth your while asking at the Information Desk which galleries are closed – an ongoing programme of development means that some galleries may be closed and only selected galleries are accessible on late night openings.

For first timers, the free introductory 'Eye Opener' tours are a painless way to find your feet – each tour lasts about 30-40 minutes and topics include 'Ancient Rome', 'Ancient Egypt', 'Art of the Middle East' and 'Early Medieval Europe'. 90-minute guided tours of the museum's highlights cost £8 – tickets are available from the Information Desk in the Great Court where a variety of audio tours can be hired for £3.50.

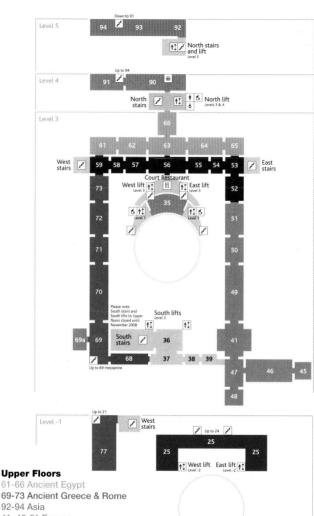

Level 5

Down to 91

94 93 92

North stairs and lift
Level 5

Level 4

Up to 94

91 90

North stairs   North lift
Levels 3 & 4

Level 3

66

61 62 63 64 65

West stairs   59 58 57 56 55 54 53   East stairs

Court Restaurant

West lift
Level 3   East lift
Level 3

73   52

35

72   Level 1   Level 1   51

71   50

70   49

Please note:
South stairs and
South lifts to Upper
floors closed until
November 2008

South lifts
Level 3

69a 69   South stairs   36   41

68   37 38 39

Up to 69 mezzanine   47 46 45

48

Level -1

Up to 21

West stairs

Up to 24

25

77   25   25

West lift
Level -2   East lift
Level -2

Upper Floors

61-66 Ancient Egypt
69-73 Ancient Greece & Rome
92-94 Asia
41, 45-51 Europe
52-59 Middle East
37-39, 68 Themes
35, 69a, 90-91 Exhibitions &
changing displays

Lower Floor

25 Africa
77 Ancient Greece and Rome

Clore Education Centre

South lifts
Level -1 & -2

Up to
Great Court   Up to
Great Court

Ford Centre for Young Visitors   Level -2

Ground Floor

26-27 Americas
4 Ancient Egypt
11-15, 17-23 Ancient Greece and Rome
33, 33a, 33b, 67, 95 Asia
6-10, 34 Middle East
1, 24 Themes
2-3 & Reading Room
Exhibitions and changing displays

KEY

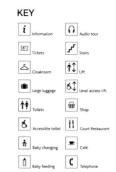

i	Information	𝖔	Audio tour
Tickets		Stairs	
Cloakroom		Lift	
Large luggage		Level access lift	
Toilets		Shop	
Accessible toilet		Court Restaurant	
Baby changing		Café	
Baby feeding		Telephone	

museums

central

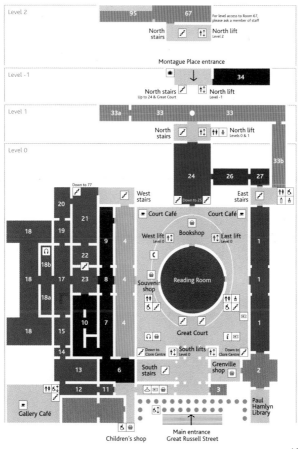

13

For those going solo, personal preference will no doubt dictate your route but, if you're feeling strong, start with the perennially popular Egyptian Galleries. Plough your way through the crowds of clipboard-carrying kids hell bent on answering the next question on their activity sheets and admire the inscrutable beauty – despite the broken noses – of the colossal Egyptian and Assyrian sculptures on the ground floor (rooms 4 and 6-10), and the world class collection of antiquities from Egypt on the upper floor (galleries 62-66). Pride of place in the ground floor sculpture galleries goes not to a statue but to the Rosetta Stone – an undistinguished-looking slab whose multilingual inscriptions helped crack the 'code' of hieroglyphics. In the upper floor galleries the evolution of Egyptian make-up palettes shows that vanity is as old as civilization, but among a host ancient artefacts and funerary finds, the real crowd pleasers here are the mummies – human as well as animal – and their richly decorated coffins. One of the most popular exhibits in the whole museum is a particularly well preserved corpse from 3,400 BC which is located in room 64, curled up and surrounded by essentials for the afterlife – including a make-up palette.

Galleries 62 and 63 explore Ancient Egyptian attitudes to death and the afterlife, covering a period of about 3,000 years, from the Old Kingdom to the 4th century AD. Among the exhibits are 1,500 year old food offerings and a heartbreakingly tiny coffin accompanied by the skeleton of a child who suffered from brittle bone disease. If ancient civilisations really are your thing, don't miss the Ancient Middle East galleries (rooms 52-59) which cover Ancient Anatolia, and Early and Later Mesopotamia. Exhibits include finds from Ninevah and Babylon, such as a fragment from a 3,000 year-old cuneiform thesaurus and artefacts excavated from the 'Great Death Pit' at Ur.

The museum is also well endowed with antiquities and sculpture from ancient Greece and Rome. On the ground floor, room 18 is devoted to sculptures from the Parthenon, aka the Elgin Marbles. Leaving aside the controversial issue of repatriation (there is a leaflet setting out the BM's position on this), these truly are marvels of craftsmanship and artistry, from the lovingly depicted tunics of the gods in the pediments, to the action packed frieze showing the Panathenaic procession in full swing. Another ancient structure, the Nereid Monument tomb – the first ever example of a temple tomb – is displayed in room 17 and more classical architectural odds and ends are littered around the lower floor (rooms 77-85) – including massive Ionic volutes from Ephesus and an elegantly draped caryatid from the Erectheum. There's plenty in the way of smaller artefacts like pottery and jewellery too – look out for the Portland Vase, a stunning example of Roman cameo work (room

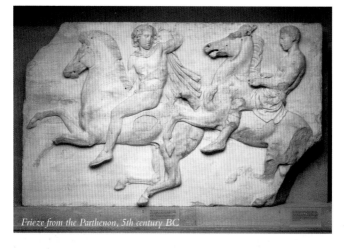

Frieze from the Parthenon, 5th century BC

70). Room 69 provides a kaleidoscopic insight into daily life in the ancient world – a 4th century BC jury ticket, a Roman dog tag and a frying pan are among the down-to-earth exhibits.

Still on a Roman theme, the Weston Gallery of Roman Britain (room 49) is a beautifully displayed collection of artefacts from the Roman Occupation. Much of the display focuses on the Roman military presence: cavalry armour, a bronze army diploma and so on – but some of the most exciting exhibits are the hoards of treasure that have been unearthed over the years. The Thetford Treasure of late-Roman jewellery includes some amazingly flamboyant finger rings, while the elegant silver tableware from the Hoxne hoard and Mildenhall treasures bespeak the ultimate in gracious living. Not to be outdone by the corpses elsewhere in the museum, room 50 (Later Bronze Age and Celtic Europe) is home to Lindow man – a sacrificial victim from the first century AD, preserved for posterity in a peat bog until he was discovered a few years ago.

Moving onto more recent European history, the applied arts in the Medieval, Renaissance and Modern collections chart the dramatic social, religious and political changes of the era. The wonderfully gnomic 12th-century Lewis Chessmen can usually be tracked down in room 42 but the diffuse range of artefacts goes right up to the 20th century with elegant porcelain, jewellery and a few curiosities like Lord Palmerston's garter thrown in for good measure. The march of time can be seen literally in the BM's horological collection, the most comprehensive in existence. The HSBC Money gallery (room 68)

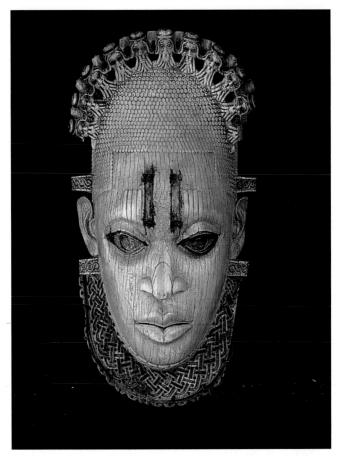

16th century Benin Mask from Benin, Nigeria

explores the history of money over the past 4,000 years through the development of coins, notes, electronic money and the systems which regulate them. It's also home to one of the 'Hands On' object handling desks that are dotted around the museum.

Flagging yet? Perhaps it's time for a coffee and a bite to eat. The museum's Gallery Café serves hot and cold light lunches while the Great Court's ground floor cafés provide a straightforward self-service experience. The posher Court Restaurant on the Upper Ellipse floor caters for deeper pockets and bigger appetites, with table service. If culture-induced claustrophobia has set in, investigate some of the local eateries and cafés in the Museum Street/Coptic Street area.

Ease back gently into the fray with a potter around room 90, which hosts temporary exhibitions organised by the Prints and Drawings Department. Manageable in size but of high quality, these are usually worth a separate visit – past shows have included Picasso linocuts, Rembrandt etchings and American prints.

Further up the North Stairs are the BM's exquisite Japanese galleries (92-4). Displays here change regularly because of the delicate organic materials of most Japanese cultural artefacts, but on my most recent visit I saw magnificent set of Edo period Samurai armour, ceramic vessels from the prehistoric Jomon period, scrolls, contemporary prints and modern ceramics crafted by some of Japan's 'Living Treasures'. The charming wooden tea house, built in situ by Kyoto craftsmen is however a permanent fixture.

The North Wing is also home to the Korea Foundation Gallery, a permanent gallery which presents an overview of Korean art and archaeology from early times to present day. As well as treasures such as royal ritual manuscripts and Buddhist sculpture, the gallery features a reconstructed sarangbang, or traditional scholar's study, designed and built by Korean architect Shin Young-Hoon. A small, changing display of top-quality contemporary Korean arts complements the historic items.

Room 33 is a vast and absorbing gallery (also just off the North Stairs) which covers China as well as South and South-East Asia. Among its jumble of exhibits are ritual vessels, Tang dynasty tomb pottery figures, statues from Jain temples, snuff bottles, Vietnamese ceramics and Buddhas galore. Tucked away at the far end, room 33a is home to relief carvings of scenes from the life of Buddha from the Great Stupa at Amaravati. Just off the Montague Place entrance, the John Addis Gallery of Islamic Art contains graphic art, weaponry, intricately patterned Iznik tiles and fabulously decorative glass mosque lamps.

Although the BM celebrated its 250th anniversary in 2003, and is one of Britain's most visited museums, it's not sitting on its laurels. The restored King's Library, just off the Great Court, reopened in 2003 as The Enlightenment Gallery a permanent exhibition devoted to discovery and learning in the 18th and early 19th centuries. This was an age of curiosity and the objects which fill this enormous room – from fossils to Easter Island ancestor figures, via classical Greek vases – tell the story of the origins of the British Museum itself, as well as the Enlightenment's urge to classify everything in sight. A Hands-On desk gives visitors young and old the chance to handle actual artefacts and learn more about them.

Equally exciting has been the return of the Ethnography Collections to Bloomsbury after years of exile at the old Museum of Mankind as well as the Mexican (room 27) and the North American (room 26) galleries. The latter stages regularly changing exhibitions about native North America – tribal costumes, pueblo pottery and walrus ivory snow goggles are among the items you might expect to see. The Mexican gallery covers the period from the Olmec culture of 1200-400BC through to the demise of the Aztecs in the 16th century. Here, the intricately carved Yaxchilan Lintels depict the bloodthirsty rituals performed by Mayan rulers; other exhibits include a 'ball game belt' from Classic Veracruz – a grisly remnant of a culture which settled political rivalries with ball game contests, in which the losers faced not relegation but decapitation.

The Sainsbury African Galleries (room 25), show how African cultures have interacted with each other and the West. Benin bronzes, ceramics, carved wood artefacts and masks are among the attractions here with audio visual presentations helping to show them in context. Contemporary art works by artists such as Sokari Douglas-Camp are the focus of temporary displays. En-route, the Wellcome Trust Gallery (room 24) offers a lively look at how people the world over deal with the harsh realities of living and dying, including how different cultures approaches the treatment of AIDS.

Retail therapy is of course the strategy of choice in the West for overcoming life's difficulties and shopaholics will not be disappointed here. A well-stocked bookshop in the Great Court caters for bibliophiles while the children's shop is filled with Egyptian themed trinkets like chocolate filled 'mummy' tins and 'colour your own papyrus kits'. The Grenville shop deals in more grown-up treats – colourful enamelled coffee spoons, replica historic jewellery and ancient statuary and reproduction Lewis chess sets.

British Optical Association Museum & Library

🖺 *College of Optometrists, 42 Craven Street, WC2*
☎ *020 7766 4353*
✍ *www.college-optometrists.org/museum*
🚌 *Charing Cross LU/Rail, Embankment LU*
♿ *Admission free (Meeting Rooms tour £5 per person)*
🕐 *Mon-Fri 09.30-17.00 (by appointment only)*

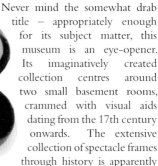

Never mind the somewhat drab title – appropriately enough for its subject matter, this museum is an eye-opener. Its imaginatively created collection centres around two small basement rooms, crammed with visual aids dating from the 17th century onwards. The extensive collection of spectacle frames through history is apparently a mecca for fashion and design students, and there's even a handy mirror so you can try some out for size. Technical apparatus like the fully deconstructible 17th-century ivory eye, a 1930's sight-testing suite and a spring loaded contact lens applicator chart the rise of optometry as a profession. Curator Neil Handley makes an enthusiastic guide, pointing out prize exhibits like the world's earliest pair of glasses with sidebars, 'wig' spectacles and celebrity curios like Leonardo di Caprio's contact lenses. Perhaps the real delight for the non-specialist visitor though is the top-notch fine and decorative art collection. Treasures here include portraits of bespectacled sitters, such as of Admiral Peter Rainier and Benjamin Franklin (whose house is just a few doors away), 18th-century satirical prints, beautifully embellished porcelain eye baths and charming fans equipped with hidden spy glasses. The museum's entertaining website is equally worthy of a visit, complete with an 'object of the month' spot and details of supernatural comings and goings at the museum.

The British Postal Museum & Archive

⌨ *Freeling House, Phoenix Place, WC1X*

☎ *020 7239 2570*

🖥 *www.postalheritage.org.uk*

🚇 *Chancery Lane LU, Farringdon LU/Rail, King's Cross St Pancras LU/Rail*

🕐 *Mon-Fri 10.00-17.00 (until 19.00 Thurs); visitors must bring ID*

💷 *Admission free*

♿ *Wheelchair access*

Sadly, the National Postal Museum closed back in December 1998 but there are plans for a new Heritage Centre, for which a permanent site is being sought. In the meantime the archive at Freeling House is open to the public and is a useful family history resource, with material such as postal staff's pension records. There's also a small exhibition space showing displays of philatelic material –that's stamps to you and me. The busy events programme includes walks, talks and film screenings. Guided tours of the museum's store in Debden, Essex take place throughout the year, but these must be booked in advance.

British Red Cross Museum & Archives

⌨ *44 Moorfields, EC2Y*

☎ *020 7877 4058*

🖥 *www.redcross.org.uk/museumandarchives*

The museum and archive records the history and activities of the British Red Cross Society from its foundation in 1870 as the British National Society for Aid to the Sick and Wounded in War. The collection includes medals and badges, first aid kits, paintings by the war artist Doris Zinkiesen, and the Changi quilt – one of only three known examples made by women interned by the Japanese in Singapore in WWII. At the time of going to press the Red Cross is in the early stages of planning a new museum and the collection is in storage. Further information about the collection can be found on their website, which is where details about the proposed new museum will also be posted. The archive is open to researchers by appointment.

The Cabinet War Rooms & Churchill Museum

🖂 Clive Steps, King Charles Street, SW1

☎ 020 7930 6961

🖉 www.iwm.org.uk

🚌 St James's Park LU, Westminster LU

🕑 Daily 09.30-18.00 (last admission 17.00)

💷 £12 (adults), £9.50 (senior citizens, students), free (under 16s)

🛍 Shop

☕ Café

♿ Wheelchair access

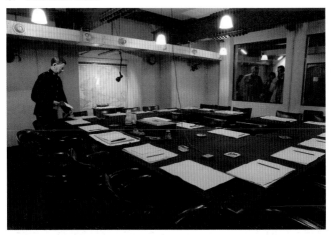

Underground Cabinet Room

Winston Churchill and his ministers spent much of World War II holed up in these underground offices, for six years a secret nerve centre for the British government and military top brass. Preserved as an historic site since 1948 and still sporting original fixtures and fittings (although now staffed by a few mannequins), the CWR are a spookily atmospheric time capsule for the years 1939-45.

Built to withstand the Nazi Blitzkrieg, the CWR now surrender themselves daily to armies of visitors who file past rooms where history was made: the converted broom cupboard from which Churchill telephoned Roosevelt, the Prime Minister's spartan office-cum-bedroom, the Map Room, as well as the inner sanctum of the whole complex – the Cabinet Room itself. Less glamourous rooms like the typing pool evoke the drudgery of war work and there are displays examining different aspects of the war.

Some rooms previously hidden from the public have recently been restored and opened to visitors and include the private rooms set aside for Churchill's wife and key members of staff, the Chief of Staff's Conference Room, as well as the tiny kitchen which kept Churchill supplied with 3 square meals a day. Free audio guides in a range of languages are issued on arrival and, lasting an hour, are essential listening for visitors who wish to explore the site thoroughly. Shorter guides are available for those with less time and there's a children's version for the under 11s. The Switch Room Café offers simple light meals of the sandwich, coffee and cake variety, served to the strains of 40s hits. The shop doesn't ration the nostalgia either, stocking a selection of goods with a wartime theme.

Time capsule they may be but the CWR certainly aren't standing still – in February 2005 the Churchill Museum opened at the site, exploring the life, leadership and legacy of the man himself and featuring material never publicly exhibited before. Divided into 5 colour coded chapters, the museum begins with Churchill's finest hour – his war years – and his transformation from political outsider to against the odds victor. Churchill's gruelling war time regime saw him working 17 hour days and notching up an incredible 40,000 'war miles' as he sought to keep his Allies on side. The displays brilliantly reflect the multi-faceted character of their subject, allowing visitors to enjoy audio excerpts from Churchill's famous speeches as well as ponder the letter from his wife reprimanding him for his deteriorating behaviour to colleagues. Other chapters look at the rest of Churchill's life, from wayward public school boy, to intrepid reporter and army officer to maverick politician, Nobel Laureate, painter and Cold War statesman. At the heart of the displays is a high spec, 15 metre touch screen time line that gives a day by day account of Churchill's life with spectacular animations for key events such as the Dambusters' Raid and Churchill's 90th birthday.

The Cartoon Museum

⌧ *35 Little Russell Street, WC1A*

☎ *020 7580 8155*

✎ *www.cartoonmuseum.org*

🚌 *Tottenham Court Road LU/Holborn LU*

🕐 *Tues-Sat 10.30-17.30, Sun 12.00-17.30 (last admission 17.15)*

💷 *£4 (adults), £3 (concessions), free (students, under 18s, Friends of the Cartoon Museum)*

✎ *Shop*

♿ *Wheelchair Access*

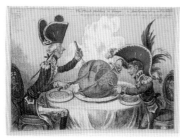

For some years a peripatetic institution, the Cartoon Art Trust has now found a home for its museum – a stylishly converted former dairy in the heart of Bloomsbury. Incredibly (given that Britain invented the art form) this is London's first cartoon museum and it is dedicated to showing the best of British cartoon art. The ever-growing permanent collection contains examples by all the big names, from the bitter satires of 18th-century exponents such as Hogarth, Gillray and Rowlandson to more recent works by current household names like Searle, Matt and Posy Simmonds. The displays cover all aspects of cartoon art, embracing not just political satire and caricature but also 'gag' cartoons, classic war cartoons, comic strips and graphic novels. Top quality temporary exhibitions make repeat visits here a must – past offerings have included a Heath Robinson retrospective, Dan Dare at 50 and Eurob★!!★@ks! – a celebration of 50 years of the European Commission. For those eager to sharpen their pencils and have a go themselves the well equipped activity room runs workshops for adults as well as youngsters, while the research library is available for those with more academic interests. Naturally, this being a 21st century museum, retail opportunities are not lacking and the museum shop features a choice selection of cartoon books, history titles and greetings cards, mugs by Simon Drew and Quentin Blake, and some rather fetching Dennis the Menace wrapping paper.

The Clink Museum

🖼 *1 Clink Street, SE1*
☎ *020 7403 0900*
🖱 *www.clink.co.uk*
🚌 *London Bridge LU/Rail*
🕐 *Mon-Fr 10.00-18.00, Sat-Sun 10.00-21.00*
💷 *£5 (adults), £3.50 (under 15s/concessions), £12 (families)*
🛍 *Shop*

This exhibition, built on the site of the original Clink prison, is more an attraction than a museum. Although a variety of authentic torture instruments are displayed, perhaps the most painful feature of the museum is reading the spelling mistakes in the wall labels. Tableaux depict the less than appealing aspects of life in the clink and, for those keen to experience the harsh character of an earlier criminal justice system more closely, some exhibits like the weighty ball and chain are hands-on.

The Clockmakers' Museum

🖼 *Guildhall, Aldermanbury, EC2*
☎ *020 7332 1868*
🖱 *www.clockmakers.org*
🚌 *Bank LU, Mansion House LU, Moorgate LU, St Paul's LU*
🕐 *Mon-Sat 09.30-16.30*
💷 *Admission free*
♿ *Wheelchair access*

Time waits for no one – especially here, at the Museum of the Worshipful Company of Clockmakers, where some 700 clocks and watches testify to man's ingenious attempts to keep tabs on this most slippery of concepts. Refurbished in 2002, the neatly ordered displays tell the story of timekeeping and watchmaking in London against a background noise of gentle ticking and hourly harmonious chimes. Some unusual timepieces lurk amongst the more elegant pocket watches and stately longcase clocks – like a macabre silver skull watch reputedly owned by Mary Queen of Scots and an innocuous-looking device which turns out to be the timer for an early nuclear weapon. There are also timepieces by Thomas Thompion ('the Father of English clockmaking') and examples of John 'Longitude' Harrison's work.

The Crypt

St Paul's Cathedral, St Paul's Churchyard, EC4M
020 7246 8348 / 020 7246 8358 (group bookings)
www.stpauls.co.uk
St Paul's LU
Cathedral Floor, Crypt & Ambulatory 08.30-16.30 (last admission 16.00); Galleries 09.30-16.30 (last admission 16.00)
£9.50 (adults), £8.50 (concessions), £3.50 (children); 'Super Tour' £3 (adults), £2.50 (concessions), £1 (children); Audio tours can be hired in English, French, German, Italian or Spanish £3.50 (£3 concessions)
Shop
Café & Restaurant
Wheelchair access (via southern transept)

Once you've done gazing at the splendid interior of Wren's Baroque masterpiece, climbed up to the Whispering Gallery, and admired Holman Hunt's *The Light of the World*, a look around the crypt is a good antidote to the cricked neck you've probably acquired. As well as being home to the splendidly kitted out OBE (Order of the British Empire) chapel, the crypt is filled with the tombs and memorials of Britain's illustrious dead – including Wellington and Nelson and of course, the cathedral's architect himself, Sir Christopher Wren. The Cathedral's 'Super Tours' reach parts of the cathedral that others can't – such as the geometrical stairs and the quire with its Grinling Gibbon carvings.

For those visitors who wish to explore online before visiting, a virtual tour is available on the website and includes 360° panoramas, maps and images. Actual visitors can purchase a guidebook for £7.99.

The Design Museum

⊡ 28 Shad Thames, SE1

☎ 0870 833 9955 (recorded information) / 0870 909 9009

🖥 www.designmuseum.org

🚆 London Bridge LU/Rail, Tower Hill LU; bus 42, 47, 78, 188, 381, 100, 225

🕐 Daily 10.00-17.45 (last entry 17.15)

💰 £8.50 (adults), £6.50 (concessions), £5 (students), free (under 12s)

🛍 Shop

☕ Café

♿ Wheelchair access

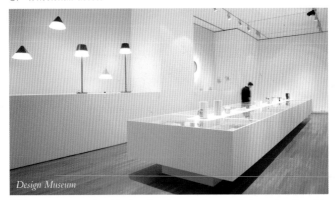

Design Museum

This museum, as its title implies, is a shrine to design. Its riverside home, a sleek white building in 1930s cruise-liner style, looks every inch the modernist icon and stands in stark contrast to the historic red brick shipping warehouses of Shad Thames.

The museum specialises in international industrial design, architecture, and the built environment; its eclectic exhibition programme reflects the breadth of its vision. Recent exhibitions have celebrated the work of designers as diverse as fashion designer Matthew Williamson, French engineer Jean Prouvé and renowned British architect Richard Rogers. The museum also features a cluster of computer screens where visitors can explore the Museum's beautifully designed website (of course you can do this from the comfort of your own home but you may not get to sit on a snazzy designer chair, as you do here). As well as containing news about the Museum's exhibitions the site is also home to an online archive with info on designers from Alvar Aalto to Michael Young. Outside, on the riverfront terrace, the Design Museum Tank hosts specially commissioned installations by both established and rising design stars

For aesthetic gratification of the take home variety, the museum shop carries tempting designer knick-knacks and a well-chosen selection of design books and magazines, with glossy coffee table tomes on fashion and design jostling for space with more technical sounding titles like 'Secrets of Digital Illustration'. The foyer coffee shop offers light refreshments while the Blueprint Café is also on-site for those with more sophisticated tastes and bigger budgets.

The Charles Dickens Museum

48 Doughty Street, WC1
020 7405 2127
www.dickensmuseum.com
Russell Square LU, Chancery Lane LU
Mon-Sat 10.00-17.00, Sun 11.00-17.00
£5 (adults), £4 (concs), £3 (children), £14 (families); Audio guide £1.50
Shop

Although Charles Dickens only lived at this address for little more than two years, the house has become something of a shrine to the writer who gave us The Pickwick Papers, Oliver Twist and David Copperfield. Displays include fragments of original manuscripts and a variety of quirky odds and ends connected with the great man – anything from his well-worn writing desk to his medicine cabinet to a grill from the Marshalsea Prison! Surprisingly perhaps for such a literary haunt, many exhibits are highly visual. Numerous illustrations to Dickens' books, and portraits of the writer and his family by eminent Victorians such as W P Frith and the gloriously named Augustus Egg are on show.

The library in the basement holds a bewildering variety of Dickens editions, and although it's the last room on the tour suggested by the guidebook, its excellent potted history video makes it well worth stopping here first. The museum also has a rolling series of exhibitions throughout the year, exploring aspects of Dickens and his work.

The basement is also home to trio of archaic domestic spaces – a still room, washhouse and wine cellar – which have all been recently opened to the public. Outside, the walled garden has been sympathetically redeveloped and replanted – and with its benches and lion's head water feature offers a pleasant outdoor sanctuary for visitors.

The small shop stocks antiquarian and new editions of Dickens' oeuvre (including a CD-Rom of his entire works) as well as the sort of kitsch which seems to be the inevitable destiny of great writers from Shakespeare onwards – this is the place to pick up that Dickens Toby jug you've always wanted.

The Michael Faraday Museum and Laboratory

⌨ *The Royal Institution, 21 Albemarle Street, W1*
☏ *020 7409 2992*
✎ *www.rigb.org*
🚌 *Green Park LU*
🕐 *Mon-Fri 09.00-17.00*
💷 *Admission free*
♿ *Wheelchair access*

Founded in 1799, this venerable scientific institution re-opened in summer 2008 after a £20 million refurbishment and its in-house museum has also been on the receiving end of some serious cash. The museum's new incarnation celebrates some of the scientific greats who worked in this building, such as Davey (he of the lamp), Dewar (he of the flask) and Michael Faraday, the London bookbinder turned experimental scientist whose discovery of electromagnetic induction paved the way for today's electrical industries and helped to shape the modern world.

The laboratory at the Royal Institution where Faraday made many important finds is still in situ but is now accompanied by a 21st century nano-tech lab, where visitors can see today's scientists at work, or perhaps having a coffee break. Displays include historic scientific apparatus, as well as the first sample of Benzene (another of Faraday's discoveries), and highlight the commonality as well as the differences between experimental science past and present. Up on the first floor, paintings and prints of famous scientists lecturing, illustrate the history of scientific communication and are displayed alongside some of the original objects depicted in the paintings.

The Fashion and Textile Museum

⌨ *79-85 Bermondsey Street, SE1*
☏ *020 7407 8664*
✎ *www.ftmlondon.org*
🚌 *London Bridge Rail/LU*
🕐 *Daily 11.00-17.00*
💷 *£7 (adults), £4 (students/concessions), free (under12s)*
🛍 *Shop*
☕ *Café*
♿ *Wheelchair access*

With its shocking pink and custard yellow façade, the FTM (designed by Mexican architect Ricardo Legorreta), is a vibrant landmark in this still rather down-at-heel part of town. This museum was the brainchild of flamboyant fashion designer Zandra Rhodes and originally opened in 2003. It was re-inaugurated in 2008, as part of Newham College, and hosts a programme of changing exhibitions exploring contemporary fashion, style and couture. A small selection of clothes by Zandra Rhodes and other designers is always on free-to-view display in the museum, which is also home to an archive of over 600 garments from 1947 to present (open by appointment). Visitors wishing to accessorize need look no further than the museum shop, which stocks funky contemporary jewellery and textiles, as well as a small selection of design books and mags.

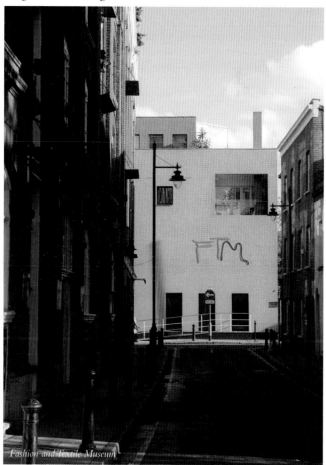

Fashion and Textile Museum

The Florence Nightingale Museum

⊡ *St Thomas' Hospital, 2 Lambeth Palace Road, SE1*

☎ *020 7620 0374*

✐ *www.florence-nightingale.co.uk*

🚌 *Lambeth North LU, Waterloo Rail/LU, Westminster LU*

🕐 *Daily 10.00-17.00 (closed Easter & Christmas); last admission 16.00*

💷 *£5.80 (adults), £4.80 (concessions), £16 (families), free (under 5s)*

🛍 *Shop*

♿ *Wheelchair access*

A legend in her own lifetime, Florence Nightingale was much more than simply 'The Lady with the Lamp', as this museum amply demonstrates. Beginning with her unfulfilled and privileged youth, it follows Florence's remarkable career through the bloodshed of the Crimean War to the energetic campaigning for health reform which occupied the remainder of her life.

Witty, intelligent, shrewd and single-minded, this ministering angel didn't mind putting a few backs up to achieve her goals, and the museum takes a commendably even-handed approach to the complexities of its subject. Some of the displays err on the side of wordiness but most of the relevant facts can be gleaned (in the comfort of the small cinema) from the audio-visual show, or you can take a guided tour (free with admission).

Original letters, nurses' uniforms and Miss Nightingale's Crimean medicine chest are among the personal artefacts on show, along with the shell of 'Jimmy', the pet tortoise at Scutari Hospital. The museum also runs an events programme as well as hosting temporary exhibitions on nursing themes. A selection of affordable souvenirs and books about nursing are available at the shop, and refreshments are served on the hospital site.

The Foundling Museum

⌖ 40 Brunswick Square, WC1N
☏ 020 7841 3600
✎ www.foundlingmuseum.org.uk
🚌 Euston Rail/LU, King's Cross St Pancras Rail/LU, Russell Square LU
🕐 Tues-Sat 10.00-18.00, Sun 12.00-18.00
💷 £5 (adults), £4 (concessions), free (children)
🛍 Small shop
☕ Café
♿ Wheelchair access

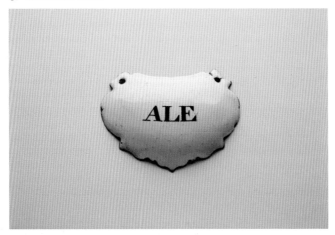

Token given by a mother, Foundling Museum

Fresh from a £4.2 million refurbishment, this museum re-opened in June 2004 and tells the story of the Foundling Hospital, London's first children's charity. It's a fascinating tale, an extraordinary blend of social injustice, campaigning fervour, creative genius and enlightened self-interest. Founded in the 18th century, at a time when over 1,000 babies a year were being abandoned, the hospital was the brainchild of Thomas Coram, sea captain and philanthropist. Illegitimacy was the main reason for children being abandoned and the museum's poignant exhibits include some of the personal tokens left by mothers with their infants as means of their identification, should they ever be reunited. New displays on the ground floor emphasise the social history surrounding the Foundling Hospital and include a range of materials such as Thomas Coram's passionate letters, prints and photographs of Foundlings in the Hospital grounds, and recorded oral histories of living Foundlings.

The museum is also home to a cracking art collection, a legacy of the days when the Foundling Hospital was also London's first public art gallery. Under royal patronage the hospital had become a fashionable attraction and the artist William Hogarth, a Founding Governor of the hospital, quickly spotted its potential as a venue for promoting the best in British art. He kick started the collection in 1740 by presenting the Hospital with a painting of its founder, Thomas Coram. This was his first portrait in the 'grand manner' (although it does feature some notably down-to-earth touches); a more typical work by the master satirist is his *March of the Guards to Finchley*, also in the collection. Other artists of the day followed Hogarth's lead and donated works, with the cream of the collection featuring paintings by Ramsay, Reynolds and Gainsborough and sculpture by Roubiliac and Rysbrack. Established in an age when art was seen as a force for moral improvement, the collection was intended to benefit the public and formed a precursor of the Royal Academy (see p. 206). These works by the hospital's early artist supporters are displayed in historic interiors preserved from the now demolished Foundling Hospital building formerly at nearby Coram's Fields.

The composer G F Handel was another of the Hospital's eminent benefactors and the museum's collection includes a manuscript copy of *The Messiah*, an early performance of which raised the then enormous sum of £7,000 for the charity. A second floor gallery displays this and Handel's will, together with books, paintings, prints and memorabilia from the world renowned Gerald Coke Handel Collection. A group of rather nifty 'musical chairs', allow visitors to sit and listen to extracts from Handel's works.

Perhaps spurred on by the newly re-invigorated Brunswick Centre nearby, the museum now also houses a sleek new café, whose menu features North African lunch specialities as well as more traditional cake, soup and sandwich options.

Benjamin Franklin House

🏠 *36 Craven Street, WC2N*

☎ *020 7839 2006*
   020 7925 1405 (booking hotline)

✎ *www.BenjaminFranklinHouse.org*

🚇 *Embankment LU*

🕐 *Wed-Sun 12.00-17.00; Entrance by tour only (shows at 12.00, 13.00, 14.00, 15.15, 16.15, ticket collection 15mins prior to these times)*

💲 *£7 (adults), £5 (concessions), free (under 16s)*

🛍 *Shop*

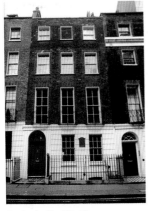

Benjamin Franklin House

Scientist, diplomat, inventor, postal pioneer, Founding Father and all-round American icon Benjamin Franklin lived at this elegant Georgian townhouse between 1757 and 1775. After years of neglect the house re-opened in January 2006, on Franklin's 300th birthday, having been carefully conserved (not restored). So don't expect fully recreated 18th-century interiors here – what you get is a rather more imaginative approach to historical interpretation. The pared down, ghostly interiors of the house are used as a blank canvas to project (quite literally) the life and times of Benjamin Franklin while an actress playing the role of landlady's daughter Polly Hewson, interacts with the pre-recorded audio visual material. Appropriately enough for the man who invented the lightning conductor, Franklin was something of a live wire himself – and each room explores the wide-ranging achievements of this 'citizen of the world'. Although his primary reason for being in London was to mediate between Britain and the increasingly fractious American colonies, Franklin still found time to invent bifocal spectacles and the glass armonica, reform the alphabet and hobnob with the leading figures of the day. Franklin led a fascinating life and although the 'Historical Experience' may sound gimmicky it proves an effective way of telling his story. For those who want to find out more, Benjamin Franklin's autobiography can be purchased in the small shop while a Student Science Centre is open by appointment.

Library and Museum of Freemasonry

Freemasons' Hall, Great Queen Street, WC2
020 7395 9257
www.freemasonry.london.museum
Covent Garden LU, Holborn LU
Mon-Fri 10.00-17.00
Admission free
Shop
Wheelchair access

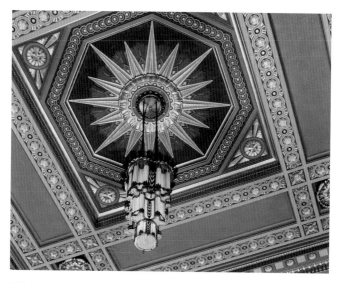

While this museum and permanent exhibition doesn't spill the beans on funny handshakes and rolled-up trouser legs, it does shed a glimmer of light on the elusive yet high profile organisation that is Freemasonry.

Housed in the intimidatingly expansive Freemasons' Hall (erected in the 1930s), the museum is itself pretty cavernous. Case after case displays the United Grand Lodge's extensive collection of masonic glass, china and silverware from lodges around the world. Insignia and regalia are also much in evidence, and with names like 'the Order of the Secret Monitor' the masons' reputation for clandestine practice seems understandable. Documents include the minutes and account books kept by PoW masons at Stalag 383, Nuremburg and a letter congratulating Queen Victoria on her escape from an assassination attempt.

34

The permanent exhibition broadly charts the 'history of English Freemasonry and its development from medieval obscurity to world-wide prominence' but, again, without giving too much away. Portraits and photographs of masons include those of Elias Ashmole, the 17th-century founder of Oxford's Ashmolean Museum, Alexander Fleming (see p.128) and Peter Sellers. Among the unusual artefacts on display are an outsized Grand Master's throne and a beautifully hand-embroidered masonic apron from the 18th century. Books, videos and regalia are available from The Grand Charity's souvenir shop on the ground floor.

The Garden Museum

▢ *St Mary-at-Lambeth, Lambeth Palace Road, SE1*

☎ *020 7401 8865*

✎ *www.museumgardenhistory.org*

🚌 *Lambeth North LU, Waterloo LU/Rail, Westminster LU; buses 3, 344, C10, 77*

◷ *Tues-Sun 10.30-17.00 (subject to change)*

💰 *Suggested donation £3 (adults), £2.50 (concessions)*

🛍 *Shop*

☕ *Café (open Tues-Sat 10.30-16.45)*

♿ *Wheelchair access*

You don't have to be a horny-handed son or daughter of the soil to appreciate this museum. With its ecclesiastical setting and intricately-planted knot garden, it's an oasis of verdant tranquillity amid the turmoil of Lambeth Bridge roundabout. Formerly known as the Museum of Garden History, the museum reopened in October 2008 with a new name and a spacious new mezzanine gallery for its permanent collection. Telling the story of gardening through the centuries, the redisplay includes plenty of unusual tools and items not previously shown while freeing up the ground floor for temporary exhibitions – such as the opening retrospective about dry gardening guru Beth Chatto. The Museum is a focal point for garden-related events and activities with a year long programme of events, talks, children's activities and plant fairs.

Out in the well-tended garden the plants (all clearly labelled) vie for attention with the churchyard's illustrious dead – William Bligh (captain of the ill-fated Bounty) and Elias Ashmole (freemason, see p. 34) are both buried here. Back inside, the shop stocks a wide range of gardening books and good quality gifts with a floral theme. Frequented by doughty horticultural ladies, the café serves vegetarian food, and its air is thick with talk of borders' bedding-out and bad backs.

The Golden Hinde

- 🏠 *St Mary Overie Dock, Cathedral Street, SE1*
- ☎ *020 7403 0123 / 0870 0118700 (bookings)*
- 🖥 *www.goldenhinde.co.uk*
- 🚇 *London Bridge LU/Rail*
- 🕐 *Phone for opening times*
- 💰 *£6 (adults), £4.50 (concessions & children), £18 (families)*
- 🛍 *Shop*

This part of London is so steeped in history that it comes as little surprise to see this full-sized replica of Sir Francis Drake's 16th-century warship moored up near Southwark Cathedral. Although describing itself as a 'museum ship', the brightly coloured vessel has clocked up over 100,000 miles and with its neatly-trimmed rigging and sturdy structure, feels very much like a working ship. Armed with a tour leaflet, the visitor has a pretty free run of the ship – from the depths of the hold, up to Drake's cabin (the only private one on board). A few sea chests and barrels aside, there's really not much to see and below decks, low ceilings and steep stairs make the going difficult for grown-ups, causing one parent of my acquaintance to rename the ship *the Golden Fleece*. Nonetheless, it's pretty atmospheric and children should enjoy the challenging terrain. Sleepovers for young buccaneers are available, and guided tours can be booked for group visits.

Grant Museum of Zoology & Comparative Anatomy

- 🏠 *Darwin Building, UCL, Malet Place, WC1*
- ☎ *020 7679 2647*
- 🖥 *www.grant.museum.ucl.ac.uk*
- 🚇 *Euston Rail/LU, Euston Square LU, Goodge Street LU, Russell Square LU, Warren Street LU*
- 🕐 *Mon-Fri 13.00-17.00 and some weekend activity days*
- 💰 *Admission free*
- ♿ *Wheelchair access (ring in advance)*

One of the pioneers of evolutionary theory and teacher to Charles Darwin, Professor Robert Grant founded this natural history museum way back in 1828. The museum retains an old fashioned feel – in true Victorian style its glass cases are crammed with skeletons and specimens suspended in jars of yellowing liquid. Arranged in taxonomic order, the displays cover the whole of the animal kingdom and feature exotic animals such as a hairy frog and a giant anteater. Among the rare specimens are three extinct species: the dodo, the marsupial wolf and the quagga. An important teaching and research resource, the museum offers 'hands-on' sessions and activity days by special arrangement.

Great Ormond Street Hospital for Children NHS Trust Museum

⊞ *55 Great Ormond Street, WC1*
☎ *020 7405 9200 (ext 5920)*
🚇 *Holborn LU, Russell Square LU*
🕐 *Mon-Fri 09.30-16.00 by appointment*
💰 *Admission free*

This rather dingy, one-room museum is housed in a 17th-century building across the road from the main hospital buildings. The exhibits illustrate the history of the hospital (the oldest dedicated children's hospital in Britain) with photographs and various pieces of vintage medical equipment enlivened, after a fashion, by curiosities such as a model ship made by inmates at HMP Dartmoor. Playwright J M Barrie gave the copyright of Peter Pan to the Hospital and the museum includes a collection of editions of the play.

The Guards Museum

⊞ *Wellington Barracks, Birdcage Walk, SW1*
☎ *020 7414 3271*
🖱 *www.armymuseums.org.uk or www.mklmodels.co.uk*
🚇 *St James's Park LU*
🕐 *Daily 10.00-16.00*
💰 *£3 (adults), £2 (students, OAPs, ex-Guardsmen), free (children under 16)*
🛍 *Shop*
♿ *Wheelchair access (telephone in advance)*

The history of the five regiments of foot guards – the Grenadier, Coldstream, Scots, Irish and Welsh Guards – in one museum. With their distinctive scarlet tunics and bearskin caps, guards are perhaps best known for their ceremonial role in the capital but have also played their part in Britain's numerous military campaigns. Uniforms include a guard's tunic worn by Edward VIII, the Grand Old Duke of York's bearskin and a Dervish chain mail shirt, while among the more unusual exhibits are souvenirs from the Battle of Waterloo, a device for tattooing deserters and the wicker picnic basket used by Field Marshal Montgomery while on campaign in Italy. For visitors inspired to play war games, the Toy Soldier Centre is close with battalions of tiny tin troops and souvenirs.

Handel House Museum

⌧ *25 Brook Street, W1 (entrance at rear in Lancashire Court)*

☎ *020 7495 1685*

✎ *www.handelhouse.org*

🚌 *Bond Street LU*

🕐 *Tues-Sat 10.00-18.00 (Thurs till 20.00), Sun 12.00-18.00*

💷 *£5 (adults), £4.50 (concessions), £2 (children);*
  children free on Saturday

🛍 *Shop*

♿ *Wheelchair access*

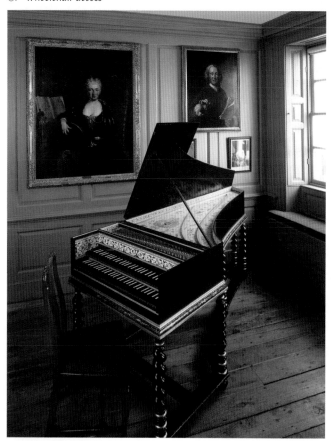

Harpsichord, Handel House Museum

G F Handel lived in this elegant town house from 1723 until his death in 1759 and it was here that he composed landmark works such as the *Messiah* and *Zadok the Priest*. The museum itself opened in 2001 and, incredibly, is the first in London to be dedicated to a composer.

Although beautifully restored and furnished with 18th furniture, paintings and prints, the restrained dark grey interiors don't try to recreate the historic house in full and are instead themed around Handel's life, work and times. Visits start on the 2nd floor with a short audio visual presentation about Handel in London – the talking heads include Timothy West, Nicholas Hytner and even a musical cab driver (proof, if proof were needed, that they really do have an opinion on everything). Handel's dressing room doubles as 'The London Room' with portraits of Georgian literati such as John Gay and Alexander Pope while the displays in Handel's bedroom (including a magnificent canopied bed) strive to get to the heart of 'Han the Man'. The combination of carefully chosen artefacts, to-the-point information sheets and friendly room stewards is surprisingly effective at bringing house and owner to life, revealing rather an endearing character who liked his grub, had a famously short fuse and was probably a very noisy neighbour.

One floor down, the focus is firmly on Handel's music: rehearsal, performance and composition. Handel's original rehearsal room explores the world of 18th-century opera and theatre with portraits of Handel's favourite artistes such as singer Susanna Cibber, and the castrato Senesino. It's very much the hub of the place and still functions as a rehearsal space and there's a chance that on your visit (as on mine) that the house will reverberate to the sound of live baroque music, perhaps played on the Museum's reproduction Ruckers double-manual harpsichord. Leading off the rehearsal room is the small room where Handel composed, overseen today by a very fine portrait of the man himself by Philip Mercier along with portraits of the composer's closest musical collaborators, his copyist John Christopher Smith the Younger and librettist Charles Jennens.

Although celebrating a long dead musician, the museum is far from moribund. The museum's events and education programme features a lively mix of temporary exhibitions, baroque music master classes, lectures and performances. Family orientated activities include a selection of trails and quizzes. Intriguingly, some of the temporary exhibition rooms are located next door at no. 23 which in 1968-9, some 210 years after Handel's death, was home to a rather different sort of musician – Jimi Hendrix.

HMS Belfast

⌨ *Morgan's Lane, Tooley Street, SE1*

☎ *020 7940 6300*

✎ *www.iwm.org.uk or www.hmsbelfast.org.uk*

🚌 *London Bridge LU/Rail, Monument LU, Tower Hill LU*

🕐 *Daily 10.00-18.00, last entry 17.15 (March-Oct);*
   10.00-17.00, last entry 16.15 (Nov-Feb)

💰 *£9.95 (adults), £6.15 (concessions), free (under 16s)*

🛍 *Shop*

☕ *Café*

♿ *Partial Wheelchair access*

Weighing in at 11,553 tonnes, HMS Belfast is Europe's last big-gun armoured warship to have seen action in World War II, and the first warship to be preserved for the nation since Nelson's *Victory*. Moored just upstream of Tower Bridge, she is boarded, in proper nautical style, via a gangplank. Once on board there are nine decks to explore, but be prepared for low-slung doorways and steep ladders. An audio guide is included in the ticket price and includes veterans' recollections and a children's quiz as well as providing the low-down on key features of the ship. For ease of orientation each visitor is given a handy map – which you will need as Belfast is a labyrinthine lady. Rather more sophisticated navigational tools can be seen on the Bridge, home of the wireless office (now manned by an amateur radio society).

Although she hasn't fired a shot in anger since the Korean War, HMS Belfast's big guns are still very much in evidence on the upper decks, while deep below the waterline are the claustrophobic shell rooms. In service from 1939-1966, the ship reflects her lengthy career, referencing her role in the D-Day landings and the sinking of the German battlecruiser *Scharnhorst*. Startlingly lifelike mannequins and sound tracks bring the living quarters to life, while the operations room reconstructs the Battle of North Cape. The attention to detail is spot on and there are even two real ship's cats who now patrol Belfast's decks.

A permanent exhibition, 'HMS Belfast in War and Peace' fleshes out the biography of the ship and those who served aboard her, charting her career beginning with her building and launch in 1938 with contemporary paintings, photographs, plans, artefacts and four historical videos. Another exhibition 'Life at Sea' reveals what life was like aboard with fascinating first hand audio accounts.

In both menu and ambience, the ship's Walrus Café offers a functional place for refreshment while back on dry land the museum shop sells model boat kits, cuddly ships' rats and a small fleet of books on naval and wartime subjects.

Household Cavalry Museum

⊡ *Horse Guards, Whitehall, SW1*
☎ *020 7930 3070*
✎ *www.householdcavalrymuseum.org.uk*
🚉 *Charing Cross LU/Rail, Westminster LU, Embankment LU*
🕓 *Daily 10.00-18.00 (except 25,26 Dec & Good Friday)*
💰 *£6 (adults), £4 (5-16 years, conc), £18 (family)*
🛍 *Shop*
♿ *Disabled access (ring for details)*

Set in an historic 18th-century building, this regimental museum is slap bang on the tourist trail between Westminster and Trafalgar Square, just opposite the Banqueting House (see p. 9). Guarded by oft-photographed mounted soldiers in scarlet jackets and shiny helmets, the Horse Guards is still the HQ of the Household Cavalry, the soldiers who guard the Queen on ceremonial occasions in London. The museum opened in 2007 and traces the origins of the regiment from its inception by Charles II (when its members paid for the privilege of guarding the monarch) to its current hard-core operational roles in Iraq and Afghanistan. The stable block setting means that visitors get a unique behind the scenes insight into daily regimental life – a clear partition allows a view (and smell) of the famous black chargers in their stalls, being mucked out, tacked up and groomed. Videos show the relentless training involved in getting men and horses ready for duty with footage of novice riders being put through their paces and troopers hard at work preparing kit for the daily inspection. Younger visitors should also enjoy the touch screen interactive quizzes and trying on the uniforms strategically placed in the empty stalls.

Moving on, the displays look at the earlier days of the regiment and include a section devoted to its role at the battle of Waterloo. Relics from this epic confrontation include the field bugle used to call for the decisive charge of the Life Guards and the artificial leg of the 18th Marquess of Anglesey who famously lost his leg watching the battle with the Duke of Wellington. A bullet stopping French dictionary from WWI and the bridle of Sefton, the horse who was injured in the 1982 Hyde Park Bomb, are sobering mementos of more recent conflicts. Packed with a marvellous array of plumed helmets, shiny breastplates and swords, the displays also trace the development of the HC into the modern, mechanised fighting force that it is today. The small gift shop offers regimental memorabilia and model soldiers for all ages.

Hunterian Museum at the Royal College of Surgeons

⊞ *35-43 Lincoln's Inn Fields, WC2*

☎ *020 7869 6560*

✐ *www.rcseng.ac.uk/museums*

🚇 *Holborn LU*

🕓 *Tues-Sat 10.00-17.00 (group visits must be booked in advance),
free public tour every Wednesday at 13.00*

💷 *Admission free*

🛍 *Small shop*

♿ *Wheelchair access (via external lift, accessible toilet)*

Packed with case upon case of anatomical and pathological specimens, human and otherwise, the Hunterian Museum is not for the squeamish. John Hunter's research into bone growth, regeneration and reproduction paved the way for modern scientific surgery and such was his reputation that his collection was purchased by the government and given to the RCS in 1799. A recent multi-million pound refurbishment has transformed the formerly old fashioned displays and a glittering 'Crystal Gallery' now houses over 3,000 of John Hunter's original 18th-century specimens. Not without their own macabre beauty, the specimen jars contain all sorts of innards and outards (many with congenital disorders) suspended in sepulchral solutions – the alimentary canal of a sea cucumber, a camel's palette and a collection of hernias are just some of the offerings. After these, it's almost a relief to look at the skeletons such as the 7ft 10in frame of 'the Irish Giant' Charles Byrne, master criminal Jonathan Wild and a solitaire (an equally defunct relative of the dodo). Other human remains include the left hemisphere of the brain of mathematician Charles Babbage and the Evelyn anatomical tables. Not content with collecting medicalia, Hunter was chummy with many of the leading painters of his day, and the museum contains some of the art works he amassed, including sculpture by Roubiliac and animal studies by Stubbs and Agasse.

Also on the ground floor, the Silver and Steel Gallery displays a menacing assortment of surgical instruments from East African 'thorn' needles to modern skin 'staplers', and some ingenious tools for removing foreign bodies (and indeed, some of the foreign bodies they removed). The McRae Gallery is a 'discovery space', on my visit filled with sketching students, but also containing toothsome treasures from the Odontological Collection. The comparative nature of the displays means that one can compare pin sharp piranha teeth with Winston Churchill's dentures, elephant molars with Anglo Saxon gnashers, and observe that, sadly, animals suffer from similar dental problems as humans.

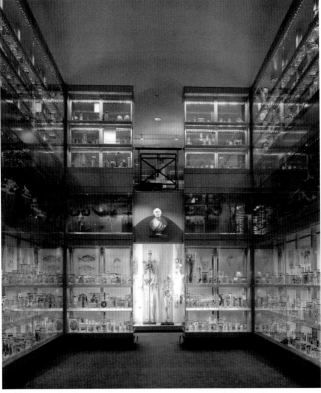

The Crystal Gallery in the Hunterian Museum at The Royal College of Surgeons

Upstairs the Moynihan Gallery explores the nitty-gritty of surgery from the gore spattered early days of do-or-die 'heroic' operations to the rise of aseptic modern techniques and developments such as open heart surgery and keyhole procedures. Regularly changing temporary exhibitions and a lively programme of events and talks complement the permanent displays. In his day Hunter used to give 'peripatetic lectures' around his collection to amuse his friends; today's visitors can take advantage of free guided tours and virtual tours of the collection, accessed via the website.

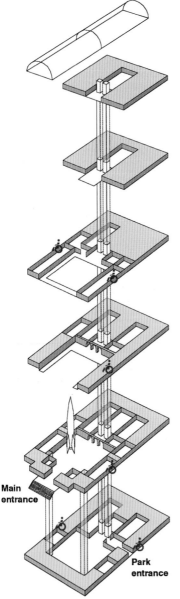

This floor plan will help you find your way around the Museum. There are direction signs on all floors to temporary as well as permanent exhibitions. Museum staff will be happy to direct you.

4 *Crimes Against Hunanity*

3 *The Holocaust Exhibition*

2 *Art Galleries*
John Singer Sargent Room
♿ *Toilets*

1 *Secret War*
Victoria Cross and George Cross
Survival at Sea: Merchant Navy
♿ *Toilet*

G *Large Exhibits*
Temporary Exhibitions
Telephone
Cinema
Shop and Café
Picnic Room (weekends & school holidays only)
♿ *Toilet*

LG *First & Second World War displays*
Trench Experience
Blitz Experience
♿ 🚹🚺 *Toilets*

Main entrance

Park entrance

Imperial War Museum

🖃 *Lambeth Road, SE1*
☎ *020 7416 5320/5321*
✎ *www.iwm.org.uk*
🚌 *Elephant and Castle LU/Rail, Lambeth North LU, Southwark LU,*
  Waterloo LU/Rail
🕐 *Daily 10.00-18.00*
🎫 *Admission free*
🛍 *Shop*
☕ *Café*
♿ *Wheelchair access*

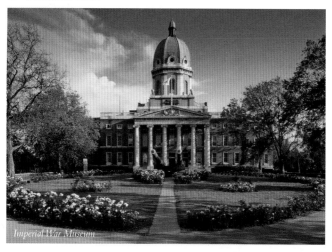
Imperial War Museum

War is often described as a kind of madness, so perhaps it's appropriate that a museum dedicated to 20th-century conflict should be housed in the former lunatic asylum known as Bedlam. The subject of an ongoing redevelopment programme, the museum's facilities and displays are top notch, taking visitors beyond just the instruments of war to focus on the people – both the perpetrators and the victims of conflict. The lofty entrance hall is dominated by the bulky hardware of modern warfare: aeroplanes, tanks, jeeps, rockets and a World War I German periscope mast, so powerful that through it you can see the dome of St Paul's, two miles away.

A permanent exhibition examining 20th-century warfare occupies the lower ground floor and is divided into four parts: World War I, the inter-war years, World War II and post-war conflicts. Displays within each section are thematic rather than strictly chronological, reducing a vast, potentially daunting subject into manageable chunks. As well as artefacts such as uniforms, equipment and weaponry, important historical documents are also displayed: letters and manuscripts from World War I poets and, more chillingly, a facsimile of Adolf Hitler's fateful directive ordering the invasion of Poland.

Personal artefacts from both well-known and anonymous soldiers shift the emphasis from the political to the personal. Recorded eyewitness accounts can be accessed through headsets and these, along with interactive videos showing archive film footage, help visitors develop an accurate picture of events. 'The Trench' and 'Blitz' participatory displays are always popular (unlike the real thing), although some people may find the 'experience' rather too voyeuristic for comfort.

New since the last edition, 'The Children's War' on the ground floor reveals what WWII was like for British children. Pretty grim by the sounds of it – rationed sweets, hand-me-down clothes and outdoor lessons were the least of children's worries in those days with parents being killed, houses being bombed and evacuation to strange parts of the country. Even if parents sent their children abroad they weren't necessarily safe as the display on the sinking of the *City of Benares* only too clearly shows. Toys, drawings, clothes, diaries and audio memories of wartime children recall this era with nostalgic clarity and there's even a walk-through recreation of a wartime semi, equipped with firebucket, taped up windows and suitably austere kitchen and bathroom arrangements.

Upstairs on the first floor, 'The Secret War' dishes the dirt on Britain's spies and has no end of nifty gadgets. Ian Fleming's 'Q' would have been chuffed with the interactive computers which let visitors sift through the files of various real-life agents and have a go at encoding messages. 'Survival at Sea' reviews the crucial role played by the Merchant Navy in WWII and recounts dramatic stories of merchant seamen like the two survivors of the SS Anglo Saxon who endured 72 days adrift on the mid Atlantic. Their 'jolly boat' is shown here along with their logbook which contains the macabre entry '2nd cook goes mad, dies. Two of us left'. On the same floor, the Victoria Cross and George Cross Gallery commemorates the bravery of individual soldiers and civilians with a display of over 40 medals and associated memorabilia.

The museum's art collection is housed on the second floor and, with holdings of 20th-century art second only to those of the Tate Gallery, merits a visit in its own right. The art displays are changed periodically but expect to see works by Stanley Spencer, Paul Nash, Henry Moore and Graham Sutherland. John Singer Sargent's unforgettable depiction of World War I, *Gassed*, has been allocated a room of its own.

The Holocaust Exhibition on the third floor tells the harrowing story of the Nazis' persecution of the Jews and other groups before and during World War II. Topics include a history of anti-Semitism, ghettoes, Jewish resistance, death marches and the discovery of the camps. A funeral cart from the Warsaw Ghetto, a deportation railcar, and a huge case of items belonging to people who were killed at Auschwitz are among the exhibits. The displays effectively convey the remorseless scale and pre-meditation of the Nazi programme of industrialised murder but never lose sight of the individuals involved, be they victim or perpetrator. Video testimonials of 18 survivors as well as photographs, letters and personal possessions such as Leibish Engelberg's prison jacket and Paul Sondhoff's toy bear ensure that the human impact of the Holocaust always stays in focus. Due to the strong content of the exhibition it is not recommended for children under 14. And if you thought mankind might have learnt its lesson from the Holocaust, a visit to 'Crimes Against Humanity' on the fourth floor should stop any complacency in its tracks. From the killing fields of Cambodia to the civil war in the former Yugoslavia, this gruelling audiovisual shows that genocide and ethnic violence remains an ongoing problem for the international community. Again, the material in this exhibit is not suitable for children.

The sheer quantity of the IWM's holdings show the extent to which conflict dominated the last century. The museum holds the national collection of 20th-century military firearms as well as having the oldest collection of wartime film in the country. Only a small proportion of these collections is on display in the public galleries but the museum stages regular film shows and visitors can use the Museum's reference departments by prior appointment. Major temporary exhibitions such as 'Camouflage' and 'Women & War' supplement the excellent permanent displays.

With such a quantity of material to see, audio tours of the museum highlights (£3.50) are a useful aide for visitors with limited time, while special family events help children get the most out of a visit – contact the museum for details and times. The pleasant ground floor café provides a convenient venue for a spot of R&R. For those in a retail frame of mind, the shop offers a good range of books and videos on 20th-century war, and souvenirs such as trendy camouflage jackets, bags and 1940s music CDs.

Inns of Court & City Yeomanry Museum

- 🖳 *10 Stone Buildings, Lincolns Inn, WC2*
- ☎ *020 7405 8112*
- 🚌 *Chancery Lane LU*
- 🕐 *By appointment*
- 💷 *Admission free*
- 🛍 *Shop*

Cunningly camouflaged among the legal buildings of Lincoln's Inn, this small military museum tells the story of two historic London regiments. Weapons, uniforms, medals, equipment and original documents follow their history to the present day, revealing the many roles the regiments have been required to play – from 18th-century riot-quelling militia to the 'Rough Riders' of the Boer War to modern communication corps. The highlight of the collection is a rare and complete set of Georgian drums of the Law Association Volunteers, dubbed the 'Devil's Own' by lawyer-phobe King George III.

The Jewel Tower

- 🖳 *Westminster (opposite the south end of the Houses of Parliament), SW1*
- ☎ *020 7222 2219*
  0870 333 1181 (customer services)
- 🖉 *www.english-heritage.org.uk*
- 🚌 *Westminster LU*
- 🕐 *Daily 10.00-17.00 (April-Oct), 10.00-16.00 (Nov-March)*
- 💷 *£3 (adults), £2.40 (concessions), £1.50 (children), free (under 5s)*
- 🛍 *Shop*
- 🍽 *Light refreshments*

Constructed in 1365, the Jewel Tower is one of the only two surviving buildings from the original Palace of Westminster. King Edward III built it as a treasure house and wardrobe but its later incarnations were distinctly downmarket: junk room, kitchen, and a testing centre for weights and measures. A smallish selection of unglamourous objects on display underline the antiquity of the site and include a 9th-century sword, part of the Tower's original elm foundations and 11th-century carved 'storytelling' stone capitals.

Mindful of its location opposite 'the Mother of Parliaments', the Tower also contains an excellent introductory exhibition about the English Parliament charting its evolution from Anglo-Saxon *'witenagemot'*, (a meeting of wise men) to today's gathering of the (ahem) same. The exhibition is arranged over the two upper floors of the Jewel Tower, and is accessible only by a steep spiral stone staircase.

Dr Johnson's House

🖥 *17 Gough Square, EC4*
☎ *020 7353 3745*
✐ *www@drjohnsonshouse.org*
🚌 *Blackfriars LU/Rail, Chancery Lane LU*
🕓 *Mon-Sat 11.00-17.30 (May-Sept), 11.00-17.00 (Oct-April)*
💷 *£4.50 (adults), £3.50 (OAPs/students), £1.50 (children), £10 (family)*
🛍 *Shop*

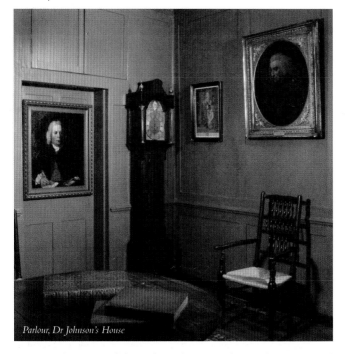

Parlour, Dr Johnson's House

It was in the garret of this early 18th-century house that Dr Samuel Johnson compiled his famous Dictionary: the first comprehensive lexicon of the English language. The house has been restored to its condition during Johnson's 11-year occupancy (from 1748 to 1759) and retains many original features – including some heavy-duty crime prevention measures and an ingenious 'cellarette' in the dining room. Arranged over several floors, the house has no shortage of stairs, but then to quote the friendly attendant, 'the chairs are for sitting on, not gawping at'.

The house has other unexpected surprises. A brick from the Great Wall of China is a tangible reminder of Johnson's unrealised ambition to visit it, while the garret is home to a model toy workshop presented to the house by firefighters in World War II. Books, paintings and memorabilia of Dr Johnson and his circle can be found throughout the house and there's an entertaining and informative video show as well as free information sheets. Changing displays and exhibitions keep things fresh for regulars while younger visitors can try on a selection of replica Georgian clothing. Cards and collections of Johnson's sayings and bon mots are available in the small shop. (Incidentally, a glance in a facsimile of the Dictionary reveals that the great man defined a museum as 'a repository of learned curiosities').

Kirkaldy Testing Museum

🖃 *99 Southwark Street, SE1 (entrance on Prices Street)*
☎ *Perry Perrin 07821337553*
🚌 *Blackfriars LU/Rail, London Bridge LU/Rail, Southwark LU, Waterloo LU/Rail*
🕐 *First Sunday of the month 10.00-16.00, other times by appointment*
💰 *Admission free (donations appreciated), £3 per person for groups*

This atmospheric museum celebrates three generations of the Kirkaldy family who worked in Southwark from 1866-1965 testing engineering and building materials. The Kirkaldy motto, 'Facts not Opinions', is inscribed above the entrance to the firm's Victorian works building, where David Kirkaldy's original all-purpose testing machine is still in place. Some 48 feet long and able to apply a load of over 300 tonnes, this mighty machine tested the chains of Hammersmith Bridge as well as the steel used to build Sydney Harbour Bridge and parts of the Comet airliner. Lovingly restored back to working order by the museum's dedicated volunteer staff, the machine is run on special open days. Regular visits last about $1^1/_2$ hours and reveal both how this extraordinary machine functioned and its role in developing quality-control techniques for construction materials.

London Fire Brigade Museum

🏠 Winchester House, 94a Southwark Bridge Road, SE1

☎ 020 7587 2894

🖋 www.london-fire.gov.uk

🚇 Borough LU

🕐 Guided tours only (by appointment) Mon-Fri at 10.30 and 14.00

💷 £3 (adults), £2 (children 7-14/concessions), free (children under 7)

🛍 Shop

Comprising one of the most comprehensive collections of firefighting equipment in the country, it's probably just as well that admission to this museum is by guided tour only. Arranged chronologically, the exhibits chart the development of the London fire service from 1666 to the present day through the use of paintings, photographs, uniforms, models and medals – including one of only three George Crosses to have been presented to a firefighter.

Equipment ranges from tree-trunk watermains, leather hosepipes and early breathing apparatus (operated by footpump!) to modern thermal imaging cameras. Larger appliances such as the 19th-century telescopic fire escape ladder and a horse-drawn 'steamer' from 1885 (immaculate in its red and gold livery) are displayed in the former Brigade HQ engine room. Particularly fine paintings of firefighting during the Blitz can be seen in the room dedicated to World War II, while the Overseas Room contains badges and helmets of fire brigades from around the world. The tours are filled with tales of bravery and even the supernatural and last between 1-2 hours. The small but choice selection of gifts in the museum shop features firemen's helmet paperweights, bronze firefighter figures and an excellent fire extinguisher water squirter.

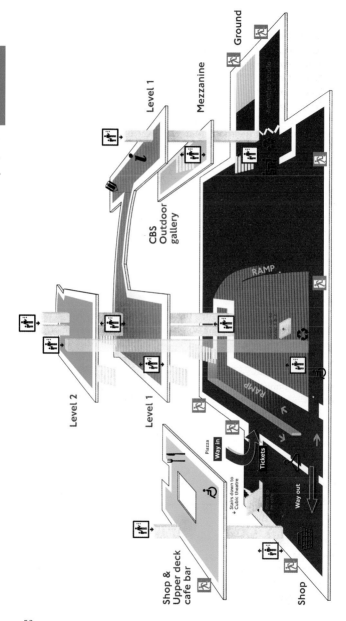

Level 1

Mezzanine

Ground

CBS
Outdoor
gallery

RAMP

Level 2

Level 1

RAMP

Piazza
Way in

Tickets

→ Stairs down to
Cubic theatre

Way out

Shop &
Upper deck
cafe bar

Shop

London Transport Museum

⊞ *Covent Garden Piazza, WC2*

☎ *020 7565 7299 (24-hour information) / 020 7379 6344 (bookings)*

✎ *www.ltmuseum.co.uk*

🚇 *Covent Garden LU, Leicester Square LU, Holborn LU*

🕐 *Mon-Thurs 10.00-18.00 (last admission 17.15),*
Fri 11.00-21.00 (last admission 20.15)

💷 *£8 (adults), £6.50 (senior citizens), £5 (students),*
free (under 16s, Freedom Pass holders)

👓 *Shop*

☕ *Café*

♿ *Wheelchair access*

Located amid the hubbub of the Piazza, and housed in a former flower market, the LTM is a must for train, tram and bus-spotters, or indeed any of the millions who travel by public transport in the capital each year. A two-year long redesign has brought the displays bang up to date, telling the story of London's transport system from Sedan chairs to Oyster cards and congestion charging. The light, airy building is still filled with the historic vehicles and machinery of old but with 1,000 new items on display it is well worth a fresh visit even if you've already visited the museum in the past.

Lumbering horse-drawn vehicles begin the display but quickly give way to the electric and motor-powered trams and buses that revolutionised transport in the capital. Sympathetically restored but retaining a slightly battered feel, the vehicles are all surprisingly atmospheric and you can watch old footage of some of them in action, listen to accounts by transport workers such as 'Cast Iron Billy' and find out why posh places like Hampstead resisted the advent of trams.

The museum follows the transport story underground with Charles Pearson's pioneering Metropolitan Railway and features an 1866 'steam' tube train, complete with carriages you can sit in and grouchy commuters you can eavesdrop on. Incidentally, Mrs Beeton (of cookery book fame) was an early female commuter, regularly travelling from Hatch End to 'town'. A reconstruction of workers digging a tube tunnel using a shield evokes the sheer hard graft and personal risk involved in bringing transport to the masses.

Moving further into the 20th century, there's a section devoted to London transport at war recalling the dark days of WWI when London buses were pressed into active service on the Western Front and the use of tube stations as air raid shelters during WWII. Misty eyed nostalgics should enjoy the 1939 electric trolley bus and more recent vehicles like the 1970s tube train, and the late lamented Routemaster bus.

While the adults take a trip down memory lane, youngsters can get stuck into the numerous hands-on exhibits with no shortage of buttons to press and handles to turn. Actors bring the exhibits to life – on a recent visit an elegant parasol twirling 19th-century omnibus traveller waylaid visitors venturing into the replica Shillibeer horse bus. Simulators give old and young a chance to get behind the wheel and are a popular attraction; 'drive' a Victoria Line train and try to align it correctly with the station platform or enjoy a driver's eye view from the cab of today's Wright Gemini bus.

From season ticket passes to London's 'intelligent' SCOOT traffic light system, the museum explores every conceivable aspect of London's transport network. A dazzling selection of London transport posters and publications pays tribute to the design geniuses behind one of the world's most famous 'brands' – head of London Underground Frank Pick, typographer Edward Johnston, architect Charles Holden, and Harry Beck, the man behind London's iconic tube map.

Although the vehicles are the main attraction, neither the social impact of public transport nor contemporary environmental concerns have been forgotten (although with a daily deposit of 1,000 tonnes of horse manure onto London's streets, things weren't too rosy in the 19th century either). A huge light-up map charts traffic congestion live as you watch and new displays flag up the challenge of climate change – a challenge the museum does its bit to meet with solar tiles, low energy lighting and natural ventilation.

If all that travel builds up your appetite, the museum's new Upper Deck café and bar is decked out with LU moquette covered seating and provides a handy pit stop for drinks and snacks. On late night openings it serves a pretty mean cocktail too – try the evocatively named 'Routemaster' or sip an 'Anorak'. For those bringing their own food, a picnic area is provided within the museum itself, handily sited next to the mini vehicles of the 'All Aboard' play area for the children.

The museum's shop is great fun although with titles like 'Slam doors on the Southern' the selection of specialist books, magazines & DVDs seems aimed squarely at the serious enthusiast and indeed on my last visit this bit of the shop was filled with actual train spotters stocking up on reading material. Posters, postcards and any amount of improbable items emblazoned with the Underground map and the LT logo should satisfy the less anorakish, with models, games and toys for younger visitors. Even pet lovers are catered for with stylish 'Mind the Yap' dog coats fashioned from tube train *'moquette'* fabric.

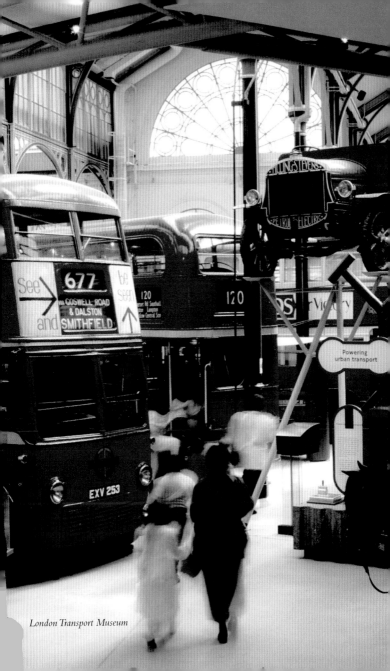

See > be see and SMITHFIELD

677
Mrs GOSWELL ROAD
& DALSTON
SMITHFIELD

EXV 253

120

120

Powering
urban transport

London Transport Museum

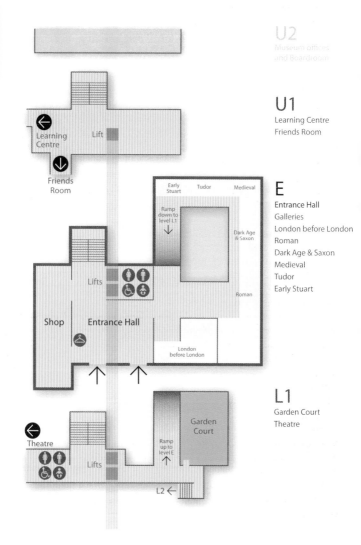

U2
Museum offices
and Boardroom

U1
Learning Centre
Friends Room

E
Entrance Hall
Galleries
London before London
Roman
Dark Age & Saxon
Medieval
Tudor
Early Stuart

L1
Garden Court
Theatre

Museum of London

📖 *150 London Wall, EC2Y*

☎ *0870 444 3851 / 3850*

🖥 *www.museumoflondon.org.uk*

🚇 *Bank LU, Barbican LU, Moorgate LU, St Paul's LU*

🕐 *Mon-Sat 10.00-17.50, Sun 12.00-17.50 (last entry 17.30)*

♿ *Admission free*

🛍 *Shop*

☕ *Café*

♿ *Wheelchair access*

Even if you think you know London like the back of your hand, the chances are that you'll see the city in a new light after a trip to the MoL. Newcomers to the capital could also do a lot worse than make this their first stop. Full of artefacts and insights, the museum offers an excellent overview of London's history from Neanderthal hunting ground to sprawling modern metropolis. The 'London before London' gallery turns the clock back to pre-history and introduces the people who lived in the Thames Valley from around 400,000BC to AD50. Exhibits such as a woolly rhino skull, found beneath Fleet Street, and flint handaxes, excavated off Piccadilly, certainly cast London's busy, built-up streets in a different light.

Things really hot up with the arrival of the Romans though and the displays succeed brilliantly in bringing *'Londinium'* to life with lots of archaeology and several reconstructed shops and interiors. The triclinium (or dining room) looks pretty luxurious even by today's standards, while a cookbook in the recreated 1st century kitchen includes tempting recipes for stuffed dormice and peacock rissoles. Modern foodies will be interested to learn that Roman London's cosmopolitan population were kindred spirits, with a taste for food and wine imported from the Mediterranean. A model of the civic centre in AD150 shows the ordered layout beloved of the Romans – no slouches when it came to architecture, they built London's first city wall, a section of which can be glimpsed from this section of the museum. With finds ranging from a skimpy leather bikini to beautifully carved heads from the Temple of Mithras, all aspects of Londinium life are here – from the nuts and bolts of transport and trade to the razzamatazz of Roman religion and entertainment.

Next up is the Medieval gallery, which spans the long and eventful period from the end of the Roman empire to Henry VIII's Reformation. London was a popular destination for successive waves of invaders – Saxons, Danes, Normans – and there's a great deal of weaponry on display, including some fearsome Viking hardware. On a

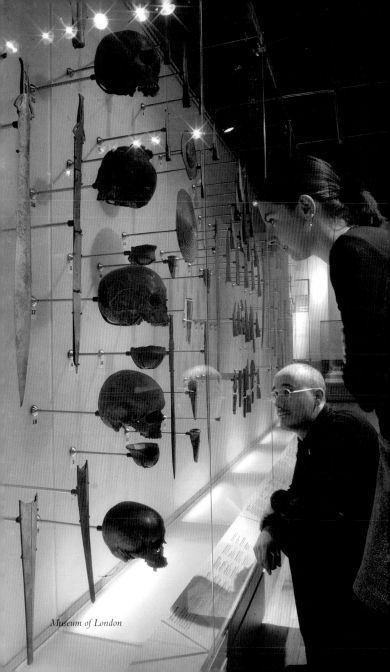

Museum of London

more domestic note, the reconstructed Saxon home looks the picture of cosiness with its glowing hearth and attractive thatched roof. Even London's geography was on the move during this period – Westminster used to be an island! But despite everything that history threw at it – famine, fire, plague and religious argy bargy – London always emerged bigger, better and stronger, becoming by the late 15th century 'the flower of cities all'. Displays are structured around key 'turning points' such as King Alfred's re-founding of London in AD886 and the Black Death in 1348 and feature more archaeological finds from old London town. Computer terminals reveal the lives of individual Londoners– such as tragic 7 year old John le Stolere, who was crushed to death by a cart. It's not all gloom and doom though – despite the sleaze, the medieval period had its own glamour, with plenty of luxury imported goods, fine dining and knights in shining armour. Medieval Londoners liked to look good too, if the displays of outlandish pointy-toed shoes and fancy head-dresses are anything to go by. The destruction of the Reformation brings this party to a close – mutilated statues, shattered glass and fragmented altar pieces illustrate the tangible results of Tudor intolerance.

At the time of going to press the Museum's lower galleries are in the throes of a £20.5m redevelopment. When they re-open in 2009 they will tell the story of London from 1666 to the 2012 Olympics (the museum's displays currently stop at 1666, with a child orientated exhibition about the Great Fire placed, annoyingly, between prehistoric and Roman London). 2009 will see the return of old favourites like the Lord Mayor's Coach, the graffitied 'Wellclose' prison cell and the Victorian walk, and there will be a showcase of the museum's art collection. A new theatre, e-learning centre, interactive exhibits and a 'coffee point' are also promised.

The Museum's shop carries a comprehensive range of books about London – from guidebooks and local history pamphlets to novels, as well as an extensive stock of general gift items and a more upmarket selection of jewellery and ceramics by London designers.

During the week this part of London – the corporate hub of the city – bristles with activity, but a weekend visit finds the area much quieter. The museum does have its own, fairly utilitarian, self-service café but the Barbican Centre and its facilities are but a short walk away if you fancy an alternative.

The Museum of Methodism

- *Wesley's Chapel & House, 49 City Road, EC1*
- *020 7253 2262*
- *www.wesleyschapel.org.uk*
- *Moorgate LU, Old Street LU, bus 43, 76, 141, 214, 271, 55*
- *Mon-Sat 10.00-16.00 (closed Thursdays between 12.45-13.30), Sun 12.30-14.00; last admission half an hour before closing*
- *Admission free (donations welcome)*
- *Shop*
- *Wheelchair access*

'Perfectly neat but not fine' was how John Wesley, the founder of Methodism, described the chapel he built in 1778, now known rather more grandly as the 'Cathedral of World Methodism'. The museum in the chapel's crypt tells the story of the Movement, with displays including original letters from John Wesley, his death mask and wooden pulpit, as well as a selection of Methodist paintings and commemorative pottery. Across the courtyard from the chapel lies Wesley's house, where he lived for the last 11 years of his life. Relics of the great man on display here include his travelling communion set, and an early electric shock machine, used by Wesley to treat cases of depression – including his own. A 'chamber horse' and 'cockfighting chair' are among the more unusual pieces of furniture in the house, while Wesley's bedroom features its own en-suite prayer room.

The Museum of the Order of St John

🏛 *St John's Gate, St John's Lane, EC1*

☎ *020 7324 4070*

🖳 *www.sja.org.uk*

🚃 *Farringdon LU/Rail*

🕐 *Mon-Fri 10.00-17.00, Sat 10.00-16.00 (guided tours Tues, Fri and Sat 11.00 and 14.30)*

💷 *Admission free (donations requested for tours)*

🛍 *Shop*

♿ *Wheelchair access (museum rooms and limited access elsewhere)*

A sturdy 16th-century gatehouse is the picturesque setting for this museum, which tells the story of the Order of St John from its foundation in the Crusades to its present day functions, including the St John's Ambulance. Warlike defender of the faith on one hand, merciful providers for the poor and sick on the other, the role of the original Order seems a tad contradictory. An exhibition on the history of the Order includes a rare chain mail outfit and coins minted by the crusaders, as well as colourful majolica pharmacy jars and a scale model of the Order's ophthalmic hospital in Jerusalem. Another display looks at the modern St John's Ambulance.

The guided tours take about an hour and are well worthwhile, giving access to the church and parts of the gatehouse not normally open to the public. As well as soaking up the archaic atmosphere, visitors can admire portraits of the Order's top brass, fine silverware and books. There are also some interesting pieces of Maltese furniture (a reminder of the Order's long association with the island), one particularly intricate cabinet contains 50 secret compartments. The gatehouse still boasts its original wooden spiral staircase and, a short distance away, the 12th-century crypt in the Order's church is home to a beautiful carved alabaster effigy of a Spanish knight. As St John's Gate is still very much the working home of the Order, visitors are strongly advised to telephone before a visit as Order business, such as investitures, require the building to be closed to the public. A major new development plan is scheduled to begin in the next few years. Heritage Lottery funding will enable, among other things, the introduction of a 'pavement museum' and a new exhibition space – but work is not expected to start until at least 2010.

The Museum of the Royal Pharmaceutical Society

⊡ *1 Lambeth High Street, SE1*

☏ *020 7572 2210*

⌨ *www.rpsgb.org/museum*

🚌 *Lambeth North LU, Vauxhall LU/Rail, Waterloo LU/Rail, Westminster LU*

🕐 *Mon-Fri 09.00-17.00; guided tours by appointment Tues 14.00 & 16.00*

💷 *Admission free*

🛍 *Shop*

♿ *Full Wheelchair access*

This specialist museum, based in the Society's headquarters, traces the long and fascinating history of medicinal drugs and their use. The collection is particularly strong on community and retail pharmacy from the 17th century onwards and among its treasures are 'Lambeth delftware' apothecary jars and glass carboys filled with brightly coloured liquid. The displays also include more sophisticated dispensary equipment such as pill-making paraphernalia, a tincture press, and devices for sugar-coating and even silver-coating pills. The first floor displays can only be viewed on a guided tour and include the Ernest Saville Peck bequest of bell metal mortars and 'Healing Science', a permanent exhibition telling the sometimes addictive story of the last 1,000 years of medicinal drugs. There are no catering facilities on-site but The Garden Museum (see p. 35)) is just over the road and has a good café.

The Old Operating Theatre Museum & Herb Garret

⊡ *9a, St Thomas' Street, SE1*

☏ *020 7188 2679*

⌨ *www.thegarret.org.uk*

🚌 *London Bridge LU/Rail*

🕐 *Daily 10.30-17.00*

💷 *£5.45 (adults), £4.45 (concessions), £3 (children), £13.25 (families)*

🛍 *Shop*

Located in the garret of St Thomas' Church, the Old Operating Theatre is perhaps London's most atmospheric museum, as well as one of its most inaccessible. A rickety wooden spiral staircase leads up to the displays, a precipitous climb unsuitable for those with restricted mobility but well worth the effort for those who can make it.

The operating theatre – the oldest in the country – is the centrepiece of the museum and a grisly remnant of pre-anaesthetic and antiseptic surgery. Built in 1822 the theatre was part of the adjoining St Thomas' Hospital but remained hidden for nearly 100 years when the hospital relocated to Lambeth, before being rediscovered in 1956.

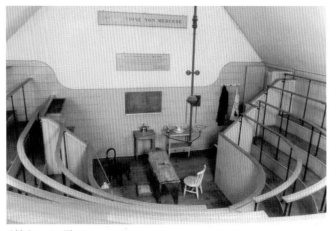

Old Operating Theatre

A semi-circular arena overlooked by raised tiers with leaning rails (from where medical students watched the bloody proceedings), it was not called a theatre for nothing – although the scarred wooden operating table looks better suited to the kitchen than the hospital. Nearby displays of surgical knives and saws, horsehair sutures and early anaesthetic equipment leave no doubt about the horrors of 19th-century surgery.

Festooned with dried herbs hanging from the wooden eaves, the adjacent Apocathary's Garret is only marginally less gruesome. Pickled human specimens are also displayed here, along with some worryingly indelicate medical instruments like amputation kits and obstetrics tools with off-putting names like 'blunt hook and crochet' and 'Smellie's perforator'. Standing as it does on the site of the original St Thomas' Hospital, the museum also has displays on medieval health care, and enterprising younger visitors can follow a 'Plague Trail' around the garret, choosing medicinal ingredients from the bowls of dried herbs liberally dotted around the garret. Contemporary artworks, scattered amongst the medicalia – created by the museum's artist in residence – are an unexpected bonus. The imaginatively stocked shop contains an eclectic range of medical books as well as amusingly macabre knick-knacks like memento mori memo pads and rubber internal organs.

Petrie Museum of Egyptian Archaeology
University College London

🏠 *Malet Place, WC1*

☎ *020 7679 2884*

🖥 *www.petrie.ucl.ac.uk*

🚌 *Euston LU/Rail, Euston Square LU, Goodge Street LU,*
Russell Square LU, Warren Street LU

🕐 *Tues-Fri 13.00-17.00, Sat 10.00-13.00*

♿ *Admission free*

✎ *Salespoint*

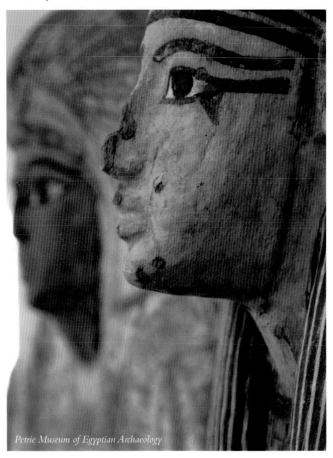

Petrie Museum of Egyptian Archaeology

Founded by the father of Egyptian archaeology, W M F Petrie, and voted one of London's Top Ten little-known museums, the Petrie is a treasure trove for Egyptophiles. With its huge collection of domestic artefacts dating from Pre-Dynastic times to the Roman era, it's the ideal place to get acquainted with the everyday life and death of ancient Egyptians and the cultural developments of one of the greatest civilizations ever known. Highlights of the collection include the world's earliest surviving dress (complete with original underarm perspiration stains), a pot burial and an exceptionally fine display of Roman mummy portraits. The well-stocked salespoint carries a good selection of Egyptology titles for both adults and children as well as jewellery, children's gifts, and other articles of Egyptiana. The collection is scheduled to be moving to a new site by 2011, so be sure to visit whilst the museum still retains its current spooky charm.

Pollock's Toy Museum

🏠 *1 Scala Street, W1T*
☎ *020 7636 3452*
🖉 *www.pollockstoytheatres.com*
🚌 *Goodge Street LU*
🕐 *Mon-Sat 10.00-17.00 (last admission 16.30)*
💰 *£3 (adults), £2 (students), £1.50 (children)*
🛍 *Shop*

With its quirky collections of toy theatres, toys, games and pastimes, this dinky museum is the perfect antidote to the increasingly slick and shiny museums of the 21st century. Two ramshackle old houses provide the setting, every available nook and cranny of which is packed with old toys; even the winding, brightly painted staircases double up as display areas, covering topics as diverse as board games, Penny Dreadfuls and war games like the short lived Falklands War Game. Many exhibits are at child height but there's plenty to enjoy for visitors of all ages – from puppets to puzzles, tin toys to Tyrolean carved animals, Victorian wax dolls to Action Man. Scattered throughout the museum are toys from around the world while Room 4 is home to group of grizzled veteran teddy bears and a collection of fine dolls houses. Named in honour of toy theatre-maker Benjamin Pollock, the museum displays a range of charming toy theatres – colourful paper and cardboard theatrical constructions which enabled children in Victorian times to 'stage' popular plays like *Aladdin* and *Cinderella* at home. Modern editions of these DIY paper theatres are available from the excellent ground floor shop, along with a nostalgic selection of good quality toys and puzzles and some brilliant old fashioned stocking filler type gifts.

Prince Henry's Room

🗔 *17 Fleet Street, EC4*
🖉 *www.cityoflondon.gov.uk*
🚌 *Temple LU*
🕐 *Mon-Sat 11.00-14.00*
♿ *Admission free*

Built in 1610 as an office for King James's eldest son, this funny little room has in its time been a tavern and a waxworks. It's worth a peek if only for the fine Jacobean plaster ceiling, wood panelling and quaint leaded light windows overlooking the bustle of Fleet Street. Prince Henry's Room is currently closed to the public – see website for further details.

The Rose Theatre Exhibition

🗔 *56 Park Street, SE1*
☎ *020 7261 9565*
🖉 *www.rosetheatre.org.uk*
🚌 *Cannon Street LU/Rail, London Bridge LU/Rail, Mansion House LU*
🕐 *Occasional open days, staged readings, and other events (see website for details). At other times the Rose can be visited by joining tours run by the nearby Globe Theatre (when matinee performances make tours of the Globe impossible, visitors are taken to the Rose), these can be booked via the Shakespeare's Globe Exhibition, tel. 020 7902 1500; exhibit@shakespeares-globe.com, or www.shakespeares-globe.org*
♿ *Wheelchair access*

The basement of an office block is perhaps not the first place you'd think of staging an exhibition. But this is an office block with a difference because it is built over the site of 'The Rose', Bankside's first purpose-built playhouse, where Shakespeare learnt his craft and for which Marlowe wrote his best plays. Tantalisingly, the theatre's remains are today buried for safekeeping, pending excavation, beneath layers of sand, concrete and water. In the meantime, underwater lighting reconstructs the exact position of the remains and visitors can enjoy a rousing audio-visual presentation, narrated by Sir Ian McKellen, star of the current Elizabethan stage, which relates the history of the theatre and its discovery in 1989.

Royal College of Physicians

🏠 *11 St Andrew's Place, NW1*
☎ *020 7935 1174*
🖱 *www.rcplondon.ac.uk/heritage*
🚇 *Great Portland Street LU, Warren Street LU*
🕐 *Mon-Fri 09.00-17.00*
💷 *Admission free (by appointment only)*
♿ *Wheelchair access*

museums
central

Founded by Henry VIII in 1518, the College is today housed in a Grade I listed icon of modern architecture by Sir Denys Lasdun. As the oldest medical college in Britain it's had plenty of time to build up its heavy weight library, archive and museum collections. The first book printed in the English language is one of the treasures of the library while the archive includes the personal and professional papers of physicians from the 16th century onwards. The museum meanwhile gives wallspace to some fine portraits of notable physicians past and present – from paintings of Sir Hans Sloane and John Radcliffe to a sculpture of Sir Raymond Hoffenberg by Dame Elisabeth Frink. Other highlights include the Symon's Collection of medical instruments, William Harvey's demonstration rod, the College silver-gilt mace (following the same design as the Commonwealth mace in the House of Commons) and six 17th-century anatomical tables fashioned from preserved human blood vessels and nerves.

Royal Fusiliers Museum

🏠 *HM Tower of London, EC3*
☎ *020 7480 6082*
🚇 *Tower Hill LU*
🕐 *Daily 9.30-17.15*
💷 *£1 (in addition to entrance fee to HM Tower of London)*
🛍 *Shop*

Having just paid a hefty entrance fee to get into the Tower, visitors may baulk at having to shell out extra to look around this small regimental museum. However, for your £1 you get a coherent, concise account of the Fusiliers' history from 1685 right up to the ongoing military operations in the Middle East. Artefacts range from the innocuous (regimental egg cups) to the deadly (some of the shot and shell fired over 'No Man's Land' in World War I). The museum has recently acquired another Victoria Cross – bringing their total of VCs to twelve.

St Bartholomew's Hospital Museum & Archive

⌑ *St Bartholomew's Hospital, West Smithfield, EC1*

☎ *020 7601 8152*

✐ *www.bartsandthelondon.nhs.uk/museums*

🚇 *Barbican LU, Blackfriars LU/Rail, Farringdon LU/Rail, St Paul's LU*

🕐 *Tues-Fri 10.00-16.00*

⊛ *Admission free*

✎ *Small shop*

♿ *Wheelchair access (by arrangement)*

Founded in 1123, St Bart's is what you might call well-established. Its small museum can be reached via the Henry VIII Gate and explores the hospital's antiquity with displays relating to the work of medical people of earlier times – the apothecary, the physician and the surgeon. A short introductory video tells the story of Rahere, the courtier turned monk who founded the hospital and church at 'Smoothfield' (today's Smithfield). Old documents on show include a hospital inventory of 1546, while early syringes, an 18th-century 'lunatic restrainer', a grisly Victorian amputation set, and a wooden head for practice trepanning are among the gory surgical items. Bart's pre-eminence is reflected in its personnel over the years – it was at St Barts that William Harvey discovered the circulation of blood in the 17th century and exhibits include a lancet belonging to surgeon John Hunter (see also The Hunterian Museum p. 42). Visitors can also glimpse two uncharacteristically grandiose paintings by William Hogarth on the Grand Staircase.

St Bride's Crypt

⌑ *St Bride's Church, Fleet Street, EC4*

☎ *020 7427 0133*

✐ *www.stbrides.com*

🚇 *Blackfriars LU/Rail*

🕐 *Daily 09.00-17.00 (ring to check first as crypt is sometimes closed for Church events)*

⊛ *Admission free*

From the top of its wedding cake spire to the depths of its crypt, St Bride's is steeped in history. Samuel Pepys was christened here, and it was here too that novelist Samuel Richardson was buried. Badly bombed in World War II, Christopher Wren's church (the eighth on the site) was restored to its former glory – but not before excavations revealed the site's previously unknown Roman origins. Some of these and later archaeological finds are displayed in the small museum in the crypt: clay pots and pipes, coins and fire-distorted fragments of the old church's bells. St Bride's was the site of the City's first printing press and although the newspaper offices have moved downriver, it remains the parish church for the industry known collectively as 'Fleet Street'. The crypt museum explores the church's connections with the print trade – from Caxton to the demise of 'Ink Street'.

Shakespeare's Globe Exhibition

🖾 *21 New Globe Walk, SE1*

☎ *020 7902 1400*

✐ *www.shakespeares-globe.org*

🚇 *Cannon Street LU/Rail, London Bridge LU/Rail, Mansion House LU, Southwark LU, Blackfriars LU/Rail*

🕓 *Daily 09.00-12.00 (May-Sept), 10.00-17.00 (Oct-April)*

🎟 *£9 (adults), £7.50 (students/seniors), £6.50 (under 15s), £20 (family)*

🛍 *Shop*

🍽 *Café & Restaurant*

♿ *Wheelchair access*

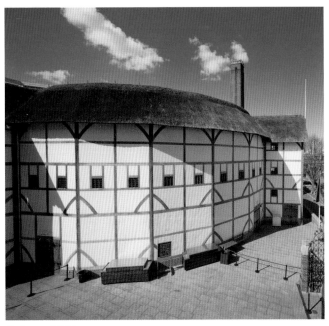

Shakespeare's Globe

A decade on since its opening season in 1997, it still comes as a bit of a jolt to see this perfectly reconstructed Elizabethan theatre in the middle of 21st-century Bankside. The first Globe Theatre burned down in 1613, the second was pulled down in 1644 and this phoenix-like reconstruction, yards from the original site, was the brainchild of American actor Sam Wanamaker who came to England in the 1940's expecting to see the theatre still standing. After nearly half a century of campaigning, the new Globe is testament to Wanamaker's vision and now every summer an international company of actors takes to the boards to perform Shakespeare's plays in the kind of theatre for which they were written. Attending a performance here is a magical theatre-going experience but if you really want to brush up your Shakespeare, then a visit to the permanent exhibition in the 'UnderGlobe' is a must.

The recently revamped exhibition offers a lively exploration of Elizabethan theatre: its architecture, actors and audience. Bravely, the displays tackle head-on the oft-debated question of 'Who was Shakespeare?' and take a good look at the days when Bankside entertainment really was down and dirty – a heady cocktail of bear baiting, drinking dens, brothels and, of course, theatres. Dressing up is such a central part of play-acting and costumes from past productions at the Globe are displayed on mannequins as well as in production photographs. Visitors can hear a designer discuss some of the problems creating period clothing in the 21st century and learn how actors cared for their costumes (a valuable asset) in an age when urine was the stain remover of the day. Another display turns the spotlight on music at the Globe and features early instruments such as the tenor sackbut (a precursor of the modern trombone) and the crumhorn. Touch a screen to have a go playing one – and touch again to hear how they sound in the hands of a professional musician. Other nifty computer animations demonstrate Elizabethan special effects such as flying, trick tables and the 'thunder run'. Would-be thespians are invited to 'Join the Cast' and make a sound recording of a scene from Shakespeare while, thanks to the National Sound Archive, visitors can listen to a host of different actors playing Shakespeare – among the mellifluous voices are those of Alec Guinness, Richard Burton and Judi Dench.

A guided tour of the Globe Theatre itself is included in the price of an entrance ticket – tours run every half an hour for individuals (groups must be booked in advance). Visitors during the theatre season (May-Sept) may be able to see the 'Wooden O' in action during rehearsals. Morning coffee, light lunches and afternoon teas are available year round in the Globe Café, while the restaurant offers à la carte, pre- and post-theatre menus. Both eateries enjoy panoramic views over the River.

The Sherlock Holmes Museum

- *221b Baker Street, NW1*
- *020 7935 8866*
- *www.sherlock-holmes.co.uk*
- *Baker Street LU*
- *Daily 09.30-18.00*
- *£6 (adults), £4 (under 16s), free (under 7s)*
- *Shop*

A museum dedicated to a fictional character does seem to stretch the definition of what a museum is and what its purpose should be. This one aims to show visitors exactly how the great detective and his sidekick Watson would have lived in their 19th-century lodgings – although as far as I recall the intrepid duo made do without a souvenir shop.

Smythson

- *40 New Bond Street, W1*
- *020 7629 8558*
- *www.smythson.com*
- *Bond Street LU*
- *Mon-Tues, Wed and Fri 09.30-18.00; Thurs and Sat 10.00-18.00*
- *Admission free*
- *Wheelchair access*

Frank Smythson Limited has been catering for the smart set's stationery needs since 1887 and for many this Mayfair emporium is still the last word in leather-bound luxury and pukka paper. Items from the company's archive are displayed in the small museum at the back of the shop: monogrammed paper, photograph albums, engraved wedding invitations and calling cards, individualised seals and luscious leather samples reflecting the tastes of clients who included maharajahs and royals. Even the shell-encrusted grotto which houses the display is impeccably well-connected, having been designed by the architect who remodelled Downing Street.

Sir John Soane's Museum

⌂ *13 Lincoln's Inn Fields, WC2*

☎ *020 7405 2107*

✎ *www.soane.org*

🚇 *Holborn LU*

🕐 *Tues-Sat 10.00-17.00, Candlelit openings are held on first Tuesday of every month 18.00-21.00*

💲 *Admission free*

🛍 *Shop*

Sir John Soane was the most original architect of his day. Luckily for us, his house was established as a museum during his lifetime and today remains much as it did when he died – a wonderfully dotty creation. The labyrinth of rooms, each one more fantastical than the last, is a testament to Soane's vision. Clearly he was a stranger to today's mania for minimalism – every available nook is home to some treasure or other. When they're not made of stained glass or smothered with mirrors, walls are encrusted with fragments of antique marble statuary. The Dome & Colonnade features larger works like a cast of the *Apollo Belvedere* – an iconic work despite the strategically placed fig leaf – and a bust of Soane himself looking uncannily like Julius Caesar.

Ingenious hinged-screen walls in the Picture Room allow over 100 paintings to be displayed in what is a modest space – amongst them Hogarth's biting political satire *The Election* and his scathing look at contemporary morals, *The Rake's Progress*. Gothic morbidity is the order of the day in the basement, which comes complete with a skeleton in the closet, a monk's cell, Pharaonic sarcophagus and a hoard of Roman cinerary urns. After all these excesses, the upstairs Drawing Room seems the model of good taste.

A guided lecture tour takes place every Saturday at 11.00 to bring order to the apparent chaos. Tickets cost £5 and are on sale from 10.30; they are limited, so arrive early to ensure a place.

Even a much loved institution such as the Soane is not immune from change; completion of new education and research facilities at No 14 in 2008 are the first steps in a project to restore the upper floors of no. 13 and to reinstate Soaneian arrangements throughout the original museum. The development process will be ongoing over the next few years.

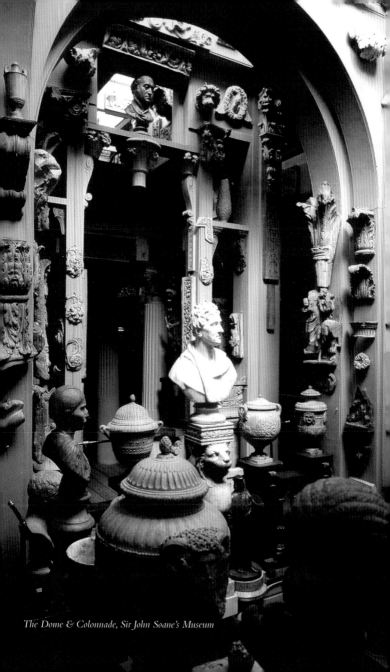

The Dome & Colonnade, Sir John Soane's Museum

Spencer House

📇 27 St James's Place, SW1

📞 020 7499 8620

🖰 www.spencerhouse.co.uk

🚌 Green Park LU

🕐 Sun 10.30-17.50 (except January & August), last tour 16.45
   (tours last approx 1 hour)

💷 £9 (adults), £7 (concessions)

♿ Wheelchair access

This private palace was originally built for the 1st Earl Spencer, an 18th-century ancestor of Diana, Princess of Wales. Thanks to a 10-year restoration programme, the building has regained its opulent neoclassical appearance. Its swanky State Rooms include the Palm Room – a positive jungle of gilded fronds and foliage – and the Painted Room, designed by James 'Athenian' Stuart and now reunited at last with the furniture he designed for it. Paintings on loan from the Royal Collection are among the art works on display. Access is by guided tour only and children under 10 years old are not admitted. The gardens are open on specific days between spring and summer each year.

The Tower Bridge Exhibition

📇 Tower Bridge, SE1

📞 020 7940 3985 (recorded information)

🖰 www.towerbridge.org.uk

🚌 London Bridge LU/Rail, Tower Hill LU

🕐 Daily 10.00-18.30 (April-Sept), 09.30-18.00 (Oct-Mar);
   last admission one hour before closing

💷 £6 (adults), £4.50 (OAPs and students), £3 (children)

🛍 Shop

♿ Wheelchair access

A triumph of Victorian civil engineering, Tower Bridge is one of London's most instantly recognisable landmarks. For those not content with admiring from a distance, a walk around the bridge's innards should be just the thing. Introductory videos and display boards tell the story of this once controversial structure and the technological achievement of its construction. Taking in both North and South Towers, the exhibition also provides access to the two glassed-in walkways which link them offering spectacular views up and down river.

Down in the Engine Rooms are two of the massive steam engine pumps that once powered the famous drawbridge. If it's 3-D souvenirs you're after, impressively small models of the bridge are under a fiver from the giftshop.

The Tower of London

⌖ *Tower Hill, EC3*

☎ *0870 756 6060 (information line) / 0870 756 7070 (advance tickets)*

🖰 *www.hrp.org.uk*

🚇 *Tower Hill LU, Tower Gateway DLR*

🕓 *Tues-Sat 09.00-17.30, Sun-Mon 10.00-17.30*

💷 *£16.50 (adults), £14 (concs), £9.50 (under 16s), £46 (families)*

🛍 *Shops*

☕ *Cafés & Restaurant*

♿ *Partial wheelchair access*

London's tourist trail wouldn't be complete without the Tower. Rich in tradition, history and the special brand of arcane ceremony that Britain does so well, the Tower attracts some 2 million visitors a year, despite the hefty entrance price. The traditional guardians of the Tower, the Beefeaters (or Yeoman Warders as they prefer to be known), double up as guides and lead regular free tours and talks, giving plenty of coverage to the bloodier goings on. For those going it alone, the buildings are well labelled and free maps are available; alternatively an audio tour, 'Prisoners of the Tower' can be hired for an extra charge. Visitors with small children should note that access to many of the towers is via narrow, spiral staircases and prams and pushchairs must be left outside buildings.

Built as a palace by William the Conqueror, the Tower has fulfilled many functions and in its time has also served as a royal arsenal, menagerie, mint and jewel house. It is though, perhaps best known as a royal prison, and several of its walls still bear the inscriptions carved by 'guests' – the astrological clock engraved in the Salt Tower by suspected sorcerer Hugh Draper is a notably elaborate variation on the 'I woz 'ere' school of graffiti. Sir Walter Raleigh's cosy apartments can be seen over in the Bloody Tower – 13 years a prisoner, Sir Walter made himself very much at home and even grew his own tobacco. The scaffold site on Tower Green – where two of King Henry VIII's wives got the chop – is commemorated with a plaque.

Although the Royal Menagerie moved to Regent's Park in 1835, the Tower's famous ravens are still in residence – tradition has it that if they leave the White Tower will fall and disaster overtake the kingdom. Part of William's original fortress, the White Tower is the oldest medieval building in the whole complex. It now contains a selection of arms and armour from the Royal Armouries. Among the suits of armour is a foot combat suit made for Henry VIII in 1540 and a boy's armour possibly made for his son Edward VI. There are also impressive displays of massed weaponry, unusual combination weapons like the deceptively-titled 'Holy Water Sprinkler' and experimental contraptions such as a 19th-

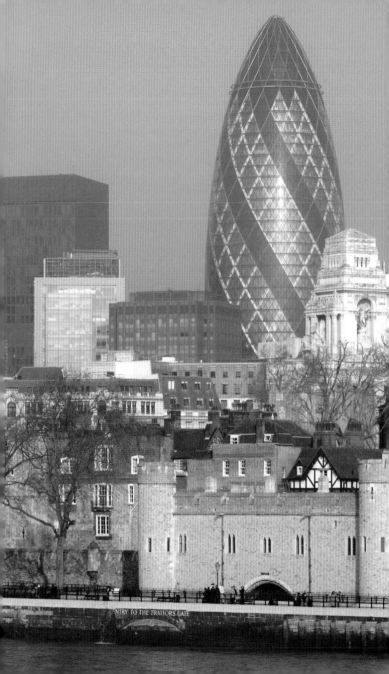
ENTRY TO THE TRAITORS GATE

century steam operated gun. An extra-long jousting lance designed to shatter on impact with its target is a rare survivor (its presence here leading one to suppose its owner wasn't too successful).

Metalwork of a different kind can be admired in the Jewel House where the coronation regalia of British monarchs makes for a dazzling display. The phrase conspicuous consumption could have been invented for the Crown Jewels: the Cullinan diamond in the Sovereign's Sceptre may not be as big as the Ritz but it isn't far off and is, in any case, the world's largest top-quality cut diamond. Another hefty sparkler – the fabled Kor-i-Noor diamond – is the jewel in the late Queen Mum's crown, while older regalia includes the St Edward's Crown and the 12th-century Coronation spoon. For those not thoroughly versed in Royal ceremonials, footage of the coronation in 1953 introduces the displays, but if you're still none the wiser there's a fully illustrated guide book.

Stout as they are, the Tower's fortifications have proved no defence against naked 21st century commercialism and with no less than five souvenir shops, cafés, and its own on-site currency exchange, retail opportunities are never very far away.

UCL Art Collections

🖾 *Strang Print Room, South Cloister, Main Building, University College London, Gower Street, WC1*

☎ *020 7679 2540*

🖰 *www.ucl.ac.uk/museums*

🚌 *Euston LU/Rail, Euston Square LU, Goodge Street LU, Warren Street LU*

🕐 *Mon-Fri 13.00-17.00*

♨ *Admission free*

♿ *Wheelchair access*

The UCL Art Collections comprise over 600 hundred paintings, 7,000 prints and drawings and some 150 sculptures. The Print Room itself is home to works by Old Masters such as Dürer, Cranach and Rembrandt and each term hosts a new exhibition of works drawn from the UCL collections. 'The French Revolution in Print' and '16th-century Vanitas images' are examples of recent shows here. The permanent collections are open by appointment and include the Slade collection, which traces the development of art education in England and includes early works by Stanley Spencer and Augustus John as well as 20th-century drawings by professors and students at the Slade School. UCL also houses the Flaxman Collection, the largest single group of works by the neo-classical sculptor John Flaxman. Forty of his full scale plaster models (mostly relief plaques) are displayed in the Flaxman Gallery along with the study for Flaxman's magnificent sculpture *St Michael Overcoming Satan*.

University College Geology Collections

⌨ *Department of Earth Sciences, UCL, Gower Street, WC1E*

☎ *020 7679 7900*

🖃 *www.ucl.ac.uk/museums/geology/*

🚌 *Euston LU/Rail, Euston Square LU, Goodge Street LU,*
Warren Street LU

🕐 *Wed lunchtimes and other times by appointment*

💷 *Admission free*

♿ *Wheelchair access*

This collection contains 40,000 geological specimens from all over the world – from fossils to meteorites and minerals. A new display, 'Infinite Possibilities', is open to the public in the aptly named Rock Room (Room 4, First Floor, South Wing). The Regional Planetary Image Facility (www.earthsci.ucl.ac.uk/research/planetaryweb) contains data from almost all of the NASA planetary missions since the 1960s, covering all the planetary bodies in the solar system which have been surveyed to date by spacecraft. This and other specialist collections may be viewed by appointment.

Wellcome Collection

⌨ *183 Euston Road, NW1*

☎ *020 7611 2222 / 020 7611 7211 (recorded information)*

🖃 *www.wellcomecollection.org*

🚌 *Euston LU/Rail, Euston Square LU, Warren Street LU,*
King's Cross LU/Rail

🕐 *Mon closed, Tues 10.00-18.00 (Library until 20.00),*
Wed & Fri 10.00-18.00, Thurs 10.00-22.00 (Library until 20.00),
Sat 10.00-18.00 (Library until 16.00), Sun 11.00-18.00 (Library closed)

💷 *Admission free*

📖 *Bookshop*

🖥 *Café*

♿ *Wheelchair access*

A hefty £30 million has been lavished on this new medical museum, which opened in June 2007 – and it shows. The previously drab entrance to the Wellcome Library on Euston Road has been transformed into a light and welcoming foyer, complete with an open plan Blackwells Bookshop and a funky café run by acclaimed bakers Peyton & Byrne. Some visitors may not in fact get beyond this point, for those that do, there's a treat in store with three sleekly designed gallery spaces exploring the nature and history of medicine.

The Medicine Man gallery introduces the visitor to the Henry Wellcome – an extraordinary character whose entrepreneurial flair

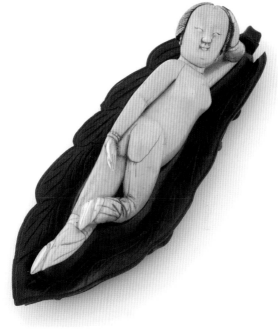

Late 19th Century Chinese ivory diagnostic doll used by female patients to indicate where their symptoms were

took him from humble American log cabin origins to millionaire pharmaceutical business giant and philanthropist. Along the way Wellcome also found time to run major archaeological digs, pioneer aerial photography and amass a 1 million strong collection of medical and cultural artefacts, 500 of which are displayed here. The offbeat cross-section of material takes in everything from serried ranks of amputation saws to 18th-century nipple shields, from Napoleon's toothbrush to a Peruvian mummy and it's hard not to conclude that Henry Wellcome must have had terrific fun amassing this stuff. Although the apparently random material is tamed into a dozen or so categories such as 'Beginning of Life', 'Understanding the Body', 'Votive Offerings' and 'Masks', there's still a cabinet of curiosity feel about the gallery which is entirely in keeping with the ethos of the collection. There's typically macabre medical humour here too – a dentist's chair and a birthing chair are displayed alongside a torture chair made from razor sharp blades, hinting darkly at the affinity between healthcare and torture. Detailed information about the exhibits are discretely tucked away behind doors set into the wooden wall panelling or in pull out drawers – a stylish and intelligent touch that lets these extraordinary objects speak for themselves first.

The adjoining Medicine Now gallery looks at science and medicine since Wellcome's death in 1936, concentrating on the key topics of obesity, genomes, malaria and the body. The exhibits here are no less fascinating, whether the bacterial colony used by Picker in the Human Genome Project, a plastinated body slice or a larger than life wax model of a malarial mosquito. Ethical dilemmas generated by scientific advances such as the de-coding of human DNA are tackled head on while a selection of contemporary art works offer a different take on the issues under debate. On the ground floor a third gallery houses a programme of challenging temporary exhibitions – tackling subjects such as 'Sleeping and Dreaming' from different scientific, social and cultural perspectives.

Wellington Arch

📖 *Hyde Park Corner W1*

☎ *020 7930 2726*

🖰 *www.english-heritage.org.uk*

🚇 *Hyde Park Corner LU*

🕐 *Wed-Sun and Bank Hols 10.00-17.00 (April-Oct),
Wed-Sun 10.00-16.00 (Nov-Mar)*

💷 *Adult £3.30 (adults), £2.60 (concs), £1.70 (children), free (English
Heritage members)*

🛍 *Shop*

♿ *Wheelchair access*

Originally conceived as an entrance to Buckingham Palace, this latter-day triumphal arch is one of London's most distinctive landmarks. Set in the midst of the busy roundabout that is Hyde Park Corner and topped by the vast bronze sculpture *Peace Descending on the Chariot of War*, the arch has been the subject of a major restoration by English Heritage and is now open to the public. Visitors can admire the vistas across Hyde Park, Green Park and Piccadilly from the viewing platforms as well as witnessing British ceremonial in action with the twice daily passage of the Horse Guards beneath the arch itself. Inside, away from the incessant roar of traffic, there is a brief exhibition about the, sometimes controversial, history of the arch together with a display about Blue Plaques in the capital. On the ground floor the shop sells a small selection of souvenirs, books and hot and cold drinks.

Westminster Abbey Museum

⌖ *Westminster Abbey, SW1*

☎ *020 7654 4831*

✎ *www.westminster-abbey.org*

🚇 *St James's Park LU, Westminster LU*

🕐 *Daily 10.30-16.00 (may be closed at short notice for state or other special events); Chapter House and Pyx Chamber daily 10.30-16.00*

💰 *Included in Abbey admission fee (see website for details)*

Compared to the hubbub of the Abbey, this museum (located in an 11th-century vaulted undercroft) is a haven of tranquillity. Its collection of royal and other funeral effigies is certainly bizarre enough to reduce even the most garrulous tourist to silence. Compelling viewing, the macabre wood and wax images, mostly dressed in original clothing, include those of Edward III, Henry VII, Elizabeth I and Charles II (in his Garter robes). Lord Nelson's effigy joins this royal company and was much admired by his contemporaries (although Nelson himself was buried in St Paul's Cathedral, see p. 25). Other items on display include a Roman sarcophagus and replicas of the Coronation Regalia used for coronation rehearsals (the real thing can be seen at the Tower of London, p. 75). The admission price also includes entry to the historic Pyx Chamber and the medieval Chapter House, which has some fine wall-paintings, an original floor of 13th-century glazed tiles and England's oldest door.

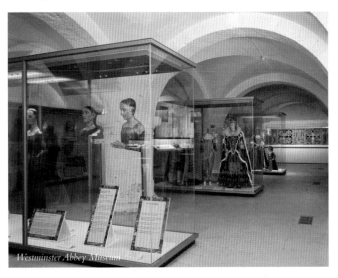

Westminster Abbey Museum

North

Arsenal Football Club Museum

🖼 *Emirates Stadium, Northern Triangle Building, Drayton Park, N5*

☎ *020 7704 4504 (stadium tours bookings)*

🖱 *www.arsenal.com*

🚇 *Arsenal LU*

🕐 *Mon-Fr 10.00-18.00, Sat 11-18.00, Sun 10-17.00 (matchdays 10.00 until 1/2 hour before kick off)*

💷 *£6 (adults), £3 (children/OAPs/students), free (under 5s)*

🛍 *Shop*

♿ *Wheelchair access*

If you're an Arsenal fan you've probably already visited the Club's swish new Emirates Stadium (opened 2006) and perhaps looked around the in-house museum, but for newcomers it's as good a place as any to be initiated into the wonderful world of Arsenal. The museum recounts the club's eventful history from its impoverished beginnings at the Royal Ordnance workshops in Woolwich to First Division glory days under Herbert Chapman's visionary management, to more recent triumphs like the Club's 'Double' win in 2001/2 and their 'invincible' 2003/04 season.

Divided, like the game itself, into two halves, the displays celebrate legendary players such as Bob Wilson, Pat Rice, and 'old baggy shorts' Alex James as well the ethos and traditions of the club. There's a whole section devoted to the club's recent move from Highbury and copious footage of goal scoring as well as a series of fun interactive quizzes to test visitors on Arsenal trivia. Club memorabilia aplenty should keep Arsenal addicts of all ages happy – there are photographs, autographed match strips and trophies galore – but (for the complete novice at any rate) the museum's lively displays offer an invaluable insight into football in general. Stadium tours also incorporate a visit to the museum but must be booked in advance.

Brent Museum

🖳 *Willesden Green Library Centre,*
   95 High Road, Willesden Green, NW10
☎ *020 8937 3600*
🖎 *www.brent.gov.uk/museum*
🚌 *Willesden Green LU*
🕒 *Mon 11.00-18.00, Tues & Thurs 09.00-20.00, Wed & Fri 09.00-18.00,*
   Sun 11.00-18.00
🏛 *Admission free*
♿ *Wheelchair Access*

This museum – newly opened in 2006 – is firmly rooted in its local community, one of the most multi-cultural in London. As if to prove the point a bust of Marcus Garvey, the founder of the pan African nationalism greets visitors as they arrive (he's buried in nearby Kensal Green Cemetary). The permanent displays tell the story of the borough from its pre-historic days submerged beneath a tropical sea to the present day, and include images of Brent past and present, a display about the evolution of shopping and industry in the district and a collection of Victorian household bits and bobs. Temporary exhibitions have included an interactive science exhibition about optics but also tap into the area's multiculturalism with community and inter-museum projects such as the recent 'Caribbean Currents'.

Bruce Castle Museum

🖳 *Lordship Lane, N17*
☎ *020 8808 8772*
🖎 *www.haringey.gov.uk*
🚌 *Wood Green LU, then 243 bus*
🕒 *Wed-Sun 13.00-17.00 (and Summer Bank Holidays)*
🏛 *Admission free*
🛍 *Shop*
♿ *Wheelchair access*

Although 'castle' is rather too generous a soubriquet, this historic building is one of only two Grade I listed buildings in Haringey. Once the manor house of Tottenham, Bruce Castle is now home to the Haringey borough archive. Illustrating Haringey's evolution from rural idyll to sprawling suburb, the displays include Roman pottery as well as material relating to World War II. Postal history is the subject of a small display, reflecting the fact that Sir Rowland Hill, founder of the Penny Post, once lived at Bruce Castle. Early postmen's uniforms and letter-writing paraphernalia help illustrate the origins of the postal service. The museum also hosts changing exhibitions.

Church Farmhouse Museum

- ⌖ *Greyhound Hill, Hendon, NW4*
- ☎ *020 8359 3942*
- ⌨ *www.churchfarmhousemuseum.co.uk*
- 🚇 *Hendon Central LU*
- 🕐 *Mon-Thurs 10.00-17.00 (closed 13.00-14.00),*
  Sat 10.00-17.30 (closed 13.00-14.00), Sun 14.00-17.30
- 🎟 *Admission free*
- 🛍 *Shop*

Ten minutes walk and a world away from the teeming traffic of downtown Hendon, Church Farmhouse is a picturesque property dating from the reign of Charles II. Once the centre of a busy dairy and hay-making enterprise, the farmhouse escaped post-war demolition by becoming Hendon's local history museum. A trio of cosy reconstructed Victorian rooms – a laundry, kitchen and dining room – are at the centre of the displays and the house itself retains the quirks of an historic building: low beamed ceilings, wonky wooden floors and narrow stairs. The museum has two spaces for temporary exhibitions with past topics including the Festival of Britain and Troika pottery. Outside the charm continues in the garden which features not only a dew pond and a well but also a brick maze, installed in 2006. Eat your heart out Hampton Court.

Fenton House

- ⌖ *Hampstead Grove, NW3*
- ☎ *020 7435 3471*
  01494 755563 (recorded information)
- ⌨ *www.nationaltrust.org.uk*
- 🚇 *Hampstead LU, Hampstead Heath Rail*
- 🕐 *Sat-Sun 14.00-17.00 (March); Sat, Sun and Bank Holidays*
  11.00-17.00 (April-Oct); Wed, Thurs and Fri 14.00-17.00 (April-Oct);
- 🎟 *House and Garden £5.40 (adults), £2.70 (child), £13 (families),*
  free (National Trust members); joint ticket with Willow Road £7.30
  (adults); Garden only £1; Garden season ticket £5.50
- ♿ *Disabled access (ground floor only)*

Known primarily for its collection of early keyboard instruments, this National Trust property also contains an interesting array of furniture, textiles, art and 18th-century porcelain. Interior design students will be intrigued to learn that the house was 'done up' by renowned decorator John Fowler in 1973, and was one of his last commissions for the National Trust. The bold tangerine coloured decorative scheme by Fowler in the Dining Room forms a vivid backdrop to a group of

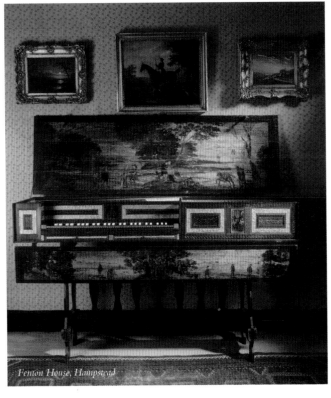

Fenton House, Hampstead

no less delectable paintings by Sir William Nicholson, newly loaned by the Bacon family. A recent bequest of 55 paintings, drawings and watercolours by the late actor Peter Barkworth are an additional draw; now on permanent display in the house they include paintings by the Camden Town School and 18th and 19th centuries watercolours by the likes of Constable, Cox and Collier.

A late 17th-century merchant's house, Fenton House has clung onto a number of original features and is still surrounded by a large walled garden, with orchard, making it a pleasant haven from Hampstead's bustling shops. Classical concerts are put on here throughout the year but if you're lucky you might hear a music student playing on one of the old spinets or harpsichords during your visit. A costume exhibition is held annually, usually in the summer, with costumes from period film & TV productions.

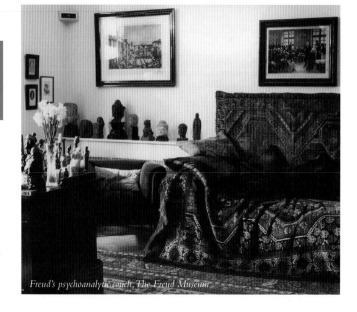

Freud's psychoanalytic couch, The Freud Museum

The Freud Museum

⌷ *20 Maresfield Gardens, NW3*

☎ *020 7435 2002*

✐ *www.freud.org.uk*

🚃 *Finchley Road LU*

🕒 *Wed-Sun 12.00-17.00*

💲 *£5 (adults), £3 (concessions), free (under 12s)*

🛍 *Shop*

♿ *Wheelchair access to ground floor, help available for access to first floor*

A refugee escaping Nazi oppression, Sigmund Freud made this house his final home. Freud's study – an almost exact recreation of the one he vacated at his apartment in Vienna – remains as it was during his lifetime. Festooned with oriental rugs and lined with books, this room in particular offers a remarkable slice of *fin de siècle* Vienna. The centrepiece of the museum, the study, is home to *that* couch as well as to the many Egyptian, Greek, Roman and oriental antiquities Freud loved to collect. Preserved by a long period of burial, these objects from the past are worth seeing in their own right – for the founder of psychoanalysis they constituted the perfect analogy to his own archaeology of the unconscious.

On the landing hangs Salvador Dali's haunting portrait of the face that launched a thousand slips and upstairs there's another couch – this one belonged to Freud's psychoanalyst daughter Anna, who lived at the house and whose pioneering work is also celebrated here. A video shows footage from the Freud family home movies and the shop is well stocked with titles covering the A-Z of psychoanalysis, along with gifts and jewellery inspired by Freudian theories.

Hampstead Museum

▯ *Burgh House, New End Square, NW3*
☎ *020 7431 0144*
✑ *www.burghhouse.org.uk*
🚌 *Hampstead LU*
🕐 *Wed-Fri 12.00-17.00, Sun 12.00-17.00, Saturdays by appointment only*
🕑 *Admission free*
👓 *Shop*
☕ *Café*

Just off Hampstead's busy, bijoux High Street, this recently refurbished local history museum is a useful first port of call for those doing the cultural pilgrimage bit around this part of London. Housed in a graceful Queen Anne building, the museum shows how Hampstead developed from Mesolithic hunting ground to 'small and lonesome village' to fashionable spa and affluent suburb. Hampstead has long since been a mecca for arty and literary types and exhibits at Burgh House include watercolours by Helen Allingham, Modernist furniture designed by Marcel Breuer and memorabilia from the High Hill Bookshop. The obligatory WWII display features evocative items such as a bed from the Belsize Park Deep Shelter while the wartime memories of Hampstead residents can be accessed via a Bakelite telephone. The small shop sells books, quality conserves and attractive studio pottery by Anthea Ryan. Down in the basement the excellent Buttery serves good home-cooked food.

Islington Museum

- 245 St John Street EC1V 4NB.
- 020 7527 2837 (gallery)
  020 7527 3235 (museum office)
- www.islington.gov.uk
- Angel LU then 19 bus
- Daily 10.00-17.00 (closed Wed and Sun)
- Admission free
- Shop
- Wheelchair access

This local history museum opened in its new premises in May 2008. Its permanent exhibition gallery explores the history of Islington from Tudor times through different themes, such as childhood, fashion, poverty, food and drink. The collections include a beautiful 1838 day dress and a silver cup from 1797 – presented to the man who set up the Islington Volunteers in the face of the invasion threat by Napoleon. Fascinatingly the collections also contain a bust of Lenin, originally erected in WWII by the then Communist run Islington Council. Lenin himself lived and worked in Islington in the early part of the 20th century, working on a revolutionary newspaper. Over the years the bust became something of a focus for political protestors and vandals – the curator's hoping that perhaps its new home at the museum will prove more tranquil. The temporary exhibition gallery will host a programme of changing exhibitions and will showcase art as well as covering historical subjects.

The Iveagh Bequest, Kenwood

- Hampstead Lane, NW3
- 020 8348 1286
- www.english-heritage.org.uk
- Archway LU, Golders Green LU (then 210 bus), Hampstead Heath Rail
- Daily 11.30-16.00
- Admission free
- Shop
- Café
- Wheelchair access (ground floor only)

With its serene neo-classical architecture, beautiful picture collection, landscaped gardens, extensive catering facilities and gift shop, Kenwood House is a favourite endpoint for many a Sunday afternoon walk on nearby Hampstead Heath.

Although its library is a good example of a lavishly-modelled interior by architect Robert Adam, Kenwood is not really one of those houses you visit for meticulously reconstructed period rooms. That said, the Music Room and Dining Room wings have both been refurbished, their décor providing an elegant and sympathetic backdrop to the real draw: The Iveagh Bequest. Gems in this world-class picture collection include Rembrandt's late, rather melancholy, self portrait and Vermeer's *Guitar Player*. Works by British artists are plentiful and feature fine pieces by the stalwarts of 18th-century portraiture: Gainsborough, Reynolds and Romney.

The Jewish Museum

- 🖃 *Raymond Burton House, 129-131 Albert Street, NW1*
- ☎ *020 8371 7373*
- ✎ *www.jewishmuseum.org.uk*
- 🚌 *Camden Town LU*
- ✺ *Shop*
- ☕ *Café*
- ♿ *Wheelchair access*

At the time of going to press the Jewish Museum is in the midst of a £9 million development programme. When it reopens in summer 2009 the museum will be greatly enhanced with larger exhibition galleries, hands-on children's displays, new education facilities, a shop and a café serving Jewish cuisine. The new museum will combine the collections and activities previously split between two sites (Camden and Finchley), featuring a history gallery telling the story of the Jewish people across the world and in particular the Jewish presence in England since 1066. The religion gallery will showcase the museum's outstanding collection of Jewish religious ceremonial items and explore Jewish ethics, values and religious festivals. Renowned for its work against racism, the museum's new Holocaust Education Gallery will focus around the poignant story of Leon Greenman, a London born holocaust survivor, anti-racist campaigner and much loved figure at the museum until his death in early 2008.

Contact details while the new museum is under construction are as follows: The Jewish Museum, 4 Shakespeare Road, London N3; telephone, same as above.

Keats House

⌦ Keats Grove, NW3
☏ 020 7435 2062
✍ www.cityoflondon.gov.uk/keats
🚌 Belsize Park LU, Hampstead LU, Hampstead Heath Rail

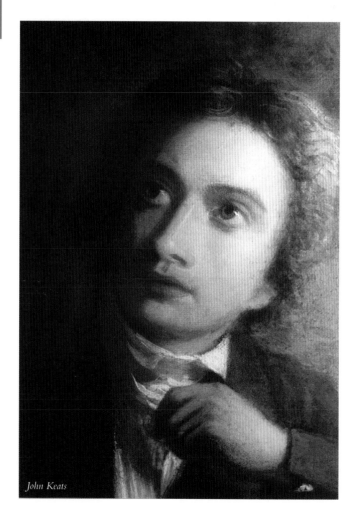

John Keats

Romantic poet par excellence, John Keats lived in this pretty Regency house from 1818-1820. Despite the onset of the TB which eventually killed him, Keats was at the height of his poetic powers during these years. It was here, sitting in the garden, that he penned his *Ode to a Nightingale* and here too that he met and fell in love with Fanny Brawne, the girl next door. They became engaged but their relationship was tragically brief – in 1820 the ailing Keats left Hampstead for Rome, where he died the following year aged just 25.

A Heritage Lottery funded refurbishment underway at the time of writing will restore the interior to 'authentic' Regency style and will enable more of the collection to be displayed. Exhibits will include paintings of Keats by Joseph Severn as well as the garnet engagement ring Keats gave to Fanny, which she wore for the rest of her life. The House – which has been closed on and off for refurbishment since 1999 – is scheduled to reopen in 2009 and visitors are advised to consult the website for details of opening hours and admission charges.

The London Canal Museum

📖 *12-13 New Wharf Road, N1*
☎ *020 7713 0836*
🖊 *www.canalmuseum.org.uk*
🚌 *King's Cross St Pancras LU/Rail*
🕐 *Tues-Sun and Bank Holidays 10.00-16.30 (last entry 15.45)*
💷 *£3 (adults), £2 (concessions), £1.50 (children); free (under 8s)*
🛍 *Shop*
♿ *Wheelchair access*

Overlooking the murky waters of Regent's Canal, the LCM celebrates the history of London's 'silent highway' from its heyday as a bustling trade route to its more recent role as a tourist trail. Visitors can experience at first hand the cramped conditions endured by canal folk in part of a restored narrowboat, admire the florid style of their decorative art and find out how canal locks work.

The building was once a Victorian ice house owned by ice-cream entrepreneur Carlo Gatti and a massive, still only partially excavated ice pit dominates the far end of the ground floor. Displays covering London's ice trade and the history of ice cream explain the pit's cavernous presence in this canalside warehouse, and upstairs in the former stables, visitors can sit back and enjoy a video trip along the canal. The shop is small but well-stocked with relevant, reasonably-priced souvenirs, including books about boats and canals and a range of colourful hand-painted canalware.

MCC Museum

Lord's Cricket Ground, St John's Wood Road, NW8 8QN

020 7616 8595

www.lords.org

St John's Wood LU

On match days entry to match spectators only; Tours of the ground (including museum) usually twice or three times daily throughout year (except major match days), see website or telephone for times

Tours £12 (adults), £7 (concessions), £6 (children aged 5-15), £31 (family)

Shop and tavern

Partial wheelchair access

Based at Lord's, the home of cricket, Marylebone Cricket Club's museum is a haven for those who love the sound of leather against willow. For those less familiar with the game, displays chart over 400 years of cricketing history. Unwieldy curved-edge bats and two-stump wickets (which often let the ball straight through) date from the days when sheep kept the pitch in trim – more recent clobber includes the pads, blazers, boots and caps of Sir Donald Bradman and Sir Jack Hobbs. Special exhibitions are mounted to mark particular anniversaries and honour visiting teams, and highlights of some of the game's great matches and performances are screened in the Brian Johnston Film Theatre. A stuffed sparrow commemorates one of the game's smaller casualties (clean bowled in 1936) but pride of place undoubtedly goes to the Ashes – a permanent fixture in the museum regardless of whether Australia or England win. More paintings and memorabilia are displayed in the Long Room, the MCC's inner sanctum. This atmospheric club room can usually be viewed by visitors on the tour. Cricket gear is stocked at the Lord's shop, along with a comprehensive selection of cricketing books and souvenirs ranging from floppy hats to pencil sharpeners. Refreshments are available at the Lord's Tavern, the ground's on-site pub.

Royal Air Force Museum

- Grahame Park Way, NW9
- 020 8205 2266
- www.rafmuseum.org.uk
- Colindale LU
- Daily 10.00-18.00 (last entry 17.30)
- Admission free
- Shop
- Café, restaurant and picnic areas
- Wheelchair access

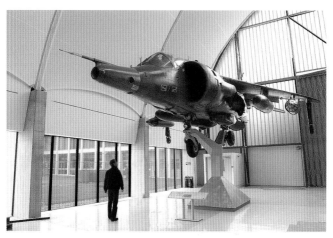

Set on 10 acres of what was once Hendon aerodrome, this is Britain's National Museum of Aviation. With over 100 historic aircraft from around the world on display, it's a plane-spotter's paradise as well as a must for those interested in 20th century history, and particularly the two world wars. The excellent Milestones of Flight exhibition was launched on 17 December 2003, the 100th anniversary of the first powered flight and makes a terrific opener to a visit. Its sleek barrel vaulted, stainless steel clad building houses a gleaming split level display of landmark flying machines from flimsy looking early pioneers like the Clarke Hang Glider of 1910 and Bleriot XI to muscular creations like the Harrier Jump Jet and a prototype Eurofighter Typhoon. Other beauties include an immaculately restored Fokker D.VII from 1917, resplendent in purple, green and black camouflage, a nippy Hawker Hart, a shiny silver American Mustang and that wooden wonder, the De Havilland Mosquito.

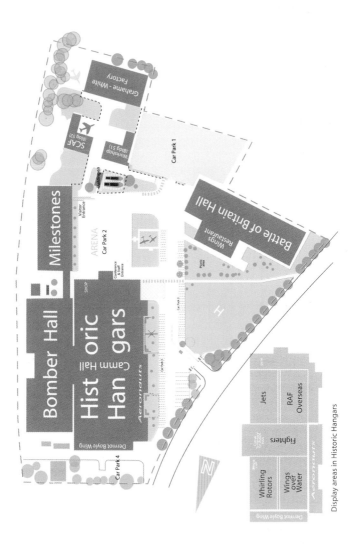

Grahame - White Factory

SCAF (Bldg 52)

Workshop (Bldg 51)

Car Park 1

Visitor Entrance

Milestones

ARENA
Car Park 2

Conference & Staff Entrance

Wings Restaurant

Battle of Britain Hall

Picnic Area

Bomber Hall

SHOP

Historic Hangars

Camm Hall

Dermot Boyle Wing

Aeronauts

Car Park 3

Car Park 4

H

N

Jets

RAF Overseas

Fighters

Whirling Rotors

Wings over Water

Dermot Boyle Wing

Aeronauts

Display areas in Historic Hangars

'Top Trumps' veterans will relish the technical specifications which can be accessed via the touchscreen computers dotted around, along with the history of each aircraft, its designers and pilots and film footage. On the ground floor level visitors can mingle with the machinery, and inspect the timeline wall with its year by year account of this century of aviation. Up in the Control Tower there's a rolling programme of short 3D aviation films and more interactives let would be air traffic controllers try their hand at managing the airways.

From 'Milestones' a covered walkway leads into Bomber Command Hall where gargantuan aircraft like the Wellington and the Lancaster make planes such as the Spitfire look like gnats. Prize for the spookiest exhibit goes to the ghostly, water-stained wreck of a Halifax bomber, dredged up from the Norwegian fjord where it had lain since the 1940s. The development of bombers and bombing is examined and a reconstruction of a bombed-out industrial plant offers a sobering reminder of the destructive capability of these giants of the air.

The museum's Historic Hangers, – so called because they are in fact two original WWI hangers, – showcase a wider variety of aircraft and are divided into Jets, the RAF Overseas, Fighters, Wings over Water and Whirling Rotors. This latter display includes the chalk and cheese of helicopters – a cumbersome looking Wessex Belvedere and a sprightly Gazelle. Air-sea rescue and maritime reconnaissance are covered in 'Wings over Water' – look out for 'A Very Gallant Gentleman', the carrier pigeon which saved a 'downed' WWI flying crew. Raised walkways allow a look inside the cockpits of planes like the inter-war Supermarine Southampton flying boat, the 'touch and try' Provost lets wannabe aviators loose on the controls of a modern jet trainer while there's a Flight Simulator for confirmed thrill-seekers. A Tornado F.3 fighter is due to be added to the line up soon.

'Aeronauts Interactive' is an extensive hands-on area with exhibits demonstrating the underlying principles of aviation such as thrust, drag, and airspeed. Aimed at younger visitors, the fun activities include pilots' aptitude tests, flying a hang-glider, and landing supplies accurately on a drop zone. Over in the Battle of Britain Hall, a sequence of tableaux explain the background to the outbreak of World War II and a sound and light show portrays the stirring story of the Battle of Britain and 'Our Finest Hour'. Many of the planes included in this hall are German models like the Junkers 88, and there's even an Italian Fiat plane. A fragment of Rudolph Hess's wrecked Messerschmitt and Herman Goering's decorations and awards are among the more unusual exhibits here. Tribute is paid to the 'Few' and the uniforms and medals of distinguished airmen are also displayed.

Amid all the hardware, the human element is never overlooked: throughout the museum are memorials and testaments to airmen and women from the Great War to the Gulf War. A quiet moment of contemplation can be sought in the prefab RAF chapel from the Falkland Islands or in front of medals won by WWI pilots. Other displays highlight the roles played by test pilots, ground staff, the WAAF, and that major contribution to air safety – the ejector seat.

Don't forget to leave time for another attraction, the Grahame-White Factory. This original aircraft factory building, dating from Hendon's early aviation days, has been restored and reconstructed at the Museum, where it makes an appropriate setting for some of the earliest aircraft in the collection. Expect to see WWI 'crates' such as the lovable Sopwith 'Pup', the Vickers FB5 and the Sopwith Triplane.

There's a lot to see but the Wings Restaurant and Wessex Café are on standby all day to banish the inevitable hunger pangs and for those bringing packed lunches, there are pleasant picnic areas inside and out. The museum shop has more Airfix models than you can shake a joystick at, and a wide range of aviation books and videos.

The Stephens Collection

🖼 *Avenue House, East End Road, N3*
☎ *020 8346 7812*
🖥 *www.london-northwest.com/sites/stephens*
🚇 *Finchley Central LU*
🕐 *Tues-Thurs 14.00-16.30*
💷 *Admission free*
♿ *Wheelchair access*

Dr Henry Stephens was the inventor of the famous 'Blue-Black Writing Fluid' and went on to become something big in ink. His son Henry Charles ('Inky') Stephens developed the family business and brought Avenue House in 1874, adding a laboratory and planting the rare trees which can be seen in the landscaped grounds today. Stephens Jnr left the house to the people of Finchley and it is now run as a charitable trust, with a room dedicated to the Stephens Collection on the ground floor. Displays are changed every 6 months or so and explore the history of writing materials and the Stephens Ink Company. Hands-on writing sessions can be arranged for groups of up to 15.

2 Willow Road

Willow Road, NW3

020 7435 6166 / 01494 755570 (recorded information)

www.nationaltrust.org.uk

Belsize Park LU, Hampstead LU, Hampstead Heath Rail

Thurs-Fri 12.00-17.00 (Mar-Oct), Sat 12.00-17.00 (March-Nov);
Entry by timed tour only 12.00, 13.00 & 14.00 (and 11.00 on Sat);
non-guided viewing 15.00-17.00 with timed entry when busy;

£5.10 (adults), £2.60 (child), £12.80 (family);
joint ticket with Fenton House £7.30; free (National Trust members)

Wheelchair access (ground floor only)

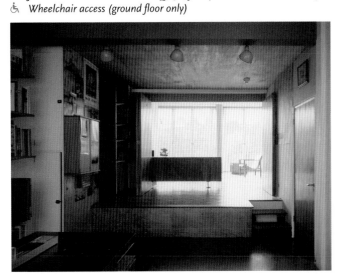

2 Willow Road, Hampstead

A Modern Movement interpretation of a terraced house, 2 Willow
Road is as about as far from the stereotype of a National Trust property
as it's possible to get. Set in leafy Hampstead, it was built by architect
Ernö Goldfinger in 1937 and remained his family home until 1994. The
stylish modernist aesthetic of the building is matched by its contents
– along with furniture and toys designed by Goldfinger are works of
art by Henry Moore, Bridget Riley, Max Ernst and Marcel Duchamp.
Goldfinger's uncompromising approach is not everyone's cup of tea –
his Trellick Tower in North Kensington remains controversial although
flats inside are still much sought after. An introductory video is shown
at regular intervals.

West

Carlyle's House

  24 Cheyne Row, SW3
  020 7352 7087
  www.nationaltrust.org.uk
  Sloane Square LU
  Wed, Thurs-Fri 14.00-17.00; Sat-Sun and Bank Holidays
  11.00-17.00 (April-Oct)
  £4.75 (adults), £2.40 (children), £11.90 (family), free (National
  Trust members)

This desirable Queen Anne residence was home to Victorian historian
Thomas Carlyle and his wife Jane. Although Carlyle's star waned in
the 20th century, he was a hugely influential writer in his day, and
visited by the likes of Tennyson, Dickens, George Eliot and Chopin
(who tinkled the ivories on Mrs Carlyle's piano). Today's visitors can
follow in their footsteps, soaking up the atmosphere of intimate rooms
which still contain their original furnishings, together with Carlyle's
books and personal effects such as the non-slip horseshoe he invented
for icy roads. All very cosy, but spare a thought for the Carlyles' maid
– who had to sleep on the bottom shelf of the dresser in the spartan
basement kitchen. The restored walled Victorian garden is also open
to visitors.

Centre for Performance History

  Royal College of Music, Prince Consort Road, SW7
  020 7591 4340
  020 7591 4842 (Museum of Instruments)
  www.rcm.ac.uk
  South Kensington LU
  Tues-Fri 14.00-16.30 (closed Christmas & Easter vacations)
  Admission free
  College cafeteria
  Wheelchair access to ground floor (by prior appointment)

The Centre brings together the RCM's museum of musical instruments
and their collection of portraits of musicians, the most comprehensive
in Great Britain. With examples dating from the 15th century
onwards, the musical instrument collection is weighted in favour of
European stringed, wind and keyboard instruments but does contain
some Asian and African examples. Exhibits range from rare early
creations like the clavicytherium right down to the humble recorder

as well as instruments touched by celebrity such as a spinet used by Handel and Haydn's clavichord. Lecture tours with live and recorded demonstrations are available and tours for groups can be made by appointment (at an extra charge).

The portrait collection is supplemented by extensive collections of general musical iconography (opera, concert hall and instrument design) and by an important history archive of more than 600,000 programmes.

The Chelsea Physic Garden

⌨ *66 Royal Hospital Road, SW3*
☎ *020 7352 5646*
🖉 *www.chelseaphysicgarden.co.uk*
🚌 *Sloane Square LU*
🕐 *Wed-Fri and Sun 12.00-17.00 (Wed until 22.00 July & August),*
   bank holidays 12.00-18.00, closed winter
💰 *£7 (adults including senior citizens), £4 (concessions)*
🛍 *Shop*
☕ *Café*
♿ *Wheelchair access*

Despite the roar of traffic from the neighbouring Chelsea Embankment, this formal historic walled garden is a magical place. Founded in 1673 as a botanic garden to promote the study of medicinal plants, the Physic Garden continues the same role today and is filled with therapeutic flora from around the world. Most specimens, from traditional medicinal plants like verbena to medicinal plants popular today such as evening primrose, are clearly labelled with their botanical classification and place of natural origin, as well as what ailments they treat. Enjoying a balmy micro-climate, the 3½ acre garden also cultivates rare and tender plants and is home to the largest outdoor fruiting olive tree in the country as well one of the earliest rock gardens in England. A profusion of benches line the scrunchy gravel paths offering an ideal place to while away a sunny summer afternoon in the city. The shop is well-stocked with gardening goodies, own produced honey and homegrown plants and seeds. The café serves delicious homemade food and is one of the nicest places in London to enjoy a traditional afternoon tea.

Chiswick House

- 🏛 *Burlington Lane, W4*
- ☎ *020 8995 0508*
- 🖉 *www.english-heritage.org.uk*
- 🚌 *Turnham Green LU*
- 🕐 *Sun-Wed 10.00-17.00 (April-Oct)*
- 💷 *£4.20 (adults), £3.40 (concessions), £2.10 (5-15yrs), free (under 5s, English Heritage members)*
- 🛍 *Shop*
- 🍴 *Refreshment kiosk*
- ♿ *Wheelchair access (telephone in advance)*

The last word in classical chic when it was built in the 1720s, Chiswick House is still a sumptuously stylish pad by any standards. Owner-architect Lord Burlington was inspired by the architecture of Ancient Rome and the austere symmetry of his villa is typical of his rigorous approach to design. The decadent-sounding Blue Velvet Room is one of several fine interiors by William Kent for which the Italianate gardens he originally designed are the perfect natural foil. The recently repainted gallery room displays furniture designed by William Kent and porphyry urns collected by Burlington on his grand tour. An audio tour, introductory film and exhibition are included in the admission charge. A major regeneration of the park got under way in April 2008 and is expected to last 18-24 months but work will be done on an area by area basis so visitors should not experience too much disruption. As part of the improvement works, the care-worn old café in the grounds will be demolished and replaced by a smarter, more architecturally appropriate facility, with a south-facing seating area. Until this opens in autumn 2009 a refreshment kiosk will be doing the honours by the cricket pavilion.

The Alexander Fleming Laboratory Museum

- 🏛 *St Mary's Hospital, Praed St, W2*
- ☎ *020 7725 6528*
- 🖉 *www.imperial.nhs.uk*
- 🚌 *Paddington Rail/LU*
- 🕐 *Mon-Thurs 10.00-13.00, and by appointment; Guided tours available*
- 💷 *£2 (adults), £1 (concessions)*
- 🛍 *Shop*

It was in this tiny, old-fashioned laboratory that Alexander Fleming discovered penicillin – a storm in a petri dish that transformed its discoverer into a national hero and earned him a Nobel Prize.

A very distant relation to today's pristine white boxes, the laboratory is an accurate reconstruction of Fleming's workplace (although his original penicillin culture plate is housed at the British Library). Volunteer guides, some of them retired medical staff who knew Fleming personally, talk visitors through the momentous – and accidental – discovery of penicillin. A concise, well-presented exhibition charts the development of penicillin from mystery mould to life-saving wonder drug and the impact of antibiotics on modern medicine. The displays also recount the details of Fleming's life and career – including reproductions of the bizarre 'germ' paintings he created. The museum has recently been designated an International Historic Chemical Landmark.

Gunnersbury Park Museum

🖼 *Gunnersbury Park, Popes Lane, W3*
☎ *020 8992 1612*
✎ *www.hounslow.info*
🚌 *Acton Town LU*
🕓 *Daily 11.00-17.00 (until 16.00 Nov-Mar)*
🐾 *Admission free*
☕ *Café*
♿ *Wheelchair access*

Local history museums don't come much grander than this. Once the home of the Rothschild family, the richly decorated rooms of Gunnersbury Mansion are now furnished with exhibitions about Ealing's and Hounslow's past. Period clothing is displayed (or can be seen by appointment when not on display), while the Rothschild's regal carriages help to illustrate transport in days gone by. A copious collection of domestic objects and the fully-restored Victorian kitchens give a 'below stairs' insight into how a large household was run. A lively and varied programme of changing exhibitions highlights particular aspects of local history – everything from market gardening to travellers in Ealing. The house is still surrounded by 160 acres of parkland with its café situated next to a pond.

Hogarth's House

📺 *Hogarth Lane, Great West Road, W4*
☎ *020 8994 6757*
🖉 *www.cip.com*
🚇 *Turnham Green LU*
🕐 *Tues-Fri 13.00-17.00 (Nov-Mar 13.00-16.00),*
   Sat and Sun 13.00-18.00 (Nov-Mar 13.00-17.00)
💷 *Admission free*
🛍 *Shop*
♿ *Wheelchair access (ground floor only)*

It requires a leap of the imagination to picture this odd-shaped house back in the 18th century when it was the country home of the painter-engraver William Hogarth. Only one room deep, and now somewhat overwhelmed by the A4 dual-carriageway that roars alongside it, the house was accurately described by Hogarth as his 'little country box by the Thames'. The charming (but overgrown) walled garden still contains a precariously propped up mulberry tree that Hogarth would have known – a doughty survivor of age and wartime bomb damage.

Often regarded as the founder of British painting, Hogarth's fame now rests on the detailed social observation and scathing moral commentaries of engravings such as *The Rake's Progress* and *The Harlot's Progress* (see entry for Sir John Soane's Museum, p. 72). These and many other of Hogarth's prints are displayed as part of an exhibition telling the story of his life and work. Although restored and redisplayed for Hogarth's tercentenary in 1997, the house is now once again in need of some TLC. Luckily the house has recently been awarded a Heritage Lottery Fund grant – the second floor will become a study space while the current temporary exhibition room will be improved to allow more changing exhibitions.

Kensington Palace State Apartments

📺 *Kensington, W8*
☎ *0870 751 5170 (information line)*
🖉 *www.hrp.org.uk*
🚇 *Bayswater LU, Gloucester Road LU, High Street Kensington LU,*
   Notting Hill Gate LU, Queensway LU
🕐 *Daily Nov-Feb 10.00-17.00, March-Oct 10.00-18.00; last admission*
   1 hour before closing
💷 *£12 (adults), £10 (concessions), £6 (children 5-16 years); Audio guides*
🛍 *Shop*
☕ *Café*
♿ Restricted wheelchair access

Kensington Palace was snapped up by monarchs William and Mary in 1689 when it was still humble Nottingham House. Remodelled by Sir Christopher Wren, this tidy red brick building (the birthplace of Queen Victoria and home of Diana, Princess of Wales) boasts illusionistic ceilings and staircase painted by William Kent, and a clutch of Old Masters in the State Apartments. 'KP' is also home to the vast Royal Ceremonial Dress Collection, which features court dress worn by members of the Royal Family and courtiers from the 18th century to the present. Outfits belonging to Diana, Princess of Wales are among the treasures, and the displays of sumptuous clothing are enlivened by a multilingual sound guide which leads visitors from dressmaker's workshop to court 'presentation'.

Leighton House Museum

⌨ *12 Holland Park Road, W14*
☎ *020 7602 3316*
✎ *www.rbkc.gov.uk*
🚇 *High Street Kensington LU*
🕙 *Daily 11.00-17.30 (closed Tuesdays), last admission 17.00*
💷 *£3 (adults), £1 (concessions/children)*

This evocative haute-bohemian pad was once home to Frederic, Lord Leighton, the great classical painter of the Victorian age. Hung with paintings by the man himself and his Pre-Raphaelite pals Millais and Burne-Jones, and with ceramics by William de Morgan (see p.130), the house was designed as a palace devoted to art, and its darkly opulent interiors are spellbinding. Leighton's vast studio dominates the upper floor but the domed Arab Hall is the centrepiece of the house: a Moorish fantasia complete with gilt mosaic frieze, antique decorative tiles, lattice-work window frames and gently playing fountain. Free guided tours take place every Wednesday and Thursday at 14.30. The lovely garden to the rear of the house was restored in 1997 and is open from April to the end of September. The house will be closed from 31 October 2008 for at least a year while major restoration and refurbishment takes place.

The Museum of Brands, Packaging & Advertising

📇 *Colville Mews, W11*
☎ *020 7908 0880*
🖊 *www.museumofbrands.com*
🚇 *Notting Hill LU*
🕐 *Tues-Sat 10.00-18.00, Sun 11.00-17.00*
💷 *£5.80 (adults), £2 (children 7-16), £14 (family), £3.50 (concessions)*
🛍 *Shop*
☕ *Tea room*
♿ *Disabled access*

This delightfully eccentric museum opened at the end of 2005 and, if you haven't been yet, is well worth a visit. The brainchild of Robert Opie, whose collection of consumer packaging it houses, the museum pays affectionate homage to 20th century consumerism or as the Wombles would have it the 'everyday things that folks leave behind'. Robert Opie's Damascene moment occurred at the age of 16 and involved, of all things, a Munchies wrapper and from this humble start the collection has grown to comprise thousands of items, including toys, games, magazines, food and drink packaging, postcards, and advertising artwork. Exhibits are laid out along a 'time line' from the 1890s to present day and provide plenty of Proustian moments for all ages, provoking delighted cries of recognition as the visitor re-encounters the toys, sweets and games of their childhood.

Nostalgia aside, the collection beautifully shows how consumerism reflects society, unerringly charting trends like our national obsessions with crisps, ready meals, DIY and washing whiter than white. Striking a chord with current concerns about over-packaging, displays also examine the technology and materials of packaging itself and the rise of containers like Tetrapak and the increasing sophistication of fizzy drinks cans. Commercial artwork is a particular strength of the collection and the flowing Art Nouveau lines of an Edwardian biscuit tin, or the striking Art Deco cover of a 1920s *Radio Times* show how directly the art movements of the day affected the look of trivial everyday items. Displays of fashions through the decades – from flapper dress to mini skirts – reflect Opie's view of clothing as the ultimate human packaging and on my visit Mr Opie himself was in evidence, happily talking to visitors about his collection. The small shop stocks engagingly nostalgic products and there's a small tea room, should looking at all those sweet wrappers make you hungry.

CHIVERS JELLY CRYSTALS

CHIVERS CUSTARD POWDER

SYMINGTONS IDEAL TABLE CREAM

PEKOE CANNINGS 2/2

FRY'S COCOA PASTE

Parkinsons
SELL MORE
Sugar Coated Pills
THAN ANY OTHER FIRM IN THE WORLD

HARRY PECK'S WILD BOARS HEAD

MADDIE'S

BLACK TREACLE

WILLIAMS MARZIPAN TEA CAKES

STOMACH PILLS Parkinsons
THE FRIEND OF PEOPLE

HEALTH SALT

KINGFORD'S

Parkinsons' VELVET Skin Tablets

Glaxo

HEALTH SALT

NEVO COCOA

MAPROVIT

CERES

PEAS

BAKING POWDER

GOLDEN SYRUP
SUNNY WEST

EDWARDS Desiccated Soup

MONK & GLASS Custard Powder

ROYAL BAKING POWDER

GREEN'S CUSTARD

EIFFEL TOWER Lemonade

VI-COCOA

HOLFORCE

MACKINTOSH'S TOFFEE DE LUXE

CHELSEA TOFFEE

RADIANCE DEVON'S CREAM TOFFEE

FRY'S COCOA

COCOA

SILVER BADGE COCOA

LYONS COCOA

GOLDEN SYRUP

Assorted Toffee

PARKINSONS BUTTER-SCOTCH

WALTER'S PALM TOFFEE

NUT JOY

TOFFEE DE LIGHT

BENSON'S SUPER-CREAM HYDRO TOFFEE

CREAMILK TOFFEE

WHITBREAD'S

RED SEAL

BENSON'S

DEVON CREAM TOFFEE

JACOB & CO

PLASMON BISCUITS

REID'S STOUT

Museum of Brands, Packaging & Advertising

The Museum of Fulham Palace

⌗ *Bishops Avenue, SW6*
☏ *020 7736 3233*
✐ *www.fulhampalace.org.*
🚌 *Putney Bridge LU*
🕐 *Sat 11.00-14.00, Sun 11.30-15.30, Mon 12.00-16.00, Tues 12.00-16.00;*
   Grounds open daily dawn to dusk
💲 *Admission free*
🛍 *Shop*
☕ *Café-Bar (open daily 09.00-17.00)*
♿ *Disabled access*

New displays opened at this small museum in 2007, telling the story of this remarkable site from prehistory to the present. The life and times of the Bishops of London were sometimes bloody and the ghost of the Bishop Bonner is said to haunt the Tudor Courtyard. More tangible exhibits take the form of archaeological remains, a scale model of the palace, a mummified rat and Bishop Winnington-Ingram's bejewelled mitre and cope. Benjamin West's pious depictions of Thomas à Becket and Margaret of Anjou are among the paintings on display. Several Fulham bishops were keen gardeners and their botanizing legacy lives on today in the charming Palace grounds, which include an 18th-century walled garden, herb knot garden, woodland and lawns. *The Bishops' Tree* carving by sculptor Andrew Frost is a recent addition to the gardens and depicts various of Fulham's prelates, among them anti-slavery campaigner Bishop Porteus. Another welcome addition to the set up is a stylish café-bar, run by Oliver Peyton, and a small gallery showing contemporary art and photography inspired by the Palace.

The National Army Museum

⌗ *Royal Hospital Road, SW3*
☏ *020 7730 0717*
✐ *www.national-army-museum.ac.uk*
🚌 *Sloane Square LU, bus 239*
🕐 *Mon-Sun 10.00-17.30*
💲 *Admission free*
🛍 *Shop*
☕ *Café*
♿ *Wheelchair access*

If you've got a thing about men – or women – in uniform this is the place for you. Unlike the Imperial War Museum (see p. 45), whose subject is 20th-century conflict, the NAM focuses on the life of ordinary British and Commonwealth soldiers and is appropriately situated next to the Royal Hospital, home of the Chelsea pensioners (see p. 115). But even if you're not barmy about the army, this well-thought out and imaginatively presented museum makes for a rewarding visit. An ongoing refurbishment programme ensures displays don't get stale, but does mean possible disruption to some galleries. If you are planning a visit to see something specific, it's probably worth checking before you set out.

Starting with the crack-shot archers at Agincourt, the permanent displays track the development of the modern soldier right up to the Cold War and beyond. The museum ably covers the period 1914-45, with uniforms, equipment, lifelike tableaux, and a walk-through trench, but also covers less familiar territory such as the wars in America and the 'Road to Waterloo'. Filled with the weaponry and uniforms you expect from a military museum, this gallery also features curiosities like a 50 metre-square model of the Battle of Waterloo with a cast of 75,000 tin soldiers, and the skeleton of 'Marengo', Napoleon's favourite charger. As elsewhere in the museum, startlingly realistic full-size models of historic soldiers bring the Napoleonic campaign to life.

'730 Days until Demob' is an enjoyable look at National Service, with insights into barrack room life, and how national servicemen contributed to campaigns such as the Malayan Emergency and the Korean War. 'The British Army Today' brings the story up to date and gives would be soldiers the chance to test their skill at map reading and target spotting as well as advising on the correct way to eat a tarantula. And if that isn't gruesome enough for you, the exhibits also include the blackened, frostbitten fingertips of Major Michael 'Bronco' Lane – the good major having parted company from them after his successful ascent of Everest in 1976. Also on the third floor, the art gallery shows off the museum's impressive collections of paintings – from portraits of soldiers such as the pub-loving Marquis of Granby to guts'n'glory battle scenes.

Special exhibitions ensure this is a museum to return to even after you've seen the permanent collections. Recent displays have included 'Task Force Falklands', 'Helmand: the Soldiers' Story' and 'Faces of Battle', the provocative and highly moving story of pioneering facial surgery on the wounded of WWI. An interactive Kids' Zone is a fun new addition on the ground floor for 10s and under, with castles to defend, monkey bars to climb, uniforms to try on and books to read.

A comprehensive selection of military books and knick-knacks can be found in the shop – deck the kids out in some trendy camo gear, pick up a military survival kit or simply award yourself a miniature campaign medal. Now run by Costa Coffee, the café is strategically placed to let you regroup your forces before doing battle with the well-heeled hordes of Chelsea.

Floor 2

Floor 1

Mezzanine

Entrance
(Exhibition Road)

Ground Floor

Earth Hall

Ground Floor

Lower Ground Floor

Central Hall

Entrance
(Cromwell Road)

West lawn

Ground Floor

Entrance
(from west lawn)

Key

🚻 Toilets
♿ Accessible toilets
👶 Baby care room
🧥 Cloakroom
ℹ Information and tickets
🎓 School Reception
🛍 Shop
🍴 Restaurant
🍷 Sandwich bar
☕ Café
🥪 Snack bar
BGS British Geological Survey
🎦 Picnic Area
🎭 Flett Events Theatre
📖 Mary Anning Room
📞 Telephones
🛗 Lifts
L1 Learning Room 1
L2 Learning Room 2

Blue Zone
Dinosaurs
Fishes, Amphibians and Reptiles
Human Biology
Jerwood Gallery
Marine Invertebrates
Mammals
Mammals (blue whale)

Orange Zone
Darwin Centre (tours only)
Wildlife Garden (entrance outside)

Green Zone
Birds
Creepy Crawlies
Ecology
Fossil Marine Reptiles
Giant Sequoia
Investigate Centre
Minerals and The Vault
Our Place in Evolution
Plant Power
Primates

East lawn

Red Zone
Earth Lab
Earth Today and Tomorrow
Earth's Treasury
From the Beginning
Lasting Impressions
The Power Within
Restless Surface

108

The Natural History Museum

🖼 *Cromwell Road, SW7*
☎ *020 7942 5000*
🖊 *www.nhm.ac.uk*
🚇 *South Kensington LU*
🕐 *Mon-Sat 10.00-17.50 (last admission 17.30)*
♿ *Admission free*
🛍 *Shops*
☕ *Cafés*
♿ *Wheelchair access (via Exhibition Road entrance)*

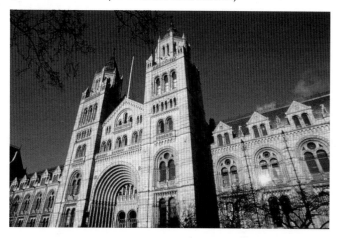

One of South Kensington's 'Big Three', the Natural History Museum has been a London landmark since 1881. Famed for its dinosaur collection, the museum was once in danger of becoming a fossil itself. Now with revamped displays in the Life Galleries and new Earth Galleries, the Museum welcomes over 3 million visitors a year and supports a 300-strong team of research scientists behind the scenes.

Purpose built by Alfred Waterhouse, the museum building is worth a visit in its own right. While its elegant Romanesque arches conceal an iron and steel framework (the last word in Victorian innovation), the exterior sculptures of plants and animals form a Gothic curtain raiser to the exhibits inside.

Dominated by the famous diplodocus skeleton, the Cromwell Road entrance hall introduces the 'wonders' of the museum. Eight exhibition bays house an item drawn from the museum's vast collection of over 68 million specimens, each accompanied by a multilingual

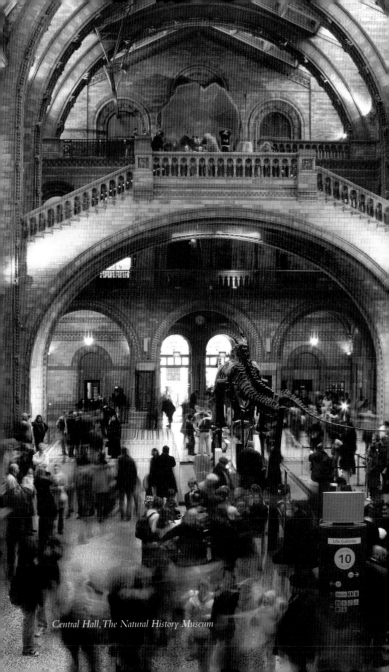

Central Hall, The Natural History Museum

touchscreen computer which tells you where to find related exhibits, as well as acting as a more general guide.

Diplodocus has been shrewdly placed: I suspect many make 'Dinosaurs' their first port of call. It can't take many dinosaurs to fill a room, but this display is chock full of overgrown skeletons who all look ready to sample some human prey. A raised walkway brings you eyeball to eyeball with 'fearful lizards' like Dromaeosaurus, Triceratops and the mighty Tyrannosaurus Rex. Vicious claws, teeth, horns and spines abound in this gallery. The animatronic model of a grumpy T-Rex guarding its kill means you can even see, and hear, one of them in action. On ground level, interactive displays ask 'What is a Dinosaur?' and look at possible reasons for their demise.

There's more animal magic, albeit of the stuffed variety, in 'Mammals'. Flying mammals and mammals with pouches put in an appearance alongside more familiar species. The life-size model of a blue whale, slung from the ceiling, makes even the giraffe and elephant look like small fry. Films and hands-on exhibits supplement the stuffed specimens (some of which are showing their age) and bring to life mammalian habitats, life cycles and evolution.

Completed in 1977, the 'Human Biology' display contributed to the NHM being made Museum of the Year in 1980 – and it's still one of the best things here. After all, what could be more interesting than us? The human life cycle and the vital roles played by our component parts are explored and, although highly educational, lots of exhibits are interactive to make the information accessible. Share a womb with a giant foetus (cheaper than a flotation tank!) or listen to a baby learning to speak.

The 'Primates' and 'Our Place in Evolution' displays put the whole process into a larger perspective, as does the cross section of a 1,300 year sequoia tree up on the second floor. Date markers chart major world events like the Battle of Hastings and the foundation of Islam against its numerous growth rings. Less cuddly creatures get a look in too – 'Creepy Crawlies' is fun, even for confirmed arachnophobes. In a highly interactive display, visitors can walk into a termite tower, see where our many-legged friends make themselves at home in our homes and find answers to tricky questions such as 'how do crabs mate?' or 'why is a millipede like a Swiss roll?'

From rainforest to desert, 'Ecology' looks at our environment, how it works and how mankind affects it. The giant 'leaf factory' shows how plants convert solar energy into food and a huge video wall follows the life cycle of water. Here you can learn about webs, pyramids and the cycles of life – and recycle a rabbit.

The Earth Galleries can be reached from the Life Galleries but also have their own entrance on Exhibition Road if you want to explore here first. These galleries, reflect the latest approach to museology: low on endless cases of sparsely-labelled specimens, high on participatory displays, sound effects and video monitors. With its six bronze statues depicting man's changing perceptions of the planet and its musical escalator leading up into a giant globe, the ground floor's 'Visions of the Earth' treads a fine line between the visionary and the naff. You can stop cringing when you get to the top of the escalator and the permanent displays like 'The Power Within' and 'The Restless Surface' get down to the nitty gritty. Stand under a volcano, 'experience' the 1995 Kobe earthquake or admire an extraordinary piece of lightning 'frozen' in desert sand. Rocks, fossils, lava: the pieces which make up this jumbo jigsaw puzzle of a planet begin to fit together in these vivacious displays. Displays in the Earth Galleries include 'From the Beginning', an exploration of the 4,560 million year-long history of the planet, and 'Earth's Treasury', a seductively glittering presentation of precious gems and minerals, including some glow in the dark specimens.

Covering some 4 billion years of the Earth's history, the NHM certainly takes the long view, and its galleries themselves are still evolving. Temporary exhibitions add some seasonal variations to the regular menu while the Darwin Centre is a state of the art scientific research building which is home to a mind boggling 22 million zoological specimens. The Centre hosts an excellent programme of free face to face events with scientists working at the Museum, including behind the scenes tours. Tours run every day with itineraries varying according to the scientist taking the tour, but tend to include the dissection room, and the 'tank room' with its macabre specimen lined walls and stainless steel 'tanks' – look out for the first barracuda to be found in British waters and some of Darwin's original specimens. To book a place on a tour ring 020 7942 5011 or go to the information desk in the Central Hall. Phase Two of the Centre is set to open in 2009 and will house the museum's insect and plant collections (28 and 6 million strong respectively) as well as a new 'communication space' named in honour of Sir David Attenborough.

As you would expect from a museum of this size and status, an extensive programme of special exhibitions, events and educational activities support the permanent displays. Families with under 7s in tow might want to pick up a free 'Explorers!' activity backpack from the Information Desk to help them get the most out of a visit. Downstairs in 'Investigate', children aged 7-14 can become a scientist for a day and explore an exciting range of seasonal specimens from the natural world

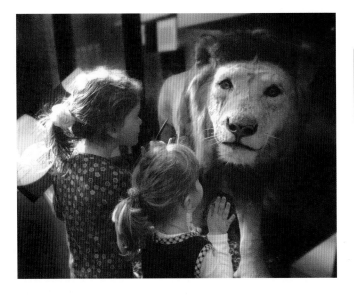

(stick insects were in residence on my last visit). Friendly explainers are on hand to guide youngsters and the atmosphere is welcoming. More flora and fauna can be see in the museum's 'outdoor gallery', the Wildlife Garden which can be accessed via the West Lawn, from April to October. Two cafés, a restaurant and a snack bar will keep any hunger pangs at bay, for a price – there's a picnic area in the basement. The museum's shops are pretty good too: if you have children the selection of dinosaur trinkets, cuddly toys, games, kits and books mean you probably won't leave empty handed – more grown-up investments could include a rather fine amethyst geode for a cool £1,200.

PM Gallery & House

⌨ *Mattock Lane, W5*
☎ *020 8567 1227*
🖰 *www.ealing.gov.uk/pitshanger*
🚇 *Ealing Broadway LU*
🕐 *Tues-Fri 13.00-17.00, Sat 11.00-17.00*
💲 *Admission free*
♿ *Wheelchair access*

Another example of Sir John Soane's inimitable architectural style (see also Bank of England Museum, p. 8, Dulwich Picture Gallery, p. 223, Sir John Soane's Museum, p. 72), Pitshanger Manor now functions as an historic house and contemporary arts venue with a lively programme of events and exhibitions. The Victorian Wing's extensive displays of Martinware pottery include a magnificent chimneypiece made for Buscot Park in Oxfordshire, and the Manor's elegant interiors are being restored to their original Regency style.

The Polish Institute and Sikorski Museum

⌨ *20 Princes Gate, SW7*
☎ *020 7589 9249*
🖰 *www.sikorskimuseum.co.uk*
🚇 *South Kensington LU, Knightsbridge LU*
🕐 *Mon-Fri 14.00-16.00 (first Sat of every month 10.00-16.00)*
💲 *Admission free (donations appreciated)*

Containing over 10,000 items, this extensive collection of Polish militaria is a valuable resource for students, particularly those of World War II. Friendly, knowledgeable volunteers guide visitors around – offering a trenchantly Polish take on events and an interactive experience in the best possible sense of the word. Each branch of the Polish armed forces is represented with memorabilia ranging from battle colours, regimental badges and weapons to photos, documents and personal effects. Exhibits include a Nazi 'Enigma machine', a submarine map drawn from memory by the crew of the Eagle when their original charts were confiscated, and the uniform in which Poland's war-time leader, General Wladyslaw Sikorski died. Military paintings and prints line the walls, among them Feliks Topolski's lively portrait of Sikorski and a dramatic depiction of the Battle of Monte Casino by Mezaj.

The Royal Hospital Chelsea Museum

  Royal Hospital Road, SW3
  020 7881 5203
  www.chelsea-pensioners.org.uk
  Sloane Square LU
  Daily 10.00-16.00 (closed 12.00-14.00); closed Sundays Oct to Mar
  Admission free
  Shop

Founded in 1682 by Charles II as a retreat for army veterans, the Royal Hospital fulfils the same function today and Chelsea Pensioners, in their old-fashioned uniforms, are a much-loved sight along the King's Road. Pensioners' uniforms and medals are displayed in this small museum, as well as photos, original documents and artefacts illustrating the institution's history. Nosey parkers will enjoy peeking into the wooden 'berth' on display. These cabin like rooms are where the Pensioners live and were designed by the Hospital's architect, Sir Christopher Wren. Originally only 6 feet square, the 'berths' today have been enlarged to a palatial 9 feet square. Alongside the military memorabilia are 17th-century 'Wren' nails found during renovation work and a button made from the oak tree in which Charles II hid. The Wellington Hall houses a vast painting of the Battle of Waterloo. There is also an excellent shop, with post office, offering well-priced souvenirs. The Chapel and Great Hall are also open to visitors and, as they were also designed by Sir Christopher Wren, are well worth a look. Conducted tours, led by Chelsea Pensioner guides and for which a charge is made, are also available – telephone for details.

Linley Sambourne House

  18 Stafford Terrace, W8
  020 7602 3316 (info and bookings)
  www.rbkc.gov.uk
  High Street Kensington LU
  Sat-Sun by guided tour only (tours start 11.15, 13.00, 14.15, 15.30
    – advance booking advised); group visits by appointment only
  £6 (adults), £4 (concs), £1 (children)
  Shop

Jam-packed with pictures, ornaments and knick-knacks of all sorts, this time capsule of a terraced house was the home of Punch illustrator and cartoonist Linley Sambourne. The artist's own photographs were the basis for many of his cartoons and can be viewed in the bathroom (which also doubled up as his dark room). With the exception of the first tour of the day, tours are led by costumed guides.

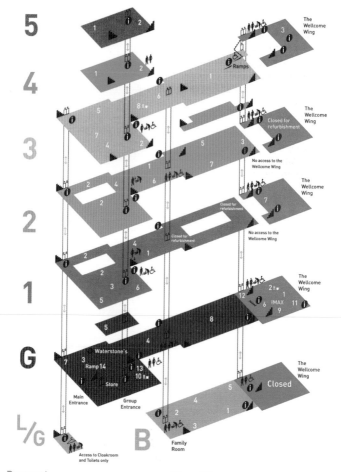

5

4

3

2

1

G

L/G

B

The Wellcome Wing

Ramps

The Wellcome Wing

Closed for refurbishment

No access to the Wellcome Wing

The Wellcome Wing

Closed for refurbishment

Closed for refurbishment

No access to the Wellcome Wing

The Wellcome Wing

IMAX

The Wellcome Wing

Waterstone's

Ramp 14

Store

Main Entrance

Group Entrance

Closed

Access to Cloakroom and Toilets only

Family Room

Basement
Eat Drink Shop, The Garden, The Picnic Terrace, The Secret Life of the Home, Things

Ground Floor
Antenna – what's new in science, Deep Blue Café, Energy Hall, Exploring Space, IMAX 3D Cinema, Making the Modern World, Pattern Pod, Revolution Café, SimEx simulator ride, The Theatre, Ticket Desk, Information Desk

First floor
Agriculture, Challenge of Materials, Telecommunications, Who am I

Second floor
Computing, Docks and Diving, Energy, Marine Engineering, Mathematics, Ships

Third floor
Flight, Health Matters, In Future, Launchpad, Launchpad City, Motionride Simulator, Science in the 18th Century, Third Floor Café

Fourth floor
Glimpses of Medical History, Psychology: Mind Your Head

Fifth floor
Science & Art of Medicine, Veterinary History

The Science Museum

Exhibition Road, SW7

0870 870 4868 (general booking and enquiries)
020 7942 4445 (Minicom)
0870 870 4771 (IMAX advance booking line; booking fee applies)

www.sciencemuseum.org.uk

South Kensington LU

Daily 10.00-18.00

Admission free

Shop

Cafés

Wheelchair access

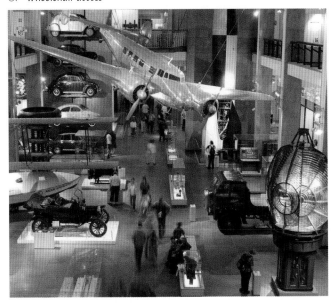

'See inside for inspiration' used to be the slogan here and although the tag line has been dropped, the sentiment remains just as true. In fact, since the 2000 opening of the £50-million Wellcome Wing there's more than ever to see and be inspired by at the Science Museum. Taking a broad view of historic and contemporary science, the museum encompasses technology, industry and medicine – everything from computing to chemistry, dentistry to deep sea diving, Foucault's Pendulum to Stephenson's Rocket.

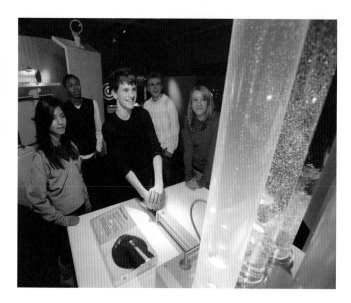

With over 200,000 historic objects in its collections, the museum also prides itself on its interactive exhibits, many of which are geared towards children. If your kids favour the hands-on approach make a bee-line for the newly re-located, re-invented 'Launch Pad' on the third floor which contains over 50 interactive experiments from the world of physics. Aimed at 8-14 year olds, it's an incredibly popular destination, on my visit in the school holidays it was positively teeming with busy little boffins. Down in the basement 'The Garden' is a marginally more tranquil exploration and discovery area for 3-6 year olds while 'Things' offers demonstrations, workshops and special events for all ages. All these galleries are supervised by 'Explainers', friendly museum staff who are on hand to answer questions, guide experiments and stage educational performances.

Also in the basement and accessible to everyone, 'The Secret Life of the Home' is an entertaining display charting man's struggle to conquer the domestic front. Given the technological wizardry on show elsewhere in the museum, what's really amazing here is just how long it has taken humans to work out an effective way of doing the housework. The evolution of the humble toilet is shown in all its glory – culminating in a frank, funny presentation of how a modern flush loo works.

'Exploring Space' is a popular draw on the ground floor covering early rocketeers, men on the moon and modern satellite communications.

The huge Black Arrow satellite launcher runs practically the length of the gallery and there's also a look at life in space – only 50 miles away – complete with astronauts' undies and a Coke can specially adapted for gravity-free conditions. Leading on from here is 'Making the Modern World', a chronological display of some 1,800 icons of the industrial world, including 'Puffing Billy' (the oldest steam locomotive), a Model-T Ford, and the Apollo 10 command module, surprisingly compact and still bearing its re-entry scars.

The first floor is home to 'The Challenge of Materials', a funky display which takes a fresh look at the manufacture, use and disposal of materials. The exhibits incorporate examples of art, architecture and fashion to challenge our perceptions. While visitors can boggle at unusual items like a steel bomber jacket, hi-tech interactive exhibits let you get to grips with how materials are developed and tested.

Contained within a vast hangar-like space, 'Flight' takes off on the third floor. Flying machines of all descriptions hang from the ceiling like Airfix models – from papery biplanes to Britain's first jet plane – while ranged along one wall is a miscellany of gleaming aircraft engines. A high-level walkway gives a bird's-eye view of the planes which include several historic exhibits from the pioneering days of flight, including the Vickers Vimy in which Alcock and Brown crossed the Atlantic in 1919. These all seem worlds away from the crowded skies of the 21st century and the paraphernalia of routine jet travel: a cross-section of a Boeing 747 and an air traffic control suite bristling with lights, switches and split-second, life or death decisions. Flight simulators – used to train pilots on the cheap – are a popular draw here, despite costing extra and promising a bumpy ride.

On a more down to earth note, the recently updated 'Health Matters' looks at how medical technology and research affect our experience of medicine. Medical hardwear on show includes a 1950s iron lung, an MRI scanner and an artificial kidney, used by Moreen Lewis, the first patient to have a home dialysis machine. Other displays look at research into community health and genetics and medicine. The top two floors of the museum, 'The Science and Art of Medicine', and 'Veterinary History' continue the gore with no end of wince-making exhibits and evil-looking instruments. Fans of hospital dramas should also enjoy the real-life reconstructions of 'Glimpses of Medical History' – visit a 1905 pharmacy, go to a 1930s dentist or (if you've got the bottle) 'drop in' on a 1980s open heart operation.

Contemporary science is the name of the game in The Wellcome Wing, the Science Museum's all-singing, all-dancing new addition. Its exhibitions handle the hottest topics in science today such as genetics, digital technology, and artificial intelligence. Billed as the world's fastest-moving science exhibition, 'Antenna' features constantly updated displays on the latest advances while 'Who am I?' is a bio-medical investigation into identity and brain science with a Live Science area with fun interactive 'bloids'. The under 8s haven't been forgotten either – the importance of patterns in science is the unusual premise for 'Pattern Pod', a multi-sensory exhibit. Looming large on the third floor, the IMAX cinema shows science films such as 'Space Station 3D' and 'Seamonsters 3D' on its five storey-high screen.

This is just the tip of the iceberg – temporary exhibitions, events and contemporary artworks are some of the other attractions on offer – but don't discount the older style galleries; just because they aren't packed with touchscreen computers doesn't mean they aren't worth a good look around. While the newer galleries can get crowded and noisy, displays like 'Time Measurement' remain havens of traditional museum hush. For quiet contemplation try 'Agriculture' on the first floor. Ponder the development of the plough and admire the old-fashioned tableaux of the changing seasons complete with model tractors and farm machinery. 'Marine Engineering', 'Ships', 'Docks' and 'Diving' are other enjoyable older-style galleries on the second floor. Simple labels let the objects speak for themselves and there's a stunning selection of model ships from across continents and through the ages.

There's a lot to see and, as with all big museums, a little pre-planning will ensure you get the most from your visit. Guided tours of the most popular galleries and outstanding objects take place every day, the museum map provides a list of highlights for those going it alone, while leaflets like the 'world wonders trail' promote a more focused visit, centred around 7 top scientific and engineering achievements. For children who just can't tear themselves away, the Museum organises 'Science Night' – a sleep-over event with demonstrations, hands-on workshops and gallery trails.

If all that thinking makes you peckish, there are two on-site cafés and several picnic sites with seating dotted about the museum. Food for the mind can be found in the bookshop, which stocks a host of relevant publications for all ages, from activity books to heavy-weight scientific tomes; while in the museum's shop, gadgets, gizmos and games are the order of the day.

Victoria and Albert Museum

- South Kensington, SW7
- 020 7942 2000
- www.vam.ac.uk
- South Kensington LU
- Daily 10.00-17.45 (Fri until 22.00, selected galleries only)
- Admission free (a separate charge applies to some exhibitions & events)
- Shops
- Café & Restaurant
- Wheelchair access

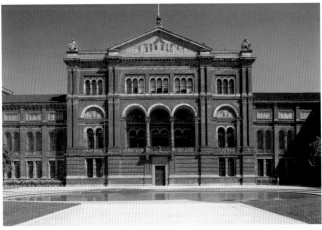

The John Madejski Garden, V&A Museum

I make no apologies for counting the V&A, the national museum for art and design, among my favourite museums. Founded in the great 19th century era of improvement, it is still a life enhancing experience. It has long been cherished by artists and designers, for whom it acts as a massive, inspirational source book. The V&A's permanent collection spans several centuries and continents and includes textiles and fashions, musical instruments, jewellery, ceramics, glass and sculpture. Although known for its decorative art, the museum also contains an interesting assembly of 'fine' art – paintings, prints, photography and sculpture.

A review of this size can't do justice to the V&A's diversity – and neither will a single visit. Little and often is the ideal approach – thank goodness that admission to this great institution is free. Free guided tours depart from the Information Desk at the Cromwell Road entrance and last an hour. Those venturing in without a guide

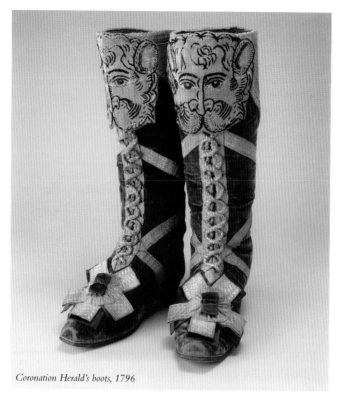

Coronation Herald's boots, 1796

– human or otherwise – shouldn't be dismayed by the odd wrong turn: the V&A is labyrinthine – but getting lost is part of the fun and you are bound to stumble across something of interest on unplanned detours. On a recent visit, wandering through 'Ironwork', I discovered the 'Melchett Fire Basket', a fabulously self-referential 1930 commission by socialites Henry and Gwen Mond, invoking the catty society gossip the couple attracted after an involvement in a menage a trois. The 'Late Views' on Friday evenings are particularly lively with regular exhibits supplemented by a programme of lectures and live music.

A word of warning though before you embark. If there is anything in particular you want to see, on arrival it's worth finding out at the information desk which galleries are closed to the public. Only selected galleries stay open on Friday evenings and implementation of the Museum's 'FuturePlan' means that some galleries may be closed while they are redeveloped. This ambitious project of renewal and restoration will reconceive the V&A as 'an indoor city' with distinct 'quarters' and promises a more logical layout. New suites of galleries for the medieval and Renaissance collections are due to open in 2009, while the William and Judith Bollinger Jewellery Gallery opened in May 2008. The Gilbert Collection (formerly at Somerset House) is also due to be relocated here in 2009. As they say, watch this space.

For the time being however, the museums collections are grouped into five major themes: Asia, Europe, Materials and Techniques (like 'Ironwork' or 'Tapestries'), Modern and Exhibitions. The magnificent, refurbished Raphael Gallery on the ground floor make a great starting point. This austere, imposing space houses the seven enormous *cartoons* or preparatory designs for tapestries commissioned for the Sistine Chapel. With their vivid colours and serene compositions they are very much works of art in their own right. On the same floor, the Far East Galleries contain the finest collections of contemporary Chinese and Japanese art outside the countries themselves. The recently opened Jameel Gallery showcases the decorative arts of the Islamic Middle East, and include a vibrantly tiled 18th-century Turkish chimneypiece, Armenian church vestments and the vast 16th-century 'Ardabil Carpet', one of the largest and finest Islamic carpets in existence.

In general, a trip to the V&A could save you an expensive jaunt to foreign climes. The vast and impressive 'cast courts' are filled with plaster reproductions of famous sculpture and architecture. Here casts of the portal from *Santiago de Compostella* and *Trajan's Column* jostle for space with medieval knights and their ladies, Michelangelo's *David* and several of his *Unfinished Slaves* amongst others.

Real sculpture isn't in short supply either and includes a fine collection of marble and bronze sculptures by Rodin (some given by the artist himself) such as his notorious *Age of Bronze*. The paintings in the refurbished Paintings Galleries also repay closer study. Look out for the first ever painting by Degas to enter a British public collection, landscape paintings by the Barbizon School and a glorious group of oil sketches by Constable including a study for *The Haywain* and some of his renowned cloud studies.

Touchscreen computers can be found in several galleries – such as the Samsung Gallery of Korean Art – and provide useful additional background information on the objects and the culture which formed them. The Glass Gallery on level 4 is a glittering celebration of a fragile yet durable substance. Artefacts range from ancient glass perfume jars to elaborate candelabra, from humble drinking glasses to the latest glass goods from Murano. A dramatic glass staircase and balcony housing the study collection supplies a fairy tale pièce de résistance.

Visitors with a magpie sensibility should dip into the Silver Galleries on level 3. Somewhat bizarrely, this collection is housed in the former ceramics galleries whose elaborate interior bears the names of famous pottery centres from around the world. A touchscreen computer recounts the history of silver in England but the real stars of this gallery are the beautifully crafted exhibits. The extensive ceramics collection charts mankind's love affair with a more down to earth material: from ancient Egyptian clay artefacts, to the work of contemporary studio potters. Currently closed, these galleries are due to re-open in autumn 2009.

Dedicated followers of fashion can trace the changing shape of clothing from the 17th century onwards in the Fashion Gallery. The collection is beautifully displayed and goes right up to the present day with designer duds by the likes of Paul Smith and Vivienne Westwood, whilst finding wardrobe space for everyday essentials such as underwear and occasionwear like wedding dresses.

And talking of well-dressed displays, the V&A's new British Galleries opened in 2001, after a £31 million refit. Comprising 15 galleries and 3,000 exhibits, the displays celebrate the best in British design 1500-1900 and examine how Britain rose from design non-entity to become the 'workshop of the world'. The displays feature five completely restored period rooms such as the 18th-century Norfolk Music Room as well as furniture, metalwork, ceramics, textiles, fine art and old favourites such as the 'Great Bed of Ware' and the 'Stoke Edith Hangings'. These new galleries include 'discovery areas' with hands-on exhibits (your chance to build an 18th century chair or try on a crinoline) and a Study Area. This latter comes equipped with interactive computers with all the gen on the many different styles in evidence in the galleries (from Renaissance to Scottish School), as well as some dangerously comfy suede chairs and a selection of appropriately themed reference books. Just don't forget to look at the exhibits.

Another recent additional is an Architecture Gallery on level 4. Showcasing the V&A and the RIBA's collections of architectural drawings and models, the exhibits include a 2004 model of Bluewater shopping mall, a preliminary sketch for Castle Howard by Vanbrugh and a startlingly modern looking 18th-century model of Fort William in India. Wall displays guide the visitor through the gamut of architectural styles from Classical to Modernist, via Gothic and Spanish Islamic. Contemporary style gurus will also want to check out the 20th Century Galleries on level 3 which have their fair share of must-haves – from iconic modernist furniture to a Dyson vacuum cleaner – but also look at graphic design and typography.

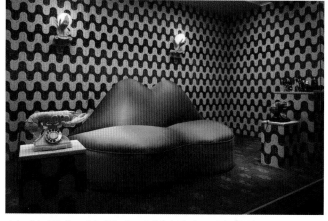

Aphrodisiac Telephone, Mae West Lips Sofa by Salvador Dali & Edward James

Temporary major exhibitions as well as ever-changing smaller displays keep things fresh exploring topics as diverse as contemporary Chinese design and Art Deco. Visitors with children under 12 should keep their eyes peeled for the Activity Cart which is parked in one of the main ground floor galleries every Sunday and offers quizzes, trails and games. On Saturdays the museum's award winning 'Back-Packs' are available to take young explorers through the collections with an innovative mix of jigsaws, stories, puzzles and hands-on.

Foodwise, the V&A offers two possibilities. The Garden Café occupies one corner of the elegantly redesigned John Madejski garden and offers light refreshments al-fresco. Enjoy the garden with its elegant, seasonally updated planting scheme and elliptical pond and see if you can spot the two small wall plaques commemorating 'Tycho' and 'Jim' two erstwhile museum dogs. Inside the Café has returned to the museum's original suite of refreshment rooms, the wonderfully over the top Morris, Gamble and Poynter rooms. Additional seating is available on the corridor overlooking the courtyard and hot and cold food is served, as well as expensive coffee. The streets around South Kensington tube station offer plenty of alternatives, if you fancy a change of scene.

The museum shop – revamped and relocated since the last edition – is as tempting as ever though and you may end up wishing you'd left your credit card at home. In addition to the usual postcards and posters, the stock here includes a discerning selection of cutting edge jewellery, ceramics and textiles by top contemporary makers as well less expensive knick-knacks and art and design books.

William Morris Society

📺 *Kelmscott House, 26 Upper Mall, W6*

📞 *020 8741 3735*

✎ *www.morrissociety.org*

🚌 *Ravenscourt Park LU*

🕐 *Thurs and Sat 14.00-17.00*

💰 *Admission free*

🛍 *Shop*

The basement and coach house of the riverside home of William Morris, now form a museum open to the public. Although by no means extensive, the displays here reflect Morris's dual role as doyen of the Arts & Crafts Movement and energetic pioneering socialist. Photographs of eminent early socialists in the coach house testify to its previous incarnation as the HQ of the Hammersmith Branch of the Socialist League while original decorative designs by Morris and exquisite embroideries by his daughter May offer a glimpse of the man's influential style. Free guided tours and slide shows are available for groups, by prior arrangement. See also William Morris Gallery p.164.

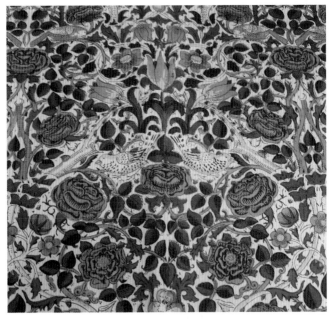

William Morris Society

South

The Brunel Museum

⬚ *Brunel Engine House, Railway Avenue, Rotherhithe, SE16*

☎ *020 7231 3840*

✐ *www.brunel-museum.org.uk*

🚌 *Canada Water LU, Rotherhithe LU (closed until July 2010);*
  bus 381, 47, 188

🕓 *Daily 10.00–17.00*

💷 *£2 (adults), £1 (concessions), free (children under 16)*

🛍 *Shop*

☕ *Café*

♿ *Wheelchair access*

It took father-and-son team Marc and Isambard Brunel eighteen years to build the world's first under-river tunnel, linking Rotherhithe on the south side of the Thames to Wapping on the north. Located in the original Engine House, this award-winning museum tells the story of their achievement in the face of floods, financial losses and human disaster. 'The Great Bore' as the project was, without apparent irony called, became known as the '8th wonder of the world' when it opened in 1843, paving the way for modern mass urban transportation. Displays explain the technological triumph of the tunnel, still used today by London Underground's East London Line, but also reveal the human side of the endeavour and the harsh lives endured by the tunnel's miners. The museum also commemorates Brunel's final project, the *Great Eastern* steamship, the world's first modern ocean liner which was launched just a few hundred yards down the river in 1858.

With its pedimented gable ends and dinky metal chimney, this modest brick building is a temple to Victorian self-belief and definitely punches above its weight. Not content with being a scheduled ancient monument and international landmark site, the Brunel Museum is taking advantage of the current temporary closure of the East London Line to create a new, enlarged museum inside the original tunnel shaft, which is due to open in 2010.

The Crystal Palace Museum

- *Anerley Hill, Upper Norwood, SE19*
- 020 8676 0700
- *www.crystalpalacemuseum.org.uk*
- *Crystal Palace Rail*
- *Sat, Sun and Bank Holidays 11.00-16.30 (last entry 16.00); other times by prior appointment*
- *Admission free*
- *Shop*

Hugely popular in its day, the Crystal Palace hosted everything from the Great Exhibition of 1851 to fun fairs and football cup finals before it burnt down in 1936. Dedicated to keeping its flame (as it were) alive, this museum is housed in the last surviving building constructed by the Crystal Palace Company. Numerous photos and artefacts tell the story of this glorified greenhouse and books and souvenirs relating to the palace are available from the museum's shop. Guided Crystal Palace Park tours, for which a charge is made, take place on the 1st Sunday of every month, starting at 12 noon from the Museum.

The Cuming Museum

- *Old Town Hall, 151 Walworth Road, SE17*
- 020 7525 2000
- *www.southwarkcollections.org.uk*
- *Elephant and Castle LU/Rail*
- *Tues-Sat 10.00-17.00*
- *Admission free*
- *Gift counter*
- *Wheelchair Access*

Hailed as a 'British Museum in miniature' when it opened in 1906, this museum is home to the extraordinary collections of father and son Richard and Henry Syer Cuming. Men of eclectic taste, their acquisitions were nothing if not diverse, encompassing natural history, ethnography, Egyptology, archaeology and the plain nutty. Now thoughtfully redisplayed in Southwark's former Town, the museum manages to combine its original Victorian 'cabinet of curiosity' feel with the best of 21st century interpretation. Living in Southwark, the Cuming's were ideally placed to pick up all sorts of goodies from around the globe – from celebrity knick-knacks like King Alphonso of Spain's tooth to Egyptian mummies, and artefacts collected on Captain Cook's voyages. Other eye-catching curios include a stuffed bear, a cow's heart from Bethnal Green as well as 'medieval antiquities' forged by 'Billy' and 'Charley', two enterprising Victorian mudlarks. Every

128

country in Africa is represented but there are also objects from Asia, the Americas and Europe. Bizarre, bygone superstitions to ensure health and wealth are the focus of the Lovett Collection, whilst among the costumes there's a picturesque dentist's cap — trimmed with several mouthfuls of human teeth — and a Hawaiian feathered cape.

The local history displays include the obligatory hands-on element for young visitors, and cover several centuries of Southwark — from prehistory to the present day. Oral reminiscences and picture books tell the stories of Southwark's multicultural communities — and there are still more curios like the 'Camberwell Beauty' butterfly and a pearly king's jacket. A temporary exhibition gallery hosts locally themed shows — a recent one looked at Hogarth's London.

Cutty Sark Visitor Centre

Cutty Sark Gardens, Greenwich, SE10 9HT
020 8858 2698
www.cuttysark.org.uk
Cutty Sark DLR, Greenwich Rail/DLR

Launched in 1869, the Cutty Sark is one of the world's most historic surviving ships — and the last remaining tea clipper. A famous speed merchant in her day she hauled not just tea but wool and a number of other cargoes. The Cutty Sark went onto become one of London's best loved sights — at least until May 2007 when a potentially devastating fire ripped through the ship. Luckily much of ship's fabric was not in situ as she was being conserved at the time and incredibly only less than 2% of her historic structure was lost. When restoration is complete the Cutty Sark will be presented in a dramatically new way: raised three metres above her current position and suspended in a glass canopy, an innovation which will create a new space underneath the ship where visitors will be able to appreciate the ship's elegant lines. Until the ship re-opens in spring 2010 there is very little to see, with the exception of a viewing platform from where visitors can observe progress on the site.

museums

south

The De Morgan Centre

☐ *38 West Hill, SW18*
☎ *020 8871 1144*
✎ *www.demorgan.org.uk*
🚌 *Putney East LU, Putney Rail; bus 37, 170, 337, 776*
🕐 *Tues-Wed 12.00-18.00, Fri-Sat 10.00-17.00*
♨ *Admission free*
🛍 *Shop*
♿ *Wheelchair access*

The De Morgan Centre opened in 2002 and those with an interest in ceramics and 19th century decorative arts will surely want to make a bee line to it, if they haven't done so already. Housed in the Reading Room of the erstwhile West Hill Public Library, the centre's permanent exhibition of William de Morgan's ceramics and his wife Evelyn's paintings offers a fascinating snapshot of a very particular moment in English aesthetics.

William de Morgan was a key player in the Arts and Crafts Movement and worked alongside William Morris while Evelyn was also something of a trailblazer, being one of the first women students to attend the Slade School of Art. A man of many parts De Morgan single-handedly rediscovered the lost art of lustre decoration, was involved in prison reform, the suffragette movement and in his last years enjoyed a second career as a novelist. It is for his pottery, though, that he is remembered today, and from the ceramics on display here it's easy to see why. Islamic pottery was a major influence and his gorgeously coloured and intricately patterned vases, bowls and tiles, decorated with fish, peacocks, boats and flowers, show how well he absorbed the lessons of his Persian and Turkish role models.

With their abundance of mournful damsels with flowing hair and robes Evelyn de Morgan's paintings in the Pre-Raphaelite style are perhaps less easy to love. A keen spiritualist and pacifist, Evelyn's work reflected her beliefs, and pictures such as the surprisingly gaudy *Daughters of the Mists* or the fanciful *Moonbeams Dipping into the Sea* seem uncomfortably fey to cynical modern eyes. However, her Botticelli inspired painting of *Flora* is lovely. A jigsaw version of it is available in the Centre's shop, which also sells a selection of upmarket De Morgan memorabilia. Visitors over the next couple of years should keep an eye on the De Morgan Centre website – expansion and a change of premises are on the cards by 2010.

Eltham Palace & Gardens

⬜ *Courtyard, off Court Road, Eltham, SE9*

☎ *020 8294 2548*

🖊 *www.english-heritage.org.uk*

🚆 *Eltham Rail, Mottingham Rail*

🕐 *Sun-Wed 10.00-17.00 (Apr-Oct), 10.00-16.00 (Nov-Dec, Feb-March), closed January*

💷 *House and gardens: £7.90 (adults), £5.90 (concessions), £4 (children), free (English Heritage members)*
Gardens only: £4.90 (adults), £3.70 (concessions), £2.50 (children), free (English Heritage members); group discounts available – booking required

🛍 *Shop*

☕ *Café*

♿ *Wheelchair access*

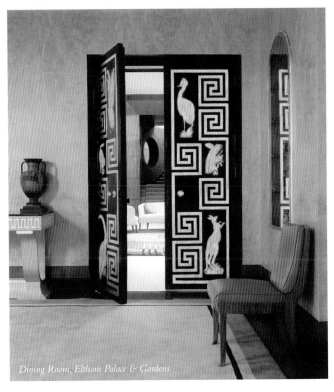

Dining Room, Eltham Palace & Gardens

A medieval royal palace with a twist. The twist being the 1930s house with stunning Art Deco interiors which is incorporated into the ruins of what was once Henry VIII's childhood home. Wealthy couple Stephen and Virginia Courtauld commissioned the house and they kitted it out in luxurious style: concealed electric lighting, a centralised vacuum cleaner and en suite bathrooms were some of the mod cons. Although most of the original artworks and furniture are no longer in place, the house has been restored to its Jazz Age opulence with replica furniture and Deco colour scheme. The Entrance Hall and Dining Room are particularly fine rooms – the former featuring marquetry panels of Italian and Scandinavian scenes (guarded by a pair of bellicose marquetry sentries), the latter with a series of black and silver doors depicting animals from London Zoo. Virginia Courtauld's onyx and gold mosaic bathroom is another essay in the Hollywood style, presided over by a classical statue of *Psyche*. In a bold juxtaposition of ancient and modern, the Great Hall of the medieval palace was rescued from picturesque decay to become the Courtaulds' Music Room, complete with underfloor heating. The relentless luxury even extended to the living quarters of 'Mah-Jongg', the Courtauld's pet lemur who, when not jet setting around the world with his owners, had use of a roomy heated cage, hand-painted with a tropical jungle scene. Old home movie footage of the Courtaulds at play with friends, family and a succession of pets, show how much they enjoyed living at Eltham. Hospitality for today's visitors comes in the form of an excellent waitress service café, housed in the pea-green former servants quarters along with an imaginatively stocked gift shop (jaunty jazz soundtracks, antique Deco jewellery and tableware). The Palace's 19 acres of gardens are being restored to their 1930s elegance and are perfect for a post cream tea stroll. Admire the stunning herbaceous border and see if you can spot the rogue goldfish among the monster carp in the moat.

The Fan Museum

- 12 Crooms Hill, SE10
- 020 8305 1441
- www.fan-museum.org
- Cutty Sark DLR, Greenwich Rail/DLR
- Tues-Sat 11.00-17.00, Sun 12.00-17.00
- £4 (adults), £3 (concessions), free (under 7s), Tues 14.00-16.30
  free entry for OAPs and disabled
- Shop
- Teas served Tues & Sun
- Wheelchair access

Set in two immaculately-restored Georgian houses, this small museum oozes gentility from every pore – from its tasteful décor and charming volunteer staff to its award-winning lavatories (the nicest I've ever seen in a museum).

As well as fans, painted fan leaves feature in the permanent display – a rare 17th-century example depicts a somewhat glum bunch of French royals at a birthday party – but the history and craft of fan-making are also explored. The fans themselves are crafted from an amazing range of materials from elaborately carved tortoiseshell, ivory and mother of pearl to Welsh slate. High profile recent acquisitions include a fan leaf painted with a landscape by Gauguin and one by Sickert featuring a music hall scene. Regularly-changing themed exhibitions are held in the upstairs gallery and showcase fans from the museum's 3,000 strong collection – past shows have included Victorian fans and ancient myths and legends. The museum also runs fan-making workshops and can even design and make fans to order for special occasions.

Fans appear in a variety of guises in the imaginatively stocked museum shop. Fan fayre on offer includes specially commissioned jewellery, as well as greetings cards, toiletries and tea cosies, plus a variety of fans. The shop also carries a range of specialist publications. Afternoon teas are served in the museum's pretty conservatory on Tuesday and Sunday afternoons; but this being Greenwich, there is no shortage of good eating opportunities within easy walking distance for those visiting on other days.

Firepower, The Royal Artillery Museum

Royal Arsenal, Woolwich, SE18

020 8855 7755

www.firepower.org.uk

North Greenwich LU, then buses 161, 422 or 472 to Woolwich; Woolwich Arsenal Rail

Wed-Sun 10.30-17.00 (April-Oct), Fri-Sun 10.30-17.00 (Nov-March)

£5 (adults), £2.50 (children), £4.50 (cons)

Shop

Café

Wheelchair access

The first home of Arsenal Football Club (see p. 82), Woolwich was also the birthplace of the Royal Regiment of Artillery. Nearly 300 years after the regiment's founding in 1716, this museum tells the story of the original 'gunners' as well as exploring the history of artillery from slingshot to supergun. Firepower features an impressive battery of weaponry including coastal and air defence guns, anti-tank guns and rockets. Displays of military hardware range from a 16th-century glass hand grenade to a fully kitted out Command Post Saracen and are backed up by archive images, personal recollections and interactive exhibits to help visitors really get a flavour of life as a gunner in both war and peace. 'Field of Fire', a noisy, seat-shaking film presentation, shows some of the museum's big guns in action. There's plenty of science on offer here too – this is the place to discover the difference between direct and indirect fire, and why 'rifling' is crucial to spin stabilisation. More than just a museum, Firepower is also a memorial to those who served in the regiment and the Medals Gallery includes decorations from just about every campaign fought by the British Army over the past 200 years. Incidentally, the museum is home to the Victoria Cross Guns – metal from which continues to be used to make Britain's most prized military honour. Things get chilly over in the East Wing Gallery with an exploration of the Cold War era to the present day, taking in topics such as the conflict in Ireland and the war(s) in Iraq. Exhibits here include ultra modern weapons such as the AS90, a self-propelled gun used in the Second Gulf War, whose range is a whopping 30km. Illustrated banners place each exhibit in a wider historical and social context and audio guides are freely available for those who require more in-depth information. The lively museum café serves simple but good hot food and a decent cappuccino.

Greenwich Heritage Centre

Artillery Square, Royal Arsenal, Woolwich SE18

☎ *020 8854 2452*

✎ *www.greenwich.gov.uk*

🚌 *Woolwich Arsenal Rail; North Greenwich LU then bus 161, 422 or 472*

🕐 *Tues-Sat 9.00-17.00*

💷 *Admission free*

🛍 *Shop*

🍴 *Refreshments*

♿ *Disabled access*

What was once Greenwich Borough Museum has amalgamated with the local history archives to become the Greenwich Heritage Centre, in the process relocating to a striking 19th-century building in the heart of the Royal Arsenal. The Centre features a permanent exhibition on the history of the Royal Arsenal, charting its roles as Henry VIII's dockyard, munitions depot, stopping off place for convicts en route to Australia, and the birthplace of the Arsenal FC. For those brave souls delving into their family history, the 'Search Room' is packed with useful resources like old census returns, electoral registers and historic maps and prints. The Centre also offers guided visits around the exhibitions and collections and walking tours around the Royal Arsenal itself. A children's Saturday Club, lectures and workshops for adults are also on the cultural menu here.

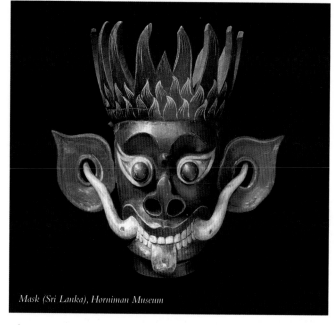

Mask (Sri Lanka), Horniman Museum

The Horniman Museum & Gardens

🗓 *100 London Road, Forest Hill, SE23*

☎ *020 8699 1872*

✎ *www.horniman.ac.uk*

🚉 *Forest Hill Rail, bus 176, 185, 197, 356, P4*

🕐 *Museum: Daily 10.30-17.30*
Gardens: Mon-Sat 7.30-dusk, Sun 8.00-dusk

🎟 *Admission free*

👓 *Shop*

🍽 *Café*

♿ *Wheelchair access*

Although firmly rooted in its South London community, the Horniman is much more than a purely 'local' museum. With displays embracing natural history, ethnography and a vast collection of musical instruments, this popular museum revels in its diversity – and its enthusiasm is catching.

The museum's in-house aquarium showcases a variety of endangered watery habitats, with the emphasis on conservation. Visitors can follow the journey of a river upstream from mouth to source, peer into the dark waters of a flooded forest pool or wonder at the brilliance and fragility of a coral reef. In these aquatic stage sets the fish – flamboyantly costumed clown fish and stately seahorses – are consummate performers and usually have a captive audience.

A veritable menagerie of stuffed animals populate the Natural History section, centred around an enormous, somewhat elderly walrus. Old style (but none the worse for that) displays explore topics such as evolution as well as Forest Hill's own flora and fauna, making the Horniman a well-structured, local alternative to the Natural History Museum.

The Horniman is also the home of Britain's first permanent gallery dedicated to African cultures and the African-influenced cultures of the Caribbean and Brazil. 'African Worlds' brings together fine and decorative arts from as far afield as Mali and Ethiopia, Egypt and Zimbabwe, with exhibits such as Benin bronzes, huge Dogon, Nufansa and Bwa masks and religious altars from Haiti and Brazil. Beautifully presented, the artefacts are accompanied by clear, informative explanatory material. Changing exhibitions on a variety of themes are shown on the balcony gallery and there is a further gallery which displays more extensive, year-long temporary exhibitions.

The museum's centenary development opened in 2002 and has greatly enhanced the original building with better access and facilities, including a shop and a pleasant café overlooking the museum's elegant Victorian conservatory. Some of the treasures collected from around the world by the museum's founder, Victorian tea tycoon Frederick Horniman, can be seen in the Centenary Gallery. The gallery tracks the changing way ethnographic collections have been displayed in the museum and looks at the ongoing collecting work of the Horniman's curators with recent acquisitions such as a Mari Lwyd hobby horse from Wales. Visitors can handle some 4,000 objects from the museum's amazing collections in the 'Hands-On Base', which is open on Saturday mornings and Sunday afternoons as well as select days in school holidays for family groups (entry by ticketed session only). The Music Gallery also promises lots of hands-on action with the chance to play a selection of instruments from an African mbira to 'paddle panpipes' (played with a pair of flip-flops!). Thanks to interactive computers, visitors can also hear what some of the other instruments in this 2,000-strong collection sound like.

The Horniman's 16 acres of well-tended gardens are also well worth a visit and are the ideal venue for a picnic. The outdoor attractions include sweeping views over London, an old fashioned bandstand and a small animal enclosure.

London Sewing Machine Museum

⌨ *300 Balham High Road, SW17*
☎ *020 8682 7916*
✎ *www.sewantique.com*
🚌 *Balham LU/Rail*
🕐 *First Sat of each month 14.00-17.00*
♿ *Admission free*

Balham is not just the 'Gateway to the South' – since July 2000 it has also been home to this specialist museum. About 550 machines are lovingly displayed here, the focus being on domestic sewing machines dating from 1850-1885 and industrial sewing machines made between 1850-1950. Built up over 40 years by one man, Ray Rushton, the collection is one of the most extensive and best of its kind in the world. The centrepiece of the display is the unique sewing machine made for Queen Victoria's oldest daughter on the occasion of her wedding.

National Maritime Museum

⌨ *Greenwich, SE10*
☎ *020 8858 4422*
✎ *www.nmm.ac.uk*
🚌 *Cutty Sark DLR, Maze Hill Rail, Greenwich Rail/DLR*
🕐 *Daily 10.00-17.00 (last admission 16.30)*
♿ *Admission free (admission charge for some exhibitions)*
🛍 *Shop*
☕ *Café & Restaurant*
♿ *Wheelchair access*

The largest museum of its kind in the world, the NMM has enjoyed something of a sea change over the past few years. Reconfigured and upgraded, the museum boasts state-of-the-art galleries whose appealing displays draw on the cream of the museum's collection to tell the story of seafaring from prehistory to present day. And the drive for modernisation hasn't stopped there – the museum is planning a £35 million new wing with more exhibition space and a new archive centre, due to be completed in time for the 2012 London Olympics.

A flashing lighthouse optic and a huge rotating propeller greet visitors as they enter – reminders of the dangers and scale of the sea. Three internal 'streets' run beneath the glass-roofed 'Neptune' courtyard to provide a dry dock for historic vessels such as a gilded royal barge and streamlined *Miss Britain III* (the first power boat to go over 100 mph) and exhibits such as a wave and vortex making tank.

Also on the ground floor (Level 1), 'Explorers' asks what possessed people to sail off on dangerous voyages into unknown waters to all

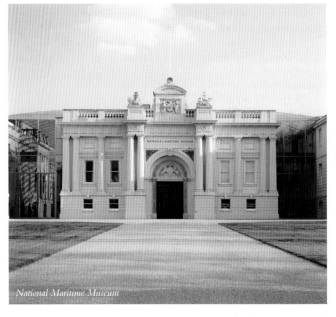

National Maritime Museum

points of the compass. Spice, gold and glory is the short answer and the displays include relics from Sir John Franklin's ill-fated voyage to discover the North-West Passage in the 1840s.

Human cargo is the subject of 'Passengers' an enjoyable exhibition about sea travel both for pleasure and as part of the mass migrations of the 20th century. Rich and poor may have travelled on the same ships but their accommodation was worlds apart – compare and contrast the cushy cabin of a 1st-class passenger with the rock-hard bunk beds and itchy blankets of 3rd-class quarters. Apparently, we haven't lost the yen to live it large at sea – the colossal *Grand Princess* cruise ship launched in 1998 and measures just 5 metres less than the Eiffel tower and contains 9 jacuzzis, it is represented here by a scale model.

As every cruise passenger knows, what to wear at sea is an important consideration. 'Rank & Style' displays a selection of maritime clobber, from a child's 'sailor suit' to serious survival gear such as the woolly pyjamas issued to the 1911 Australasian Antarctic Expedition and the garish orange survival suit worn by capsized yachtsman Tony Bullimore. Naval costumes weren't always effective in protecting their wearers as Nelson's bullet-holed, bloodstained coat (on show in the Nelson Gallery) demonstrates, but they sure could make a man look important

– check out the gold braid and epaulettes on King Edward VIII's full dress uniform as the Admiral of the Fleet.

A small exhibition on level 1 examines various aspects of 'Maritime London', such as pomp and pageantry, shipping and shipbuilding, commerce and cargoes. The original scale model of Nelson's column (minus the pigeons) is one of the exhibits here.

'Art & the Sea' (level 2) is awash with powerful images of the ocean, displaying paintings as varied as *The Battle of Texel* by Van de Velde or *L'Avant Port, Marseilles* by Edward Wadsworth and sea-borne films such as Noël Coward's *In which we Serve*.

The Upper Deck overlooking the Neptune Court deploys over 300 objects from the NMM stores to represent a snapshot of the Museum's core collections. Jolly ships' badges, ingenious navigational aides and curatorial curiosities are typical of the displays here. A small adjacent gallery – 'Your Ocean' – tackles topical sea-borne issues such as global warming, pollution and modern day piracy.

Up on Level 3, 'All Hands' is aimed squarely at young sea-dogs and is great fun, with some genuinely hands-on exhibits. Aspiring admirals can signal to each other using flags, morse code or two-way radio, learn what it's like to work deep underwater in total darkness or discover what Vikings ate on their 'cruises'. Equally interactive is 'The Bridge', where visitors can learn how to 'read' a hydrographic chart, bark instructions down a 'loudaphone' or attempt to park a ferry at Dover docks. 'Oceans of Discovery' recounts the 4,000 year old story of man's endeavour to explore the sea, both on and below the surface. A replica Polynesian map using shells and sticks to denote ocean currents is one of the navigational aids shown, and considerable space is devoted to underwater exploration, from the early days of cumbersome diving suits to the snazzy remote control deep water submersibles of today.

Level 3 is also home to 'Nelson', a permanent exhibition on one of Britain's most enduring naval heroes and 'Ship of War', the museum's collection of 17th and 18th-century models of warships. Often mind-bogglingly intricate, these miniatures include the *Royal George*, an 18th-century flagship, which inexplicably sank while at anchor in 1782. Special exhibitions expand on aspects of the permanent displays while 'New Visions' brings the world of contemporary art to the museum, with changing installation of new art works exploring the significance of the sea.

The NMM is handily placed for the amenities of Greenwich, but does boast its own on board restaurant as a café on the Upper Deck; if you've brought your own rations, a picnic area is available. The gift shop stocks nautical books and novelties across the price range.

The Pumphouse Educational Museum/ Rotherhithe Heritage Museum

🖼 *Lavender Road, SE16*
☎ *020 7231 2976*
🖱 *www.thepumphouse.org.uk*
🚇 *Canada Water LU, Surrey Quays LU, Rotherhithe LU; bus 225, 381*
🕐 *Mon-Fri 9.00-16.00*
💷 *Public entrance by donation*
🛍 *Shop*
🍽 *Lunch area*
♿ *Wheelchair access*

Artefacts found along the Thames' foreshore recount the story of one of London's oldest villages at this local history museum. The result of 10 years of beachcombing by local man Ron Goode, the collection includes an enjoyably random array of everyday objects dating from Roman to modern times. Items include medieval flea combs, 17th-century wig curlers, 19th-century pencil sharpeners and dockers' tools. In the first floor gallery, semi-permanent displays on the 1950's and 20th-century domestic artefacts bring the Rotherhithe story more up to date. Somewhat reminiscent of a glorified jumble sale, these low-frills displays have the unexpected bonus of an original 50s jukebox so visitors can soak up the nostalgia while enjoying the yesteryear sounds of Buddy Holly, Connie Francis, and Tommy Steele. Housed in the Lavender Pond Pumphouse, the museum is surrounded by a nature park complete with trails, assorted wildlife and a pond.

The Queen's House

- Greenwich, SE10
- 020 8858 4422
- www.nmm.ac.uk
- Cutty Sark DLR, Maze Hill Rail, Greenwich Rail/DLR
- Daily 10.00-17.00 (last entry 16.30)
- Admission free
- Wheelchair access

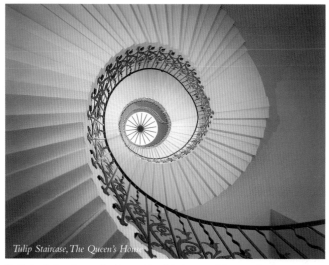

Tulip Staircase, The Queen's House

Built by Inigo Jones for James I's wife, Anne of Denmark, this gracious residence holds the double distinction of being the first classical building in England and the first to boast a flight of cantilevered stairs. The Queen's House now serves as a glorified art gallery having been redesignated as the National Maritime Museum's Fine and Decorative Arts Centre. Even without their historic furnishings the rooms are impressive – the balconied Great Hall and 'tulip stairs' are the must sees here – and the NNM's art collection of mainly maritime art is also top of its league. Displays are changed regularly and on a recent visit the images included some atmospheric 19th-century photographs of the Arctic. On the ground floor the Orangery is flanked by two galleries showing 17th and 18th century marine art by the likes of the Van de Veldes and the aptly named Isaac Sailmaker. The friendly room staff willingly share their knowledge and go out of their way to engage the visitor – a refreshing alternative to the increasingly ubiquitous audio guide.

Ranger's House

🏠 *Chesterfield Walk, SE10*

☎ *020 8853 0035*

🔗 *www.english-heritage.org.uk*

🚉 *Blackheath Rail, Cutty Sark DLR, Greenwich Rail/DLR*

🕐 *Sun-Wed 10.00-17.00 (April-Sept); pre-booked tours only
(Oct-Dec, March)*

💷 *£5.50 (adults), £4.40 (concessions), £2.80 (under 16s),
free (under 5s/English Heritage members)*

🛍 *Shop*

♿ *Wheelchair access to ground floor*

This imposing Georgian house has recently been on the receiving
end of an extensive refurbishment courtesy of English Heritage. Its
once again gracious interiors have also become home to the 'Wernher
Collection' – an opulent assembly of objets d'art put together by self
made millionaire Sir Julius Wernher. Wernher made it big in the South
African gold and diamond industries and you can certainly see where
he spent his cash – the suite of 12 display rooms are stuffed with bronze
statuary, medieval ivories, Old Master pictures, Renaissance jewellery,
Sèvres porcelain and maiolica ceramics.

The Red Room has been kitted out as it would have been at Bath
House (the Wernher's Mayfair residence). The rich ox-blood red walls
are hung with Old Masters such as Memling's *Mother & Child* and *Rest
on the Flight to Egypt* by Filippino Lippi, while its displays of Renaissance
ivories and medallions are densely packed in 19th century connoisseur
style. No labels intrude on the ambience in this room – if you want
to know what you're looking at, you can refer to information sheets,
housed in smart leather bound folders. If the Red Room is an exercise
in masculine self-expression, the Pink Drawing Room downstairs
bespeaks an altogether more feminine sensibility. This was Lady
Wernher's domain and it's characterised by deeply pink wallpaper, pretty
portraits of 18th-century beauties by the likes of Hoppner, Romney and
Reynolds, sugary Sèvres porcelain and curvaceous French furniture.

Reminiscent of the Wallace Collection (see p. 215), albeit on a
smaller scale, the collection offers a similarly revealing insight into what
makes a collector tick. Its highlights include the jewellery closet which
contains beautifully crafted Renaissance and Antique pieces, the 'private
devotion room' (mainly Medieval items), the Limoges room (painted
enamels and fine metal work) and the Green Silk Room (Dutch and
English landscape paintings). The collection concludes in The Gallery,
hung with 17th century French tapestries and overseen at the far end
by a dazzling white marble sculpture of angels by Bergonzolli.

Royal Observatory Greenwich and Peter Harrison Planetarium

Greenwich, SE10
020 8858 4422
www.nmm.ac.uk
Cutty Sark DLR, Maze Hill Rail, Greenwich Rail/DLR
Daily 10.00-17.00 (last admission 16.30)
Admission free
Shop
Café (at the Planetarium)
Wheelchair access (ring 020 8312 6608 for details)

A short sharp walk up the hill from the Queen's House and Maritime Museum brings you to a cluster of buildings which look more like a stable block than an observatory (although the big green 'onion' dome is a bit of a giveaway).

Straddling the meridian line (at 0 degrees longitude) and home to Greenwich Mean Time, the Observatory can claim to be 'the centre of time and space'. Visitors line up to photograph each other with one foot in the East, the other in the West. The 'Camera Obscura' is much more entertaining: a revolving panorama of Greenwich projected live onto a table in the middle of the room. Next door, Flamsteed House contains the spartan apartments of the Astronomers Royal and the Octagon Room, a rare example of an interior by Sir Christopher Wren. Instruments for measuring time and space are also on display and include the watch which solved the navigators' problem of assessing longitude. If you get to the Observatory before 1pm, look out for the 'Time Ball' which drops at that exact time each day to enable ships on the Thames to set their chronometers.

Over in the new Weller Astronomy Galleries at the Planetarium, there's no need to wish for the moon, when you can have the stars as well. Crammed with high-tech interactive gizmos, these engaging displays aim to unravel the secrets of the universe, revealing, amongst other things, why telescopes are like time machines and giving visitors the chance to build their own virtual space probe. It's mind-boggling stuff so it's good to see included among all the highfaluting quotes by Plato, Newton and their ilk, Douglas Adams' laconic observation, 'Space is big'. If you want to feel really insignificant, buy a ticket (£6 adults, £4 children) to one of highly enjoyable shows in the Planetarium to follow the birth and life of a star and for guidance from a real astronomer on what to see in the sky that night.

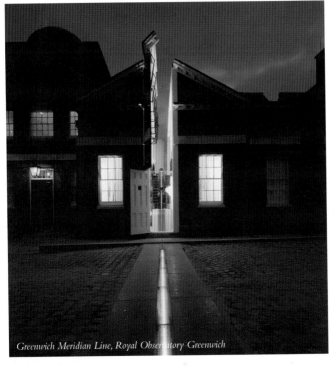

Greenwich Meridian Line, Royal Observatory Greenwich

Southside House

3-4 Woodhayes Road, Wimbledon Common, SW19

020 8946 7643

www.southsidehouse.com

Wimbledon LU/Rail

Visits by guided tour only: Wed, Sat, Sun and Bank Holidays 14.00, 15.00, 16.00 (Easter to Oct)

£5 (adults), £2.50 (children), £10 (family), £4 (student))

Wheelchair access – please phone in advance

Anybody who is anybody seems to have featured in the colourful history of Southside House: Lord Byron, Emma Hamilton, and Axel Munthe are just some of the names associated with the house, built in the Dutch Baroque style by Robert Pennington in 1687. Its contents are equally well-connected and include souvenirs of two beheaded queens (Anne Boleyn's vanity case and Marie Antoinette's pearl necklace) as well as portraits by Van Dyck, Hogarth and Angelica Kauffmann.

The Wimbledon Lawn Tennis Museum

🏛 *Museum Building, The All England Lawn Tennis Club,*
   Church Road, SW19

☎ *020 8946 6131*

🖲 *www.wimbledon.org/museum*

🚌 *Wimbledon LU/Rail then bus 493, Southfields LU then 15mins*
   walk or bus 493

🕐 *Daily 10.30-17.00 (last entry 16.30) (during the Championships*
   open only to those visiting the tournament)

💷 *£8.50 (adults), £7.50 (concessions), £4.75 (children)*

🛍 *Shop*

☕ *Café*

♿ *Wheelchair access*

It's hard to believe it now, but lawn tennis was once just a glorified garden party game, rejoicing in the preposterous brand name of 'Sphairistiké'. This museum, based at the famous All England Lawn Tennis Club, follows the development of the sport from its monastic origins to genteel Edwardian pastime to mega-bucks international industry – all thanks to the invention of the lawn mower and the bouncy rubber ball. Naturally the museum also celebrates the unique sporting event that is the Wimbledon Championship and, thanks to a recent relocation and redesign, displays are top-notch with plenty to enjoy, whether you're a die-hard tennis nut or a casual armchair aficionado.

Tableaux recreate the early days of tennis – from the quaint 1920's Gentlemen's Dressing room to a 1930's racquet makers' workshop complete with woodshavings – while comprehensive displays of tennis equipment show how the game evolved into today's hi-speed, hi-tech sport. Interactive consoles allow visitors to test their response time in the face of a 150 mph serve, interview the head groundsman or try their hand at a traditional Wimbledon pastime – pulling the rain covers over the court. Touchscreens show footage of tennis stars past and present in action, providing the opportunity to see just how leisurely the game seemed in the days of Rene Lacoste, 'Bunny' Austen and Fred Perry – the last British player to win the men's singles. Footage of Wimbledon television coverage over the decades is also nostalgic fun with no shortage of net-leaping, trophy-kissing finals action.

Tennis has always been about looking the part and the on-court fashions shown here range from full-length white cotton dresses to a gold lamé micro-mini worn by our very own Sue Barker, Roger Federer's natty white blazer kit and a bodyhugging Lycra 'corset' dress designed for Venus Williams. One of the highlights of the museum is the 'Pepper's Ghost' illusion of John McEnroe, talking about the heroes

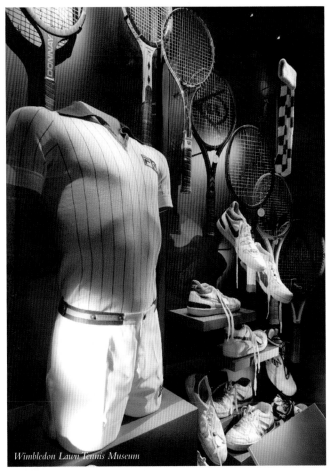

Wimbledon Lawn Tennis Museum

of men's tennis and his Wimbledon years in a recreation of the 1980's locker room he once used. The pressures and rewards of today's 'Circuit' are also explored while the science of playing tennis is explained in the 200° Cinema.

Wimbledon's glittering prizes – the Ladies' Singles salver and Mens' Singles cup – are among the closing exhibits, along with a display about the most recent Championships. Tennis themed souvenirs and equipment are the order of the day in the shop and the well-appointed Renshaw café serves light lunches and traditional cream teas.

The Wimbledon Society Museum of Local History

- 22 Ridgway, SW19
- 020 8296 9914
- www.wimbledonmuseum.org.uk
- Wimbledon LU/Rail
- Sat and Sun 14.30-17.00 (at other times by appointment)
- Admission free
- Shop

Famous today for its international tennis tournament (see previous page), Wimbledon has not always been the haunt of white clad tennis pros. Neanderthal hunters once prowled its open spaces and in Victorian times Wimbledon became the venue for popular rifle shooting competitions. There must be something competitive in the air because it was here too in 1798 that the prime minister William Pitt fought a pistol duel. These and other aspects of Wimbledon's 3,000 year long history are recounted at this small local museum, which boasts an extensive archive of paintings, prints, objects, maps and manuscripts.

Wimbledon Windmill Museum

- Windmill Road, Wimbledon Common, SW19
- 020 8947 2825
- www.wimbledonwindmill.museum.org
- Putney LU (then bus); Wimbledon LU/Rail
- Sat 14.00-17.00, Sun and Bank Holidays 11.00-17.00 (April-Oct)
- £1 (adults), 50p (children/concessions)
- Shop
- Café
- Wheelchair access (ground floor only)

What better place to tell the story of windmills and windmilling than in a windmill itself? Working models, original machinery as well as films, bring the narrative to life, revealing the development of windmills from ancient Persia to modern wind farms. There are hands-on activities for young millers but if it's all too much of a grind, the café's just next door.

East

Dennis Severs House

🖃 18 Folgate Street, E1

☏ 020 7247 4013

🖉 www.dennissevershouse.co.uk

🚌 Liverpool Street LU

🕓 Every Monday evening, by candlelight, times vary according to the
season and booking is necessary; first and third Sunday of each month
12.00-16.00 (no booking required); the Monday following the first
and third Sunday 12.00-14.00 (no booking required)

💷 £12 (Mon evening openings), £8 (Sun openings), £5 (Mon openings)

♿ No disabled access

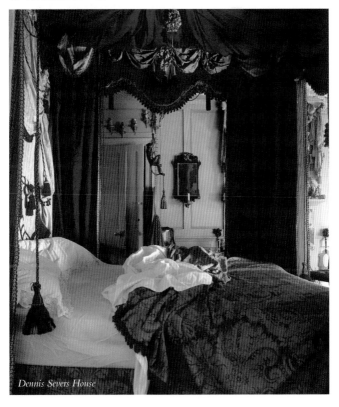

Dennis Severs House

149

Dennis Severs House is a real one-off – neither museum nor historic house it is perhaps best approached as piece of unique installation art. Created by Dennis Severs, an Anglophile Californian who died in 1999, the house is an 18th-century terraced dwelling whose candlelit rooms have been furnished and arranged as a series of atmospheric period 'still-life dramas', in which the visitor travels through the picture frame into the painting itself. Mr Severs had strong views about how his creation should be experienced, reminders of which are dotted around the house; visitors are expected to be seen but not heard and a very museum-like approach to looking but not *touching* is enforced. Talkative, tactile folk may find this constricting but restraint is worthwhile – it's hard for the magic to come alive if all you can hear is inane chatter. In the old days Mr Severs would summarily eject visitors who transgressed in this way.

The conceit is that the house is still lived in by a family of Huguenot silk weavers, and going around the house the visitor continually enters rooms they have apparently just left. Subtle recorded sound effects and authentic touches such as brimming bedside chamber pots, unmade beds and half-eaten meals help create the Marie Celeste effect but the house remains an engagingly leaky time capsule. Period pedants may disapprove but playful anachronisms abound, including poignant reminders of Mr Severs' own occupancy – a NY Yankees baseball jacket draped over the back of a chair, a pair of highly polished English gent's shoes tucked away in a bedroom. The house evokes several time periods, following successive generations of the Jervis family on a picaresque journey from genteel Hanoverian prosperity to the Dickensian hard times evoked by the squalid top floor garret. Taking the idea of painterly drama even further the 'smoking room' recreates the debauched interior of Hogarth's painting *A Midnight Modern Conversation* – x marks the spot on the floor where the visitor is invited to stand to become part of the painting.

Severs' motto was 'You either see it or you don't', and for those willing to suspend disbelief the experience he created is captivating – but don't forget to keep the noise down …

The Geffrye Museum

Kingsland Road, E2

☎ 020 7739 9893

☎ 020 7739 8543 (recorded information)

✎ www.geffrye-museum.org.uk

🚃 Dalston Kingsland BR; Liverpool Street LU/BR, then 149 or 242 bus;
Old Street LU, then 243 bus or 15 mins walk

🕐 Museum: Tues-Sat 10.00-17.00, Sun and Bank Holidays 12.00-17.00
Almshouse: 1st Sat of the month, admission by timed entry 11.00,
12.00, 14,00, 15.00

💷 Admission to museum free; Admission to almshouse £2 (adults)

✎ Shop

🍽 Restaurant

♿ Wheelchair access

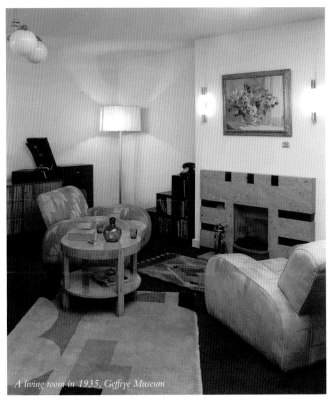

A living room in 1935, Geffrye Museum

Set in 18th-century almshouses the Geffrye is one of London's more charismatic museums, offering visitors a voyeuristic treat by inviting them to go 'through the keyhole' and explore interiors from times past. From the oak-panelled simplicity of the 17th-century to the cool elegance of the early-Georgian drawing room and the oppressive clutter of the Victorian parlour to the modern lines of art deco and contemporary warehouse 'loft' space; the museum's series of fully-furnished period rooms presents the ever changing face of English interior decoration. A kind of walk-through, 3-D source book of past taste, the Geffrye is just as revealing about the way we live now as it is about domestic history. In December the period rooms are decorated in keeping with the festive season, while in the summer the walled herb garden and period garden 'rooms' are an added attraction, echoing their counterparts indoors. A smart new extension, opened since the first edition of this guide, incorporates a venue for special exhibitions such as the recent two part 'Home & Garden' as well as housing the Design Centre, which hosts exhibitions of local contemporary design in a range of media. A real gem.

Hackney Museum

📖 *Technology & Learning Centre, 1 Reading Lane E8*
☎ *020 8356 3500*
🖥 *www.hackney.gov.uk*
🚃 *Hackney Central Rail*
🕐 *Tues, Wed, Fri 9.30-17.30; Thurs 9.30-20.00, Sat 10.00-17.00*
💷 *Admission free*
🛍 *Shop*
♿ *Wheelchair access*

This community museum explores the reasons why people have flocked to Hackney over the last 1,000 years. Its permanent displays include a very rare Anglo-Saxon log boat, a Victorian nursery-cum-contemporary flat and oral histories from people living in the area, interspersed with sculptures by local schoolchildren. Regularly changing temporary displays explore aspects of local history and the museum also runs a vibrant programme of events and activities. Installed in the smart modern premises of the Technology and Learning Centre, the museum has attracted rave reviews from the museum press and has proved a real hit with families, older visitors and those notoriously difficult to please folk, teenagers.

Museum of London Docklands

🏛 No. 1 Warehouse, West India Quay, Hertsmere Road, E14

☎ 0870 444 3856

🖱 www.museumindocklands.org.uk

🚇 West India Quay DLR, Canary Wharf LU;
Bus 227, D3, D6, D7, D8, 115

🕐 Daily 10.00-18.00 (last admission 17.30)

💷 £5 (adults), £3 (concs), free (under 16s, NUS cardholders &
disabled carers)

👜 Shop

☕ Café

♿ Wheelchair access

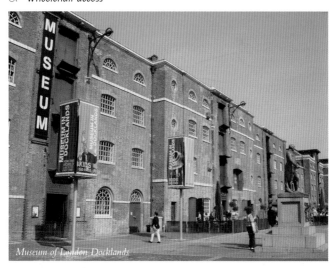

Museum of London Docklands

Woefully underused today, the river Thames permeates almost every aspect of London's history. This museum tells the story of London's river, ports and people and their role in shaping the city. An outpost of the Museum of London (p. 57) the setting for this enterprise couldn't be more appropriate: an early 19th century warehouse at West India Quay, in the heart of Docklands and in the shadow of the glittering skyscrapers that dominate Canary Wharf.

Visits start on the third floor and work down but before you get stuck in, a word of warning. The museum tackles a huge subject and is packed with things to see and enjoy – archaeological finds, historical documents, model ships (such as the remarkably difficult to launch

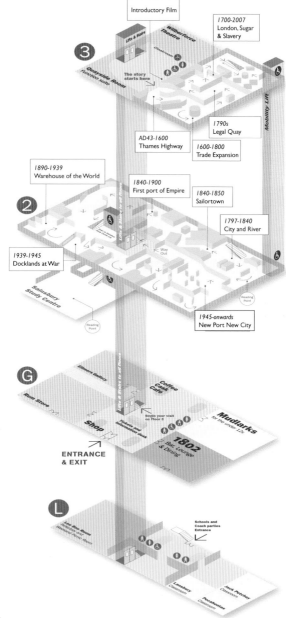

Introductory Film

1700-2007
London, Sugar
& Slavery

Wilberforce
Theatre

③

Quayside Room
Function suite

The story
starts here

1790s
Legal Quay

Mobility Lift

AD43-1600
Thames Highway

1600-1800
Trade Expansion

1890-1939
Warehouse of the World

1840-1900
First port of Empire

②

1840-1850
Sailortown

1797-1840
City and River

1939-1945
Docklands at War

Way
Out

Sainsbury
Study Centre

Reading
Point

Reading
Point

1945-onwards
New Port New City

G

Ilmera Gallery

Coffee
Creek
Café

Rum Store

Shop

Begin your visit
on Floor 3

Tickets and
Information desk

Mudlarks
for the under 5s

1802
Bar, Lounge
& Dining

ENTRANCE
& EXIT

L

Lea Bar Room

Schools and
Coach parties
Entrance

Lansbury
Classroom

Jack Petchey
Classroom

Pocahontas
Classroom

154

HMS Northumberland) and artworks. You'll certainly need to pace yourself if you want to do it in one go, but tickets are valid for a year so you can return as often as you like within that period if you prefer to dip in and out at your leisure.

London was a successful port from the word go and the museum's opening display charts the relentless comings and goings on 'the Thames Highway'. Roman *Londinium* became Anglo Saxon *Lundenwic* which in turn gave way to the 3rd century port of *Lundenburgh* and not even Boudicca or Viking marauders could dent London's pre-eminence. An audio visual presentation by Time Team's Tony Robinson sets out the whole sequence of events very clearly and boasts some neat interactives encouraging younger visitors to 'dig deeper' and find out what archaeologists really get up to. Archaeology has been crucial in shaping our understanding of London's long lost early ports and discoveries such as Roman pottery, Anglo Saxon loom weights and a Viking battle axe bring this history to life. Another highlight is a magnificent double sided model of old London Bridge showing the bridge in Medieval and Tudor times respectively. Other displays look at trade expansion and the rise of the merchant class and there's the first of the reconstructed interiors which are such a feature of the museum, this one being of a 'legal quay' from the 1790's, complete with a human treadmill crane, a counting house and a gibbet.

Still on the third floor, a new gallery (opened 2007) tells the ignoble story of London's part in the slave trade and the sugar industry from the 1700s onwards. The museum's location in the West India Docks – the construction of which was financed by London's sugar barons and which were used by slave trading ships – brings the subject painfully home. Portraits of wealthy merchants such as George Hibbert are displayed alongside the brutal instruments of slavery as well as the product which drove the trade: a sugar loaf. Slavery in Britain was finally abolished in 1833 but the repercussions continue to be felt, and the gallery brings the story up to date with contemporary artworks exploring the subject while headphones allow visitors to listen to the stories of colonial subjects in postwar London.

Moving down a floor, 'City and River' looks at the Thames in the Regency period and its role as a whaling and coal port, and the emergence of the docks. It wasn't all hard graft though as the displays highlighting the colourful rituals associated with the river show – watermen's races and barge processions involving opulent City Barges.

'Sailor Town' is an enjoyable, faintly spooky, reconstruction of the East End in the 19th century. Visitors walk down dimly lit cobbled alleyways flanked by a pub, a lodging house and shops dealing

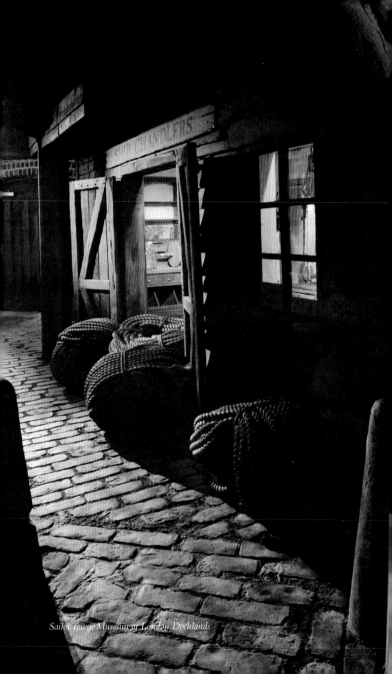

SHIP CHANDLERS

Sailor Town, Museum of London Docklands

in everything from prints to wild animals. Other reconstructed interiors such as the bottling vault and tobacco weighing station recall when London truly was 'the Warehouse of the World' – the goods once handled at North Quay's warehouses ranged from almonds to tulipwood, along with pepper, rice, rum, tea, tin and teak.

All this relentless trading was fuelled by raw manpower – as the number of ship builders', dockers', stevedores' and porters' tools on display powerfully demonstrate. Not for nothing was the quayside outside the museum known as 'Blood Alley' from the damaged hands and backs of dockers who lugged commodities from dockside to warehouse. Life in the docks was tough and there's a section devoted to the 1889 Dock Strike in which visitors can 'interview' participants on both side of this bitter dispute.

Things got even tougher during the Second World War when the Docklands became a target for Nazi bombers. Film footage showing the devastation wreaked on 'black Saturday' still has the power to move and shock, as do a series of original canvases by war artist William Ware. The wartime exhibits include a claustrophobic 'consul' air raid shelter and a mobile canteen and reveal some of the secret work carried out in Docklands, such as the development of 'Pluto' – the pipeline which carried fuel under the Channel to Allied troops in France. An area of quiet contemplation with stained glass panels by artist John Patsalides is a reminder that for some people this perilous time is not just history, it is part of their lives.

Before you get too carried away on a high tide of nostalgia the museum turns its scrutiny to the recent regeneration of the docklands after years of what seemed terminal decline. This chapter of London's history was not without its turbulent moments either and features the controversial London Docklands Development Corporation, yuppies, the Wapping newspaper dispute, as well as major engineering feats such as the Millennium Bridge and the Jubilee line extension.

On your way down to the ground floor, the mezzanine 'Thames Gallery' has been replaced by the 'Sainsbury Study Centre', which contains the Museum in Docklands and the PLA Archives as well as the Sainsbury Archive. On display are photographs of early Sainsbury stores and examples of Sainsbury's own brand packaging. The 'Mudlarks Gallery' on the ground floor lets the under 12s engage in educational fun activities such as 'tipping the clipper', tying nautical knots, and getting to grips with block and tackle technology. There's plenty of nick-nacks in the small museum shop as well as books about London and the Thames. The café serves a simple menu and a decent cappuccino while the '1802' bar and restaurant offers more substantial fare.

museums

east

Museum of Immigration and Diversity

⊞ *19 Princelet Street, E1*

☎ *020 7247 5352*

✎ *www.19princeletstreet.org.uk*

🚇 *Liverpool Street LU/Rail, Aldgate East LU*

🕐 *Scheduled days only – see website or phone for details;*
for group visits, book in advance

♨ *Admission free (donations appreciated)*

♿ *Wheelchair Access – ground floor only*

Based in a battered, unrestored 18th century house, this multicultural museum celebrates diversity and is the first of its kind in Europe. From Huguenot silk weavers' (whose garrets can still be glimpsed on the top floor) to 19th century Jewish settlers from Eastern Europe who built their own synagogue in the garden, the house is a witness to the waves of immigrants who have made their home in this part of London. A site specific exhibition 'Suitcases and Sanctuary' explores the continuing history of immigration to Spitalfields to the present day, through the eyes of children living in the area today. The fragile condition of the house means that the museum can currently only open a few days a year. Despite the limited opening hours, a shortage of funding and the fact that it is run by volunteers, thousands of people every year visit 19 Princelet Street – an indication of the resounding relevance and popularity of this 'museum of conscience'.

North Woolwich Old Station Museum

⊞ *Pier Road, E16*

☎ *020 7474 7244*

✎ *www.newham.gov.uk*

🚇 *North Woolwich Rail*

🕐 *Sat and Sun 13.00-17.00 (Jan-Nov); daily 13.00-17.00 (during*
Newham school holidays)

♨ *Admission free*

🛍 *Shop*

♿ *Wheelchair access*

Railway engines, carriages, photographs and models from the now mythic 'golden age' of rail travel are the main attractions at this museum, housed in an old station. Displays about Newham's railway industry and workers strike a more local note and there are activities and quizzes for kids to enjoy, along with a Brio train set and a virtual train to drive.

The Ragged School Museum

⊞ 46-50 Copperfield Road, E3

☎ 020 8980 6405

✎ www.raggedschoolmuseum.org.uk

🚌 Mile End LU

🕐 Wed and Thurs 10.00-17.00, first Sunday of the month 14.00-17.00

💷 Admission free (donations appreciated)

🛍 Shop

☕ Café

♿ Wheelchair access (ground floor only)

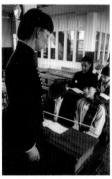

Staffed by enthusiastic, friendly volunteers and set in an old canalside warehouse, this is a charismatic little museum. The site of London's largest Ragged (free) School, the museum focuses on the work of Dr Barnardo and education in London but its displays also explore the lives and history of East Enders over the last two centuries. Many of the volunteers are locals and they help to bring the past to life in a memorable way.

Decked out in the cream and maroon livery specified by Dr Barnardo and furnished with wooden desks, writing slates, abacus and 'butterfly' blackboard, the reconstructed 1880s schoolroom makes an atmospheric centre piece. Each year thousands of primary school children take part in the popular re-enacted 'Victorian' lessons held here. On the first Sunday of the month lessons are open to everyone, whatever their age. There is also a reconstructed domestic kitchen, kitted out as it would have been in 1900, and complete with utensils for visitors to handle. The museum shop stocks local history publications as well as a selection of traditional-style toys and games. Snacks and drinks are sold in the peaceful Towpath Café.

Royal London Hospital Museum

⊞ St Philip's Church, Newark Street, E1

☎ 020 7377 7608

✎ www.bartsandthelondon.nhs.uk

🚌 Whitechapel LU

🕐 Mon-Fri 10.00-16.30

💷 Admission free (donations welcome)

🛍 Shop

♿ Wheelchair access

Located in the crypt of the former Hospital Church, this museum has an interesting selection of historic documents, medical equipment and nurses' uniforms as well as original artworks by William Hogarth and Sir John Lavery. The displays recount the history of the hospital from its founding in 1740 and highlight some of the medical developments it has witnessed like X-rays and Keyhole surgery, and the work of pioneers like Frederick Treves and Edith Cavell. There's also a small display about the hospital's most famous resident, Joseph Merrick (the 'Elephant Man'). Books and cards are sold at the shop and a digital video facility is available to visitors.

Sutton House

⊞ *2 and 4 Homerton High Street, (corner of Isabella Road), E9*
☎ *020 8986 2264*
✑ *www.nationaltrust.org.uk*
🚆 *Hackney Central Rail, Homerton Rail*
🕓 *Thurs-Sun 12.30-16.30 (Feb-Dec) (check website as times vary)*
💰 *£2.80 (adults), 70p (children), £6.30 (family ticket), free (NT members)*
🛍 *Shop*
☕ *Café*
♿ *Disabled access ground floor only*

Tudor houses aren't exactly ten a penny in the capital these days and Sutton House is a rare survivor. Built in 1535, it is in fact the oldest domestic building in the East End and its occupants have included Henry VIII's Secretary of State, Sir Ralph Sadleir, squatters in the 1980s, and its current owners, the National Trust. Although on the receiving end of later additions and alterations, the house still contains early features like linenfold panelling, stone fireplaces and 17th-century wall paintings. Hinged panels dotted throughout the house enable visitors to literally peel back the layers of history and see changes made to the fabric of the house for themselves. Located in Hackney, one of London's most arty boroughs, the house also has a gallery which hosts exhibitions of work by local artists. But if contemporary art isn't your bag, the small gift shop sells the usual array of National Trust tea towels, mugs and preserves as well as a selection of books about London history. The licensed café serves delicious light lunches and teas.

V&A Museum of Childhood

- Cambridge Heath Road, E2
- 020 8983 5200 (switchboard)
- 020 8980 2415 (recorded information)
- www.museumofchildhood.org.uk
- Bethnal Green LU, bus D6, 106, 253, 309, 388
- Daily 10.00-17.45 (last admission 17.30)
- Admission free
- Shop
- Café
- Wheelchair access

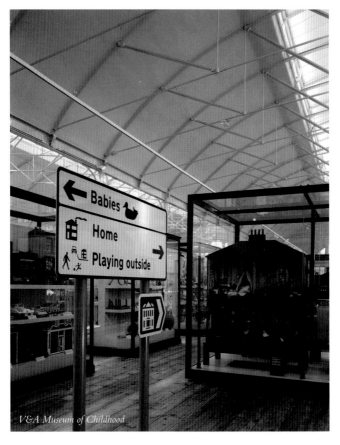

V&A Museum of Childhood

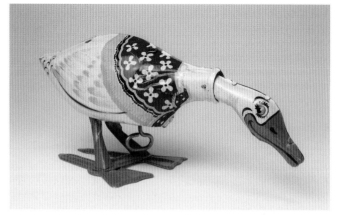

Gertie the Galloping Goose, 1930 (USA))

You don't have to have a sprog in tow to enjoy this museum. If anything, its vast hoard of toys from different eras makes it just as appealing for nostalgic adults. With a fine collection of children's clothes and paraphernalia like high-chairs and prams, the museum also illustrates the social history of childhood – but few will be able to resist embarking on a voyage to rediscover the toys and games of their youth.

The museum re-opened in 2006 after a major redevelopment which saw the airy Victorian cast iron interior restored and a welcome upgrade to visitor facilities, including a chunky new entrance lobby and better toilets. Once inside, there's no particular starting point to the displays – just start with whatever takes your fancy and follow the 'road signs' that point the way. If you are visiting with youngsters, there are ample opportunities for participation – be it messing around in the sandpit or a ride on the ever popular rocking horses.

Up on the first floor the Childhood Galleries get off to a positive start with 'Good Times' – party games like pin the tail on the donkey, an authentic 'Punch and Judy' booth and seaside accoutrements from saggy hand-knitted bathing costumes to vintage buckets and spades. More toys and games follow – the plethora of scaled down tool kits, lawnmowers and kitchens richly bearing out Roland Barthes' assertion that toys are a microcosm of the adult world.

The collection of children's clothing begins in the 18th century, when children were dressed as mini adults, and runs right up to the present day, on the way revealing how 'Lucy Locket,' of nursery rhyme fame, could have lost her pocket. Pride of place on this floor though must go to the dolls houses, executed in every possible permutation of architectural style and degree of grandeur: from the lavishly furnished Nuremburg House of 1673 (the oldest in the museum) to Betty Pinney's House, complete with lift and roof garden. The multicoloured 2001 Kaleidoscope House brings this section right up to date – perfect for today's brand-savvy youngsters.

Plenty of space too has been given over the museum's extensive collection of puppets from around the world, the centrepiece of which is an 18th century marionette theatre and its *commedia dell'arte* puppets. The theme of animation continues with a display of 'moving toys' which seem to encapsulate the unrestrained energy of childhood. Every form of propulsion is represented here from simple pull-along toys (although this category does include an avant garde beach buggy by Modernist designer Gerrit Thomas Rietveld), wind powered yachts, battery driven cars, wind-up tin toys, and self propelled items like rocking horses and space hoppers. The extensive Hornby train layout however is powered exclusively by 20p pieces. A large collection of eye-bending optical toys completes this section – from zoetropes to space invaders.

As you might expect, the museum is very child-friendly. The open plan galleries are spacious and well laid out and a team of activity assistants run daily drop in art and craft, story telling, games and puppet sessions for children. The toilets are equipped for nappy-changing and the new lobby incorporates a capacious buggy park. The centrally placed ground floor café offers a kids' menu as well as tempting coffee and cakes – if you don't mind being surrounded by wailing infants. Over by the entrance the shop sells a selection of reasonably priced toys and books, many with a retro flavour and a sure hit with visitors of all ages.

Vestry House Museum

- *Vestry Road, E17*
- *020 8509 1917*
- *www.walthamforest.gov.uk*
- *Walthamstow Central LU/Rail*
- *Thurs & Fri 12.00-16.00, Sat & Sun 10.00-17.00, Wed (school holidays only 12.00-16.00)*
- *Admission free (donations welcomed)*
- *Shop*
- *Wheelchair access (ground floor, garden and toilets only)*

An exploration of the history of Waltham Forest and its people. Locally-made produce on show ranges from tin plate toys to the star exhibit, the Bremer car of 1894 – the first petrol driven British automobile. The Victorian parlour may be a reconstruction, but the police cell is the real thing and although built in 1840, still has its original privy intact. Examples of clothing from the 18th to the 20th century can be seen in the Costume Gallery, which also contains some fine 16th-century panelling from the now demolished Essex Hall. Outside, the large garden is inspired by Vestry House's earlier role as a workhouse and is stocked with plants that would have been known to its inmates. The museum also houses Waltham Forest Archives, Local Studies Library and Photographic Collection (access by prior appointment only). The community room in the garden can be hired for functions.

William Morris Gallery

🖵 *Lloyd Park, Forest Road, E17*
☎ *020 8527 3782*
✐ *www.walthamforest.gov.uk*
🚌 *Walthamstow Central LU or Blackhorse Road LU then bus 123*
🕑 *Thurs & Fri 12.00-16.00, Sat & Sun 10.00-17.00,*
   Wed (school holidays only 12.00-16.00)
🎟 *Admission free*
🛍 *Shop*
♿ *Wheelchair access (ground floor)*

A visit to this museum is a life-enhancing experience. Designer, writer and socialist, William Morris lived in this gracious Georgian house when he was young. Now its beautifully presented galleries illustrate the man's life and achievements and contain a comprehensive collection of richly decorative artefacts designed by both Morris and his cronies in the Arts & Craft Movement.

Glowing stained glass panels, rustic furniture and textiles dense with flora and fauna encapsulate Morris's distinctive vision – among the treasures here is a copy of the *Kelmscott Chaucer*, the crowning achievement of the Kelmscott Press (see entry for The William Morris Society p. 126). Wallpaper and fabrics are shown alongside the labour intensive equipment used to make them in a vivid display on the processes behind the products and Morris's dislike of mass production. More personal exhibits include the canvas satchel he used for carrying Socialist literature and some of his desk knick-knacks.

Upstairs is found Sir Frank Brangwyn's gift of paintings and drawings featuring works by Burne-Jones, Rossetti and Ford Madox Brown. Ironically though, it's Brangwyn's own vibrantly coloured, gutsy paintings which steal the show, making the Pre-Raphaelite imagery appear trite and mannered. A selection of Morris merchandise is available at the shop – the wipe-down PVC apron is a cunning commercial interpretation of his famous dictum 'have nothing in your house that you do not know to be useful, or believe to be beautiful'.

Outskirts

Bethlem Royal Hospital Archives & Museum

🖃 *Monks Orchard Road, Beckenham BR3 3BX*

☎ *020 3228 4307 / 4227*

✐ *www.bethlemheritage.org.uk*

🚌 *Eden Park Rail, East Croydon Rail*

🕙 *Mon-Fri 09.30-16.30 (telephone before visiting to check times)*

🎟 *Admission free (donations welcome)*

♿ *Wheelchair access*

This museum houses a distinguished collection of paintings and drawings by artists who have suffered from mental disorder. Space limitations mean that the display is small but well chosen and includes work by Richard Dadd (some of whose work is also at Tate Britain) and *The man who drew cats*, Louis Wain. The museum holds one of the best, and still growing, collections of Richard Dadd's watercolours as well as the only substantial collection of work by Jonathan Martin (who tried to burn down York Minster in 1829). The famous statues of *Raving and Melancholy Madness* from the gates of 17th-century Bedlam are part of the museum's historical collections. The archives document the history of Bethlem Royal, the Maudsley and Warlingham Park Hospitals and are open by appointment only. The complete art gallery (see Bethlem Gallery p.228) and the archives catalogue can now be viewed on line.

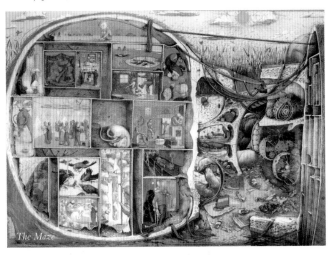

The Maze

165

museums

outskirts

Bourne Hall Museum

📰 *Spring Street, Ewell, Surrey KT17*

☎ *020 8394 1734*

🖉 *www.epsom.townpage.co.uk*

🚍 *Ewell West Rail*

🕑 *Mon-Sat 9.00-17.00*

💷 *Admission free*

🛍 *Shop*

☕ *Café*

♿ *Wheelchair access*

Bourne Hall is the local history museum for the Borough of Epsom
and Ewell, and is housed, not as its rather grand name suggests in an old
mansion, but a circular 1960s building, topped by a transparent dome.
There's plenty of local history for the museum to explore – Henry VIII's
'Nonsuch Palace' was nearby and Epsom Common was the site of the
first English spa. Perhaps Epsom's greatest claim to fame though is as
the venue for the Derby, held here since 1780 and one of the world's
most famous horse races. The museum duly obliges with changing
displays of Derby memorabilia, jockeys' silks and lightweight racing
saddles. Larger exhibits include a hansom cab used by Prime Minister,
Lord Roseby, and a primitive fire engine. Displays are continually
changing, and there is always an art exhibition on show.

Brooking Collection of Architectural Detail

📰 *University of Greenwich*

☎ *020 8331 9309*

🖉 *w3.gre.ac.uk/schools/a-and-c/*

🚍 *Greenwich DLR (for workshops)*

🕑 *Open by appointment*

💷 *Admission free (there is a charge for workshops)*

House detectives will love this fascinating reference collection of
architectural features dating from 1525 to present day. Its fixtures and
fittings, sourced from a huge variety of buildings, include fireplaces,
fanlights, staircases, rainwater heads, sash windows as well as material
removed from Windsor Castle after the 1992 fire, and the doors to the
royal suite of the late Wembley Stadium. A small proportion of the
collection is now housed at the University of Greenwich Maritime
Campus and is open by appointment and for regular workshops led by
Charles Brooking himself.

166

The Crossness Engines

🏠 *Thames Water Treatment Works, Belvedere Rd, Abbey Wood, SE2*

☎ *020 8303 6723 (contact) / 020 8311 3711 (to arrange visits)*

🖱 *www.crossness.org.uk*

🚇 *Abbey Wood LU (2 miles)*

🕐 *By appointment one Tuesday and one Sunday per month*

💷 *£4 (adults), free (under 16s), £5 (steam days)*

🛍 *Shop*

♿ *Wheelchair access (limited)*

You name it – somewhere, somehow there's a museum about it. This Victorian sewage pumping station, built by Sir Joseph Bazalgette in the 1860s, is no exception. Part of the vast sewer system that bought sanitation to London in the last century, the works contain four massive beam engines, capable in their day of raising 6,237 litres of effluent at a stroke. One of these monsters has been completely restored by a team of dedicated volunteers and can be seen 'in steam' about 5 times a year. If you think that's impressive, the building itself is a rare example of a Grade I listed industrial building that features some exuberant Romanesque style cast-iron work. The in-house Museum of Sanitation Engineering History contains decorative examples of Victorian and Edwardian toilet pans.

Dorich House Museum

🏠 *Kingston Vale, SW15 3RN*

☎ *020 8547 7519*

🖱 *www.kingston.ac.uk/dorich*

🚇 *Kingston Rail then bus 85, K3*

🕐 *Admission by pre-booked guided tours only (see website for details)*

💷 *Admission free*

This imposing Modernist house was the home of Russian sculptress Dora Nadine and her diplomat/collector husband The Hon. Richard Hare. Designed by the couple in 1936, the house and its collections were bequeathed to Kingston University on Nadine's death in 1991, and a major restoration programme was undertaken to bring the house back from dereliction. Now restored to its former glory and open on selected days, the house holds an important collection of Dora Nadine's sculpture and associated drawings, as well as the collection of Russian Imperial art (including paintings, icons, porcelain, glass, lacquer work, metal work and furniture) amassed by the couple. Austere on the outside, the house has elegant, often Chinese influenced interiors and includes Dora Nadine's sculpture studio, a light-filled gallery as well as living space.

Down House

- Luxted Road, Down, Kent, BR6
- 01689 859119
- www.english-heritage.org.uk
- Orpington Rail, Bromley South Rail
- Gardens: Wed-Sun 10.00-17.00 (April-June), Daily 10.00-18.00 (July-Aug)
  House: Wed-Sun 11.00-17.00 (April-June), Daily 11.00-17.00 (July/Aug)
  – check website or telephone for admission times as these change yearly
- £7.40 (adult), £5.60 (concessions), £3.80 (children), £18.50 (family),
  free (under 5s/English Heritage members)
- Shop
- Café
- Wheelchair access

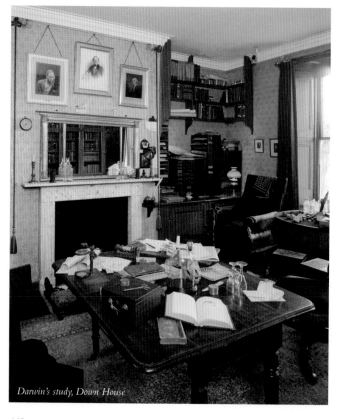

Darwin's study, Down House

Originally built as a farmhouse in the 18th century, Down House became the home of scientist Charles Darwin in 1842. It was here that he wrote *On the Origin of Species by Means of Natural Selection*, a controversial book which became one of the defining documents of the Victorian era.

The house remains much as it did in Darwin's day and the ground floor rooms, including Darwin's book-filled study, have been returned to their 1870s appearance. One of the key exhibits is Darwin's huge journal of his epic 5-year voyage on *HMS Beagle*; other treasures include his data-gathering instruments and mementos from his travels. Evidently a man able to take a joke against himself, Darwin kept the *Punch* cartoons and *Vanity Fair* caricatures which mocked his ideas and are also on display.

An interactive exhibition helps visitors get to grips with the theory of evolution while out in the restored Victorian gardens they can literally follow in the great man's footsteps by walking along the 'thinking path' he trod daily. The exhibition will be updated and changed in 2009 to celebrate the 200th anniversary of Darwin's birth, and a programme of special events is also in the offing.

Embroiderers' Guild

- *Apartment 41, Hampton Court Palace, Surrey KT8 9AU*
- *020 8943 1229*
- *www.embroiderersguild.com*
- *Hampton Court Rail, Richmond LU/rail (then bus) or by river launch from Kingston, Richmond, and Westminster, or 30 min. direct from Waterloo Station with South West Trains*
- *Mon-Fri 10.00-16.30 by appointment only*
- *Admission free*
- *Bookshop*

The Guild has a stored museum collection of embroidery from around the world, which may be accessed by the public by appointment. The collection was begun in the 1920s as a resource for information and inspiration, a function that it still fulfills today. Truly global in scope, the embroideries take many forms including costume, furnishings, functional and decorative textiles. Fragments of Coptic embroidery are the earliest pieces in the collection, while work by contemporary embroidery artists such as Audrey Walker, Rachael Howard and Paddy Killer are among the modern works. The Guild holds annual embroidery exhibitions and also has a specialist library and bookshop.

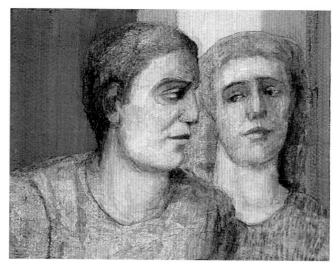

Encounter by Audrey Walker, Embroiderers' Guild

Forty Hall Museum

Forty Hill, Enfield EN2

020 8363 8196

www.enfield.gov.uk/museum

Gordon Hill Rail, Turkey Street Rail

Wed to Sun 11.00-16.00

Admission free

Café

Wheelchair access (ground floor only)

Paintings and furniture are among the historic local exhibits in this museum, which is located in an imposing 17th-century pile, Forty Hall. A grade I listed, the house is packed with period details including ornate plasterwork ceilings and fireplace. Three upstairs rooms are devoted to Enfield history while the Raynton Room and Exhibition Gallery provide a venue for local artists' work. The hall is surrounded by pleasant informal gardens and a 264-acre estate composed of parkland and a working farm.

Garrick's Temple and Lawn

- Hampton Court Road, Hampton TW12
- www.garrickstemple.org.uk
- Hampton Court Rail (then bus), Hampton (then bus)
- Temple open Sun 14.00-17.00 April-Sept, Lawn open daily dawn-dusk
- Admission free (to arrange special visits for small parties/schools contact Orleans House Gallery tel: 020 8831 6000)

Hero-worship doesn't come much more picturesque – or literal – than this, a dinky classical temple built by actor-manager David Garrick in 1756 to honour his idol, William Shakespeare. The pleasure garden that surrounds it was originally laid out with advice from landscape designer Lancelot 'Capability' Brown. Both temple and lawn have been the subject of restoration in recent years and the temple is now home to a replica of the life-size statue of Shakespeare by Roubiliac which was commissioned by Garrick for the temple. Regular events such as concerts and poetry readings enliven proceedings during the summer months and visitors wishing to arrive by waterborne transport can catch the Hampton Ferry from Molesey Hurst.

Ham House

- Ham, Richmond, TW10
- 020 8940 1950
- www.nationaltrust.org.uk
- Richmond LU/Rail
- House Sat-Wed 12.00-16.00 (Mar-Nov); Garden 11.00-18.00 (all year),
- House & Garden: £9 (adults), £5 (children), £23 (families), free (National Trust members)
  Garden only: £3 (adults), £2 (children), £8 (families), free (National Trust members)
- Shop
- Café

A 17th-century house on the banks of the River Thames. Built in 1610 and extended in 1670, Ham House is a unique example of Jacobean architecture and its imposing, perfectly symmetrical, south front makes an implacable statement about the power and taste of its occupants. Much of the Duchess of Lauderdale's extravagant 1670s redecoration is still in place and the lush interiors include fine textiles, furniture and paintings. The Duchess – a famous political schemer in her day – is said to haunt the house and ghost tours are held regularly (booking essential). The 17th-century gardens are currently being restored and feature a maze-like wilderness and formal lavender parterres as well as intriguing outbuildings such as an ice-house, dairy and the earliest known still-house.

Hampton Court Palace

🖼 *Surrey, KT8 9AU*

☎ *0870 752 7777 (general information)*

🖥 *www.hrp.org.uk*

🚌 *Hampton Court Rail, Richmond LU/Rail (then bus) or by river launch from Kingston, Richmond, and Westminster*

🕐 *Daily 10.00-18.00 (Mar-Oct, last admission 17.00), Daily 10.00-16.30 (Oct-Mar, last admission 15.30)*

💷 *£13 (adults), £10.50 (concessions), £6.50 (under 16s)*

🛍 *Shops*

☕ *Cafés*

♿ *Disabled facilities*

So vast is Henry VIII's Thameside palace that visitors are advised to allow 3 hours to do it justice. Architecturally speaking, the palace has something of a split personality. On one hand its expansive red brick sprawl is a stunning example of Tudor architecture with all the crenellations and turrets you'd expect from a royal palace. On the other, it's a stately

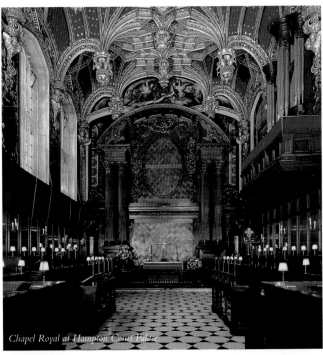

Chapel Royal at Hampton Court Palace

Baroque masterpiece designed (but never completed) by Christopher Wren. Inside it's not so bad either – from the State Apartments and Renaissance picture gallery (featuring important works from the Royal Collection) right down to the vast Tudor kitchens. Costumed guides and audio tours help interpret life in the royal household over the centuries while a new permanent exhibition explores the myths surrounding the young Henry VIII and reveals the reality behind them.

The gardens – all 60 acres of them – are as famous as the palace and include a wilderness, the recently restored 18th-century Privy Garden, the Great Fountain Garden and the Maze (although, depending on your navigational skills, you'll need to allow extra time to negotiate this famous feature). The palace is also home to The Great Vine which, planted in around 1768, is the oldest and largest known vine in the world. Although there are two cafés for hungry history hunters to choose from, picnickers are welcome and can use any of the benches around the palace courtyards or the gardens.

Harrow Museum

Headstone Manor, Pinner View, Harrow HA2 6PX
020 8861 2626
www.h18th arrow.gov.ukv
Mon, Wed, Thurs, Fri 12.00-17.00, Sat & Sun 10.30-17.00
Harrow & Wealdstone LU/Rail then walk or bus H9
Admission free
Café
Shop

This local history museum is based in a group of historic buildings, centred around Headstone Manor. Partially restored, the manor house dates from the early 14th century, comes complete with water (and duck) filled moat and is the earliest surviving timber building in Middlesex. Its bare but historically interesting interiors can be seen by guided tour every weekend during the summer. The handsome 16th-century 'tithe' barn that once used to store grain and stable horses now accommodates the museum's temporary exhibitions, events (including children's activities), café and shop. Aptly named, the diminutive 'Small Barn' dates, like the manor, back to the 14th century and houses a permanent display about the history of the site, on which prehistoric and Roman remains have also been found. Permanent exhibitions about Harrow's rural and industrial past can be found in the 18th-century Granary, with a collection of old agricultural equipment and displays reflecting local industry: Whitefriars glass, Kodak cameras as well as a giant paintbrush from Hamilton's brush factory.

Kew Bridge Steam Museum

📭 *Green Dragon Lane, Brentford, Middlesex, TW8*
☎ *020 8568 4757*
🖊 *www.kbsm.org*
🚌 *Gunnersbury LU then 237 or 267 bus, Kew Bridge Rail*
🕐 *Tues-Sun & Bank Hol Mon 11.00-16.00 (last admission 15.30)*
🎟 *Admission-weekday: £5 (adults), £4 (concessions), free (under 16s)*
   Admission-weekend (engines in steam); £8.50 (adults), £7.50
   (concessions), free (under 16s)
🛍 *Shop*
☕ *Café (open weekends only), Picnic area*
♿ *Wheelchair access*

Opposing elements they may be, but fire and water are inextricably linked in this magnificent Victorian pumping station, which once supplied water to the west of London. The gargantuan Cornish beam engines are still in situ in their original pump houses and can be seen 'in steam' on selected weekends. Other, lovingly maintained rotative engines fill the Steam Hall and are in steam most weekends. More modern engines can be admired in the evocatively scented Diesel House, and train buffs young and old can enjoy a ride on the resident 'Wren' type steam locomotive every Sunday from March to November. Special events are regularly held throughout the year.

The 'Water for Life' gallery takes a close, sometimes microscopic, look at the history of London's water supply and doesn't fight shy of talking dirty. With the emphasis on interactivity and fun, visitors are invited to sift through a cesspit and walk through part of the Thames Water Ring Main. As well as the ubiquitous rat, London's sewers have supported a colourful range of wildlife from eels to red-eared terrapins as well as succession of different professions – from medieval 'gongfermors' to Victorian 'flushers' and 'toshers'. Other exhibits include Roman toilet spoons, medieval ice skates and a modern sewage worker's protective clothing. One of the best exhibits is the 'wall collage' of domestic appliances showing our ever-increasing demand for water.

The engines here may be steam driven but this dynamic museum itself runs on volunteer power – and a dedicated bunch they are too, maintaining the engines to a meticulous standard and even finding time to develop a lovely garden, complete with wildlife area, benches and wartime allotment. The café is only open at weekends but for weekday visitors in need of a cuppa, the Musical Museum (see p. 181) is just a short walk away and has a very pleasant tea room.

Kew Palace

🏛 *Royal Botanic Gardens, Kew, TW9*
☎ *020 8332 5189*
✎ *www.hrp.org.uk*
🚌 *Kew Gardens LU, Kew Bridge Rail*
🕐 *Daily Mar-Sept 10.00-17.00 (Mons 11.00-17.00); see website for opening times, as these change yearly*
💷 *£5 (adult), £4.50 (concs), £2.50 (child), £13 (Family up to 5) – tickets only available with tickets to the Royal Botanic Gardens, Kew)*
🛍 *Shop (at Welcome Centre)*
☕ *Cafés (Kew Gardens Orangery, Pavilion)*
♿ *Wheelchair Access*

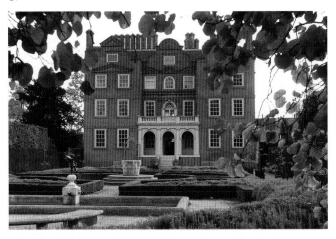

This red brick, Dutch style 17th-century house was the family home of King George III and his family, and a place of sanctuary for the king during his 'madness'. The smallest royal palace, it recently underwent a major restoration and reopened to the public in 2006. Visitors can admire the ornately decorated and furnished rooms and see family artefacts such as the elaborate dolls house made by George III's daughters. The unrestored second floor is open to the public for the first time in its history. Entrance is only possible as part of a visit to Kew Gardens, so you'll need to pace yourself if you want to combine horticulture with history. At the weekends from June to September Queen Charlotte's Cottage is open, too (see p. 184).

Kingston Museum

📠 *Wheatfield Way, Kingston upon Thames, KT1*
☎ *020 8547 6460*
🖱 *www.kingston.gov.uk/museum*
🚆 *Kingston Rail*
🕐 *Daily 10.00-17.00 (closed Wed and Sun)*
💷 *£1 (adults), free (under 16s)*
🛍 *Shop*
♿ *Wheelchair access*

As befits a royal borough, Kingston's museum is a pretty classy affair: a Grade II listed property, built with money donated by American benefactor Andrew Carnegie. Refurbished in recent years, the museum tells the story of the 'town of kings' from ancient times and also has a gallery dedicated to the photographic pioneer Eadweard Muybridge. The art gallery hosts national and local exhibitions.

London Ambulance Service Museum

📠 *London Ambulance Service NHS Trust, North East Sector HQ,*
   Aldborough Road South, Ilford, IG3 8HQ
☎ *020 8557 1711 (curator Terry Spurr)*
🖱 *www.londonambulance.nhs.uk/aboutus/history/history.html*
🚆 *Newbury Park LU*
🕐 *By appointment*
💷 *Admission free (donations appreciated)*
♿ *Disabled access*

A small but absorbing museum telling the story of London's ambulance service from its origins in the 1870s to the present. The collection includes vintage vehicles and old radio equipment, wartime memorabilia and a photographic and document archive, but it's the heartwarming personal stories of livesaving on the streets of London that really bring the hardware to life. The vintage vehicles include a horse-drawn ambulance of 1870 and one of the first paramedic motorcyles from the 1990s but also includes more glamourous vehicles like the centrally heated 1920s Du Cros ambulance. Several of the vehicles have a sprinkling of star dust too, having featured in film and TV productions from the *Carry On* films to *The Professionals* and *Minder*, *Poirot* and *Emergency Ward 10*.

Marble Hill House

⌖ *Richmond Road, Twickenham TW1*

☎ *020 8892 5115*

✐ *www.english-heritage.org.uk*

🚌 *St Margaret's Rail, Twickenham Rail, Richmond LU/Rail*

🕙 *Sat 10.00-14.00, Sun & Bank Hols 10.00-17.00 (April-Oct); tours Tues-Wed 12.00 & 15.00*

💷 *£4.20 (adults), £3.20 (concessions), £2.10 (children), free (under 5s/English Heritage members)*

🛍 *Shop*

🍽 *Café*

♿ *Wheelchair access (ground floor)*

The serene symmetry and perfect proportions of its façade give Marble Hill House the appearance of a scaled-up doll's house. In fact this elegant building, set by the Thames in 66 acres of parkland, was built by George II as a rural hideaway for his mistress. The Great Room is regally decorated with lavish gilding and the house contains early Georgian paintings and furniture along with architectural paintings by Panini and a collection of chinoiserie.

Merton Heritage Centre

⌖ *The Canons, Madeira Road, Mitcham, CR4 4HD*

☎ *020 8640 9387*

✐ *www.merton.gov.uk/libraries*

🚌 *Mitcham Tramlink, Morden LU (then bus), Wimbledon LU (then bus); bus 118, 127, 152, 200, 201, 264, 270, 280, 355*

🕙 *Tues-Wed 10.00-16.00, Fri and Sat 10.00-16.30*

💷 *Admission free*

🛍 *Shop*

♿ *Wheelchair access*

A programme of temporary exhibitions at this 17th-century house tells the story of Merton and its people. With the emphasis on making local history accessible to all ages the centre also organises lectures, craft workshops and reminiscence sessions. Exhibitions regularly feature hands-on displays. The Canons history extends back to Norman times and visitors can still see the carp pond and dovecote that were part of the grange farm complex that previously occupied the site. The small sales point offers local history publications and assorted gifts.

The Museum of Domestic Design & Architecture

🖃 *Middlesex University, Cat Hill, Barnet, EN4*

☎ *020 8411 5244*

✐ *www.moda.mdx.ac.uk*

🚌 *Cockfosters LU, Oakwood LU (take university shuttle bus direct to MoDA)*

🕑 *Tues-Sat 10.00-17.00, Sun 14.00-17.00*

💷 *Admission free*

🛍 *Shop*

♿ *Wheelchair access*

Redecorating? Perhaps a visit to MoDA is in order. Housed in a sleek Lottery-funded building, MoDA has an extensive holding of British domestic design from 1850-1960. Its six core collections include the famous Silver Studio Collection which alone features some 40,000 designs, 5,000 wallpaper samples and 5,000 textile samples, dating from the 1880s-1960s. There's also an archive relating to the work of typographer and designer Charles Hasler and the entire contents of the London studio of artist and designer Peggy Angus.

A permanent exhibition, 'Exploring Interiors: decoration of the home 1900-60' offers a chronological display of furnishing fabrics, wallpapers, trade catalogues and photos of interiors. Although it is on the small side it covers some interesting ground – the irresistible rise of DIY, changing attitudes to the kitchen – and offers the chance to compare the glossy catalogues with the interior decoration people really chose. Temporary exhibitions exploring aspects of domestic design and architecture in greater detail are held in the upstairs gallery.

Material not on display and the reference library may be consulted by appointment in the Study Room (Tues, Wed, Sat 10.00-16.00, tel 020 8411 5445). Alternatively, more of the collection can be accessed using the MoDA electronic catalogue, which is also available via the website.

MoDA's shop stocks an appealing range of gifts and books relating to the collection, including some particularly attractive postcards of fabric and wallpaper designs. For those requiring more than just aesthetic nourishment there's a cafeteria and snack-bar on campus (weekdays only).

Museum No. 1

🏛 *Royal Botanic Gardens, Kew, TW9*

☎ *020 8332 5655 (24-hour information)*

🖎 *www.kew.org*

🚌 *Kew Gardens LU, Kew Bridge Rail*

🕓 *Daily 09.30 onwards (telephone for closing time)*

💰 *Admission included in entrance to Kew Gardens: £13 (adults),*
  £12 concessions, free (under 16s)

🛍 *Shop*

🍽 *Cafés & Restaurant*

♿ *Wheelchair access*

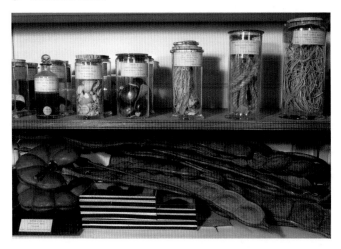

It doesn't have to be lilac time to make a trip to Kew worthwhile – with over 30,000 different types of plants in the Gardens, it's always horticultural heaven. The recently restored Museum No.1 is an extra incentive for going. Its fun and interactive 'Plants + People' exhibition shows how reliant humans are on plants for food, medicine, clothing and even personal hygiene! Intriguing exhibits include a cannibal fork and dish, a deadly bamboo blowpipe and gramophone needles made from cactus.

Museum of Croydon

🗒 *Croydon Clocktower, Katharine Street, Croydon, CR9*
☎ *020 8253 1030 (box office)*
☎ *020 8253 1022*
🖥 *www.museumofcroydon.com*
🚌 *East Croydon Rail, West Croydon Rail, George Street Tramlink*
🕐 *Mon-Sat 10.30-17.00*
💷 *Admission free*
☕ *Café*
♿ *Wheelchair access*

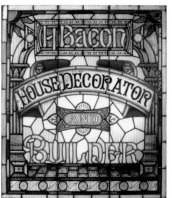

Formerly the Lifetimes Interactive Museum, the Museum of Croydon reopened in 2006 with a name change and a new, award winning design. With the focus on the objects and memories of local people, the displays explore Croydon's history from 1800 to the present day. Touchscreen kiosks allow visitors to listen to the reminiscences of residents as varied as a Sikh WWII fighter pilot, Squadron Leader Pujji, and a local Chinese food store owner. A 3-wheel 'Trojan' bubble car is one of the most popular exhibits – a genuine 1960s icon, made in Croydon. The Riesco Gallery houses a unique collection of Chinese ceramics dating from prehistory to the 19th century. Collected and donated by local business man Raymond Riesco, the exhibits include Tang Dynasty models and Ming dynasty bowls. The museum also hosts a varied programme of temporary exhibitions (both touring and self-developed) as well as events for all ages. Some exhibitions and events may carry an admission charge, although there are often 'happy hour' slots when entry is free.

Museum of Richmond

🖼 *Old Town Hall, Whittaker Avenue, Richmond, TW9*

☎ *020 8332 1141*

🖉 *www.museumofrichmond.com*

🚇 *Richmond LU/Rail*

🕐 *Tues-Sat 11.00-17.00*

💷 *Admission free*

🛍 *Shop*

♿ *Wheelchair access*

This local history museum celebrates Richmond's heritage as well as hosting regular exhibitions. The varied collection spans from prehistoric times to present day and includes such highlights as Regency actor Edmund Kean's snuff box and a 'Mickey Mouse' gas mask from 1939.

The Musical Museum

🖼 *399 High Street, Brentford, TW8*

🖉 *www.musicalmuseum.co.uk*

☎ *020 8560 8108*

🚇 *Gunnersbury LU (then 237 or 267 bus), South Ealing LU (then 65 bus), Kew Bridge Rail*

🕐 *Tues-Sun 11.00-17.30 (last admission 16.30)*

💷 *£7 (adults), £5.50 (concessions), free (children under 16)*

🛍 *Shop*

☕ *Café*

♿ *Wheelchair access*

In these days of iPods, downloads and radio it is hard to imagine life without wall to wall recorded music. With its world class collection of self-playing musical instruments the Musical Museum recaptures that far off era, when a pianola in a pub or a humble street barrel organ were how people accessed the popular music of the time. The huge variety of instruments ranges from vast ornate pipe organs to sophisticated reproducing pianos and tiny music boxes to more recently fangled contraptions such as an electronic organs and juke boxes. Regular demonstrations allow visitors to hear the instruments in action, and – as in the case of the 1813 pipe organ – literally listen to the sound of history. Guided tours of the collection take place at weekends and there are special 'Monkey Trails' for children to follow. Newly re-housed in a smart purpose built venue the museum offers not only an excellent tea room with river views, but also a concert hall complete with a 1920s 'Mighty Wurlitzer' organ, which rises majestically from the floor for concerts and silent film screenings. The imaginatively stocked shop sells music themed gifts such as 'Chopin' boards as well as vintage sheet music and music rolls.

Old Speech Room Gallery, Harrow School

⌨ *Church Hill, Harrow on the Hill, HA1*
☎ *020 8872 8205*
✐ *www.harrowschool.org.uk/org*
🚇 *Harrow on the Hill LU*
🕓 *Term-time daily (except Wed & exeat days) 14.30-17.00*
🎟 *Admission free*
🛒 *Salespoint*

Once a chamber for public speaking, the Old Speech Room was converted into a gallery in 1976 and now houses Harrow School's varied collection of Egyptian, Roman and Greek antiquities, and British watercolours and paintings. The school policy is to show its collection via themed exhibitions but works by Romney, David Jones and Old Harrovian Winston Churchill are among the works that visitors are likely to see here.

Osterley Park

⌨ *Jersey Road, Isleworth, Middlesex, TW7*
☎ *020 8232 5050*
☎ *01494 755566 (info line)*
✐ *www.nationaltrust.org.uk*
🚇 *Osterley LU*
🕓 *Wed-Sun 13.00-16.30 (March-Nov), Sat-Sun 12.30-15.30 (Dec),
(check website as these times may change yearly)*
🎟 *House & Garden: £8 (adult), £4 (child), £20 (family)*
☕ *Café*
🛒 *Shop*

A fine red brick Tudor manor house built by Sir Thomas Gresham and remodelled inside and out for the upwardly mobile Child family in the 18th century by John Adam. Stunning Georgian interiors include the austere Entrance Hall of 1767 and the tapestry room, hung with crimson coloured Boucher medallion tapestries specially commissioned from the Gobelin factory in Paris and lovingly tended over the years by the owners and family retainers. Clocking in at 130 feet, the 'Long Gallery' is aptly named and is now hung with an assemblage of 17th and 18th-century Venetian paintings. The house is set in 357 acres of parkland and gardens with lakes and featuring a collection of various species of oak tree.

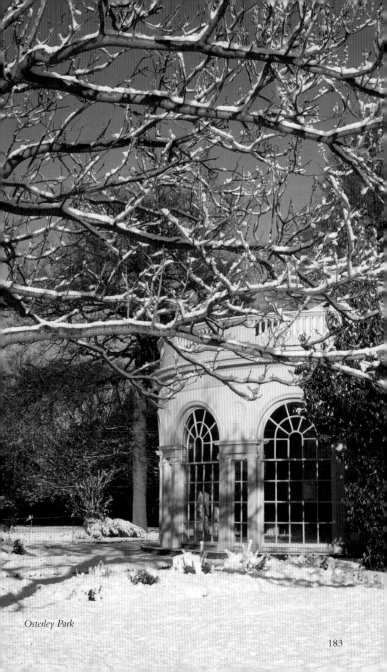

Osterley Park

Queen Charlotte's Cottage

- *Royal Botanical Gardens, Kew, TW9*
- *020 8332 5655*
- *www.hrp.org.uk*
- *Kew Gardens LU, Kew Bridge Rail*
- *Weekends & Bank Holidays 10.30-16.30 (June-Sept)*
- *Admission free with ticket to Royal Botanical Gardens*
- *Café*

Queen Charlotte's whimsical thatched cottage provided a scenic spot for the Hanoverian royal family's picnics as well as a convenient place from which to admire the exotic inhabitants of their menagerie. Set in the southwest corner of the Botanic Gardens, the Cottage is at its best in springtime, when it is surrounded by a sea of bluebells. Kew Palace, George III and Queen Charlotte's official home, is nearby and is also open to the public (see p. 175).

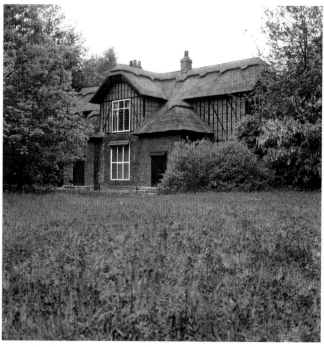

Queen Charlotte's Cottage

Redbridge Museum

Central Library, Clements Road, Ilford, IG1 1EA

☎ *020 8708 2317*

✐ *www.redbridge.gov.uk*

🕓 *Tues-Fri 10.00-17.00, Sat 10.00-16.00*

🚌 *Ilford rail then 10 mins walk*

🏛 *Admission free*

🛍 *Shop*

♿ *Wheelchair access*

This local museum opened in 2000 and takes a multi-sensory approach to the history of the London borough of Redbridge. Visitors can inhale the heady smells of the borough (from farmyard fragrance to freshly baked fruitcake) and listen to a WWII air raid siren and the reminiscences of local residents such as Irish dancer Kathleen Maguire and children from Ilford Jewish primary school. A small display commemorates local MP Winston Churchill while the presence of mammoth remains found in the neighbourhood attests to the long history of the area. Room displays such as an early 1930s kitchen and a 1901 living room bring daily life of the past to life, aided by a 'video wall' and hi-tech touch screen computers covering different areas of the borough. Regularly changing temporary exhibitions on local subjects are held on the 1st floor, complemented by an events programme for children and families.

The Royal Military School of Music Museum

Kneller Hall, Kneller Road, Twickenham, TW2

☎ *020 8898 5533 ext 8652*

✐ *www.armymuseums.org.uk*

🚌 *Whitton Rail, Twickenham Rail*

🕓 *By appointment only*

🏛 *£4 (guided tours only)*

🍴 *Café*

🛍 *Shop*

♿ *Wheelchair access (limited)*

A private collection of musical instruments, uniforms, medals and other objects with a military connection. Noteworthy exhibits include a bugle boy's book of music, found beside his body at the Battle of Waterloo, and a battle-scarred trumpet that was used in the 'Charge of the Light Brigade'. The collection also features a large variety of antique military musical instruments and is housed in a handsome 17th-century building, once the country home of the celebrated court painter Sir Godfrey Kneller.

Tithe Barn Museum of Nostalgia

- *Hall Lane, Upminster*
- *07855 633917 Malcolm Cullen (Curator)*
- *www.upminstertithebarn.co.uk*
- *Upminster LU and Rail; bus 248 (from Upminster town centre, direction Cranham)*
- *First weekend in every month 10.30-17.00 and other times by appointment (see website for further details); guided tours of barn, inside and out, available by appointment*
- *Admission free*

A 15th-century thatched barn is the unlikely but rather charming venue for this collection of domestic and agricultural artefacts dating from Roman to more recent times, amassed by the local history society. Some 14–15,000 items are crammed in beneath the barn's mighty eaves, and range from lightbulbs to signposts to old delivery bikes.

The Twickenham Museum

- *25, The Embankment, TW1*
- *020 8408 0070*
- *www.twickenham-museum.org.uk*
- *Twickenham Rail (then 10 mins walk); Richmond Rail/LU then bus H22, R68, R70, 290, 490*
- *Tues & Sat 11.00-15.00, Sun 14.00-16.00*
- *Admission free*

Housed in a pretty 18th century house overlooking the Thames and Eel Pie Island, this museum is the history centre for Twickenham, Whitton, Teddington and the Hamptons. These Thames-side villages once formed the Borough of Twickenham and their story is told through an ongoing programme of exhibitions at the museum and on the museum's excellent website.

The Wandle Industrial Museum

⌷ *The Vestry Hall Annexe, London Road, Mitcham CR4*
☎ *020 8648 0127*
✎ *www.wandle.org*
🚊 *Mitcham Tramlink*
🕐 *Wed 13.00-16.00, first Sun of the month 14.00-17.00*
💰 *50p (adults), 20p (concessions)*
🛍 *Shop*
♿ *Disabled access by arrangement*

The ultimate goal of this museum is to establish a riverside site at Ravensbury Mill in which to explore the Wandle Valley's industrial heritage. In the meantime, exhibitions at their current venue explore some of the area's better-known industries including snuff, tobacco and textiles as well as local figures such as William Morris and Arthur Liberty. Displays change annually.

World Rugby Museum

⌷ *Twickenham Stadium, Rugby Road, Twickenham, TW1*
☎ *020 8892 8877*
✎ *www.rfu.com/museum*
🚊 *Twickenham Rail*
🕐 *Tues-Sat 10.00-17.00, Sun 11.00-17.00 (closed match & post match days)*
💰 *Museum & Stadium Tour £10 (adults), £7 (concessions), £34 (family) (advance booking recommended)*
🛍 *Shop*
♿ *Wheelchair access*

Situated in the East Stand of Twickenham Stadium, this museum charts the history of Rugby Football from a schoolboy game into an international sport. Many exhibits were donated by ex-rugby players and visiting teams – personal mementos include a mascot belonging to Robert Dibble who played for England between 1906 and 1911. More recent exhibits include one of the rugby balls kicked by Jonny Wilkinson in the 2003 World Cup final, and a replica of the World Cup trophy. Visitors can also admire reconstructed period rooms, trophies such as the Calcutta Cup (made from melted-down silver rupees), pictures and rugby memorabilia. Test your strength on the scrum machine or sit back and enjoy some great moments from the game in the audio-visual theatre. The guided tour take visitors around the home of English Rugby and includes a look at the England changing room and a walk through the players' tunnel to admire the hallowed turf.

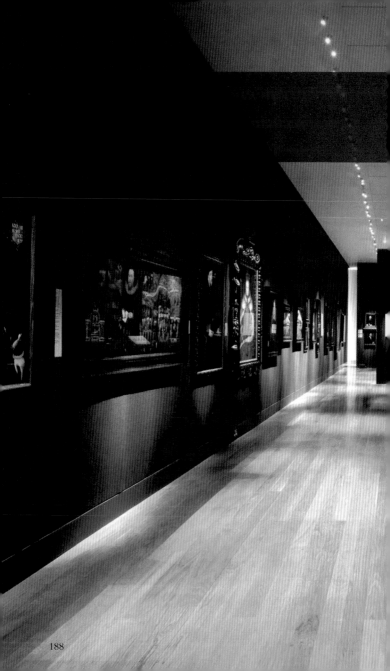

Galleries

Central

Barbican Art Gallery

🖼 *Gallery Floor, Level 3, Barbican Centre, Silk Street, EC2*

☎ *020 7638 8891 (Box Office)*

🖰 *www.barbican.org.uk*

🚌 *Barbican LU, Moorgate LU*

🕐 *Gallery: Mon, Thurs, Fri, Sat, Sun 11.00-20.00; Tues, Wed 11.00-18.00, 1st Thurs until 22.00*
The Curve: Daily 11.00-20.00, 1st Thurs until 22.00

💷 *£8 (adults), £6 (concessions)*

🛍 *Shop*

☕ *Cafés & restaurants*

♿ *Disabled access*

Set in the heart of the Barbican maze (Europe's largest multi-art venue), the Barbican Art Gallery hosts an eclectic range of photography, design and contemporary art exhibitions. The Centre's concourse, known as 'The Curve', is the venue for free exhibitions of contemporary art, specially commissioned for the site.

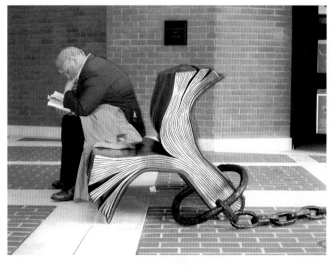

The British Library

The British Library

🖼 *96 Euston Road, NW1*

☎ *020 7412 7332 (Visitor Services Enquiries & Box Office)*

🖳 *www.bl.uk*

🚇 *Euston LU/Rail, King's Cross St Pancras LU/Rail*

🕐 *Mon, Wed-Fri 09.30-18.00; Tues 09.30-20.00; Sat 09.30-17.00;*
   Sun and Bank Holidays 11.00-17.00

💳 *Admission free (charge for some exhibitions)*

🛍 *Shop*

☕ *Café & Restaurant*

♿ *Wheelchair access*

Nestling in the shadow of a revitalised St Pancras, the British Library is a remarkable achievement – the largest UK public building of the 20th century. Housing millions of books, the 'Sound Archive' and a large daily influx of readers, this is now indisputably the UK's national library. As well as its superb research facilities, the library has several exhibition galleries, and regular tours of the building itself, as well as the recently opened Centre for Conservation.

'Treasures of the British Library', the permanent exhibition in 'The John Ritblat Gallery', is a bibliographic tour de force. With books and manuscripts spanning some three thousand years, this is the place to pore over historic documents like the Magna Carta, Shakespeare's First Folio or Captain Scott's last polar diary. Early maps offer insights into our ancestors' world view and there is a copious selection of sacred texts such as the *Golden Haggadah* and the *Luttrell Psaltar*. The Literature section includes some rare manuscripts, Lewis Carroll's meticulously handwritten copy of *Alice in Wonderland* and James Joyce's manuscript of *Finnegans Wake* among them. A Leonardo da Vinci notebook, written in his signature 'mirror writing', is one of the gems in the small Science section while over in Music, Beatles' pop songs share the limelight with Handel's *Messiah*.

Unsurprisingly, given the priceless nature of the exhibits the lighting is low and items are kept safely behind glass. Ingeniously interactive, 'Turning the Pages' gets around the restrictions of display – its touchscreen computers let you leaf through four of the library's most distinguished manuscripts at your leisure. A programme of special exhibitions in the Pearson Gallery and the Folio Society Gallery completes the picture.

For those with ambitions to build a library of their own, the bookshop on the ground floor is well stocked with books, books about books, mugs about books, bags for carrying books, and bookish gifts and games. And if intellectual stimulation just isn't enough, the library also has an in-house café and restaurant.

County Hall Gallery

🖵 *Riverside Building, County Hall SE1*

☎ *020 7450 7603*

🖉 *www.countyhallgallery.com*

🚌 *Waterloo LU/Rail, Westminster LU*

🕓 *Daily 10.00-18.30 (last entry 17.30)*

💷 *£12 (adults), £10 (concs), £8 (children over 12), free (children under 12), £30 (family)*

🛍 *Shop*

♿ *Wheelchair access*

Three exhibition spaces in one at the former HQ of the GLC. Picasso and Dali are the headline names here, with two separate permanent exhibitions devoted to these Spanish masters of modern art. The 500 or so exhibits in 'Dali Universe' include the canvas backdrop painted for the dream sequence in Hitchcock's film *Spellbound*, a Mae West Lips sofa, sculptures, as well as numerous lithographs and etchings produced by Dali to illustrate books as diverse as *Don Quixote* and *The Bible*. Printed works on paper also form the backbone of *Picasso: Art of a Genius*, but as there wasn't much the great man couldn't turn his hand to, the show also includes ceramics and wall tapestries. Contemporary, London-based artist Nasser Azam makes up the County Hall triumvirate, his work being represented by a changing exhibition of his paintings and bronze sculptures.

The Courtauld Gallery

🖵 *Somerset House, Strand WC2*

☎ *020 7848 2526*

🖉 *www.courtauld.ac.uk*

🚌 *Covent Garden LU, Holborn LU, Temple LU (not Sundays)*

🕓 *Daily 10.00-18.00 (last admission 17.30)*

💷 *£5 adults, £4 concessions, £22 (annual ticket), (free under18s, students, unemployed & on Mondays 10.00-14.00)*

🛍 *Shop*

☕ *Café*

♿ *Wheelchair access*

Comprising a series of 11 different bequests, The Courtauld is that rare creature: a display of world-class art with the intimate feel of a private gallery. Its collections include those of Austrian aristo Count Seilern and of Samuel Courtauld, textile impresario and the man who gave his name to the Institute of Art. Displayed to reflect its identity as a 'collection of collections', the Courtauld Gallery has the distinct advantage of being the ideal size to while away a morning or afternoon without having to

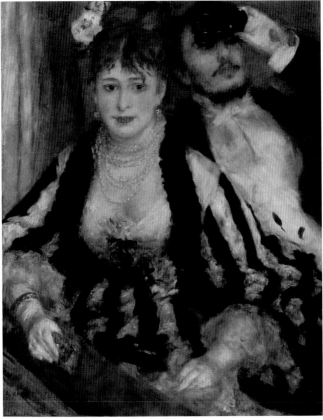

Pierre-Auguste Renoir, La Loge 1874, Courtauld Gallery

resort to military-style route planning. Free entrance on Mondays 10am until 2pm makes the whole experience even more satisfying.

It doesn't take long to see why the collection is so renowned. Works by early masters Bernardo Daddi, Borghese di Piero and Nicola di Maestro Antonio d'Ancona are among the gleaming gold 'n' gesso treasures of the Gambier Parry Collection displayed in the ground floor gallery. The medieval enamels, ivory carvings and ceramics which share this gallery in a series of changing displays are less immediately eye-catching but just as rewarding.

The first floor galleries contain some of the finest 18th-century interiors in London (look up at the ceilings) and are home to Samuel

Courtauld's collection of Impressionist and Post-Impressionist paintings. For many, this will be the highlight of their visit and it's difficult not to reduce this to a litany of famous names and iconic works: Van Gogh's *Self Portrait with Bandaged Ear*, Manet's enigmatic *Bar at the Folies-Bergères* and Gauguin's melancholic, mystical masterpiece *Nevermore* are a few of the treasures. There are some notable works by Cézanne (including *Man with a Pipe* and the sublime *Lac d'Annecy*) while landscapes in a more purely impressionistic vein can also be found by Monet, Pissarro and Sisley. Compare the uptight pointillism of Seurat with the languid sensuality of Modigliani's *Female Nude* which in turn points up the bawdy vivacity of Toulouse-Lautrec's *Tête à Tête Supper*, in which the viewer becomes the dinner date.

Also on the first floor are the Lee Collection and the Princes Gate Collection. It was Viscount Lee of Fareham, not Courtauld, who actually came up with the idea of a specialist history of art institute – and it's perhaps ironic that as a collector he was wary of 'experts'. His adventurous, sometimes speculative approach to buying art, was to the Institute's gain, his collection includes pieces such Cranach's sublime take on the Adam and Eve story.

Count Seilern's collection (known as the 'Prince Gate Collection') features a stunning roll call of works by Rubens. Popularly known for his lardy ladies, what is striking here is the sheer emotional and physical force of works like *The Descent from the Cross* and *The Conversion of St. Paul*. In contrast *Landscape by Moonlight* reveals Rubens in more tranquil mood whilst his affectionate portrait of *The Family of Jan Breughel the Elder* shows the artist in yet another light. Count Seilern also appreciated the beauty and energy of unfinished works, here represented by a series of airily exuberant oil sketches by Tiepolo, a Parmigiano Virgin and Child and a landscape by Cezanne; such works were also valued as an important tool for studying artists' working methods.

The second floor galleries are given over to the 20th Century with important long term loans from various private collections and works by modern masters such as Alexej von Jawlensky and Raoul Dufy, Derain and Vlaminck. Roger Fry's collection of Britain's answer to Post Impressionism can be found in Room 11 and includes his portrait of Nina Hamnett and works by 'Bloomsberries', Vanessa Bell and Duncan Grant. Room 15 on this floor provides the venue for a programme of temporary exhibitions.

For those in search of refreshment after their exertions, the Courtauld has a café looking out upon the fine courtyard of Somerset House. At the building's entrance is the gift shop which offers a selection of books and gifts relating to the collection.

Guildhall Art Gallery

📇 *Guildhall Yard, EC2V 2EA*

☎ *020 7332 3700*

✎ *www.cityoflondon.gov.uk*

🚇 *Bank LU, Mansion House LU, Moorgate LU, St Paul's LU*

🕐 *Mon-Sat 10.00-17.00, (last admission 16.30), Sun 12.00-16.00 (last admission 15.30), NB ceremonial events at Guildhall may require occasional closure of the gallery, telephone for details*

💷 *£2.50 (adults), £1 (concessions), free (under 16s), free on Fridays & daily after 15.30*

👓 *Shop*

♿ *Wheelchair access*

The Guildhall Art Gallery is home to the Corporation of London's collection of paintings and sculpture, begun in the 17th century and still growing today. Its posh City premises, designed by Richard Gilbert Scott, were officially opened to the public in 1999 by the Queen and have four distinct display areas. In 1987 it was discovered that the building was sited on top of London's Roman amphitheatre, the extent of which is marked out in the paved area outside the Guildhall; remains of the arena can be admired in situ in a basement gallery.

Portraits of Royalty and Lord Mayors of London preside over the Main Gallery, among them Alderman John Boydell whose magnificent full-length portrait by William Beechey accurately reflects the sitter's civic clout. Eighteenth-century paintings presented to the Corporation by the good Alderman are displayed in two galleries on the ground floor; the Boydell Room features a dashing portrait of old sea dog Horatio Nelson, while the highlight of the Copley room is a vast painting of the Siege of Gibraltar by American artist John Singleton Copley. The remarkable story of the restoration of this huge canvas and its gargantuan frame is told in a nearby display.

Temporary exhibitions permitting, the ground floor galleries focus on the 'places and faces' of London. The pageantry of the capital city is captured in paintings such as such as *The Opening of Tower Bridge* by W L Wyllie and William Logsail's atmospheric depiction of the Lord Mayor's Procession in 1888.

The collection also contains a good selection of 19th-century paintings and sculpture. Displayed in the Undercroft Galleries, these include gloriously over the top evocations of the ancient world by artists such as Alma-Tadema and Lord Leighton as well as famous Pre-Raphaelite paintings like Holman Hunt's *The Eve of Saint Agnes*. J J Tissot's acutely observations of 19th-century society and Tuke's evocative trio of swimmers, *Ruby, Gold and Malachite* are other treasures

galleries

central

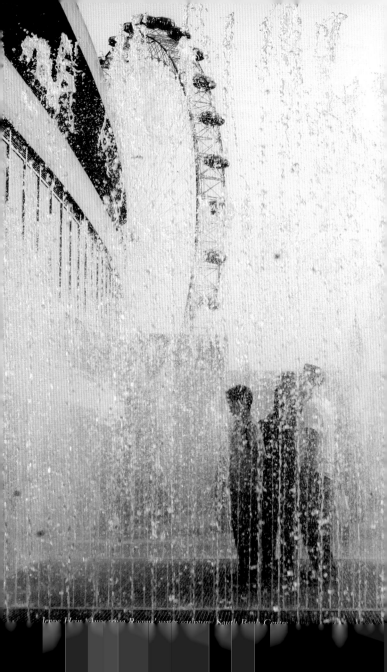

worth seeking out here, along with a powerfully expressionistic full-size oil sketch of Salisbury Cathedral by John Constable.

Splendid as the galleries are, they can only hold a small proportion of the whole collection and displays are changed regularly to explore different themes. It is possible however, to view the entire collection on COLLAGE, the Corporation's data base which contains thousands of images of works of art in the collection and which may be accessed either using the gallery's own terminals or on the internet (http://collage.cityoflondon.gov.uk). The Guildhall Gallery also hosts a regular programme of changing exhibitions.

Hayward Gallery

◻ *South Bank Centre*
☎ *08703 800400*
⌀ *www.haywardgallery.org.uk*
🚌 *Embankment LU, Waterloo LU/Rail*
🕐 *Daily 10.00-18.00 (Fri until 22.00 during exhibitions)*
💲 *Admission charge (varies according to exhibition)*
🛍 *Shop*
☕ *Café*
♿ *Disabled access*

Squatting snugly in the concrete cultural complex that is the South Bank Centre, the Hayward is not the most alluring exhibition space in town despite its love-it-or-loathe-it Brutalist bulk having acquired a glass fronted entrance foyer in recent years. Nevertheless, it puts on a quality show – recent ones have featured sculpture by Antony Gormley and the photography of Alexander Rodchenko. The gallery celebrates in 40th anniversary in 2008 with an exhibition of work by 10 artists that promises to change the gallery space inside and out. For regular visitors, the Hayward's Membership Scheme starts at £25 and offers a range of perks.

Institute of Contemporary Arts

🗓 *The Mall, SW1*

☏ *020 7930 3647 (box office)*

✐ *www.ica.org.uk*

🚇 *Charing Cross LU/Rail, Piccadilly Circus LU*

🕐 *Mon 12.00-23.00, Tues-Sat 12.00-01.00, Sun 12.00-22.30;*
   Galleries open daily 12.00-19.30 (Thurs until 21.00)

💷 *Day membership (included with any ticket purchase) Mon-Fri £2,*
   Sat and Sun £3, £1.50 (concessions weekday), £2 (concessions
   weekend), free (ICA members)

📖 *Bookshop*

🍽 *Café, Bar*

♿ *Limited wheelchair access*

For those who prefer their culture right slap bang up-to-the-minute, the ICA provides a potent programme of art exhibitions, literary events, cinema and live events from gigs to theatre. You may have to take out day membership to get in but that's a small price to pay to keep up with the zeitgeist. The bookshop does a nice line in trendy art mags while the Peyton & Byrne café offers more readily digestible fodder.

Jerwood Space

🗓 *Jerwood Space, 171 Union Street, SE1*

☏ *020 7654 0171*

✐ *www.jerwoodspace.co.uk*

🚇 *Borough LU, Southwark LU*

🕐 *Mon-Fri 10.00-17.00, Sat & Sun 10.00-15.00*

💷 *Admission free*

🍽 *Café*

♿ *Wheelchair Access*

Set in a beautifully refurbished Victorian school building, this exhibition space hosts a year-round programme of contemporary fine art shows, including the renowned Jerwood Contemporary Painters and the Jerwood Artists Platform. The acclaimed Café 171 offers good value, seasonal food in a relaxed environment. Ring ahead or view website to check exhibition programme.

The National Gallery

🏛 *Trafalgar Square, WC2*

☎ *020 7747 2885*

✐ *www.nationalgallery.org.uk*

🚌 *Charing Cross LU/Rail, Embankment LU, Leicester Square LU*

🕐 *Daily 10.00-18.00, Wed 10.00-21.00*

💷 *Admission free (a charge is made for some exhibitions)*

✎ *Shops*

☕ *Café & Restaurant*

♿ *Wheelchair access*

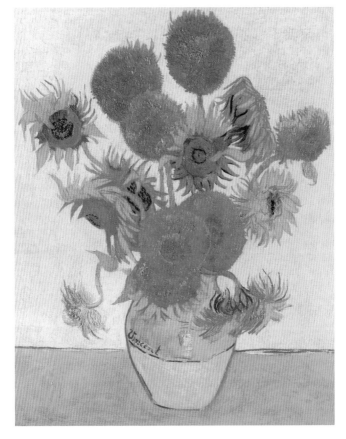

Vincent van Gogh, Sunflowers, 1888, The National Gallery

Frequented by pigeons, rollerskaters and New Year revellers, Trafalgar Square is also a favourite haunt of art lovers, being home to Britain's National Gallery. A top-notch permanent collection of over 2,300 paintings spanning 700 years of Western European art history (from 1260-1900), the NG is the jewel in London's cultural crown. Some of the world's most famous paintings are housed here, among them van Gogh's *Sunflowers*, van Eyck's *The Arnolfini Marriage*, Leonardo da Vinci's *Virgin of the Rocks* and the ever-popular *Haywain* by Constable.

The paintings (no wacky installations or performance art here – unless you count your fellow visitors) are arranged chronologically, the earliest paintings (1260-1510) being shown in the Sainsbury Wing, the newest and sleekest part of the gallery. Designed by American architect Robert Venturi, it opened in 1991 and its calm, monochrome interior provides an ideally neutral backdrop for the glistening gold leaf and vivid pigments of early Renaissance works like the *Wilton Diptych*. Christian iconography predominates but alongside the Annunciations, Nativities and Crucifixions are beautifully-observed portraits like Albrecht Dürer's *The Painter's Father* and Giovanni Bellini's *The Doge Leonardo Loredan*. Scenes from secular life include Uccello's *The Battle of San Romano* whose composition reflects the artist's struggle with the laws of perspective while Botticelli's languid *Venus and Mars* epitomises the Renaissance love affair with the classical past.

Moving back into the main building, the West Wing (coloured maroon on the gallery plan) displays painting from 1500-1600 and includes works by Cranach, Bronzino, Titian and El Greco along with Michelangelo's unfinished 'Entombment' and Veronese's flamboyant set piece 'The Family of Darius before Alexander'. Holbein's recently restored 'The Ambassadors' is one of the highlights here, its ultra-realism managing to accommodate a smattering of symbolism and hidden meanings (stand to the side of the painting to view the death's head – an effect achieved by distorting perspective).

Northern European artists 1600-1700 dominate the North Wing (orange on the gallery map) which is home to Vermeer's enigmatic *Young Woman Standing at a Virginals*. The gallery's Rembrandts are concentrated here and, looking at his self-portraits, it's hard not to be moved by the artist's searing self-analysis and his descent from cocksure, successful thirty-something to dissolute, world weary 60 year-old. Among the works by Southern European artists, visitors can admire the curvaceous *Rokeby Venus*, Velasquez's 17th-century pin up, the darkly passionate fervour of Zurbarán's meditating St Francis or enjoy the gothic frisson of Caravaggio's *Boy Bitten by a Lizard*.

The East Wing (green on the plan) brings the collection up to

1900. Hugely popular, the Impressionist and Post-Impressionist galleries always seem to be crowded – among the show-stoppers are a late Monet, *The Water Lily Pond*, Seurat's *Bathers at Asnières*, and Renoir's *Parapluies*. Escape the crush in Room 42, an intimate space hung with small, loosely painted *'plein-air'* sketches by the likes of Boudin, Corot and Degas. The wing's less fashionable galleries have treasures equally worth exploring – from frothy creations by Fragonard to landscapes by Constable and Turner to the Neo-Classicism of Ingres and David and the Romanticism of Delacroix.

Space restrictions ensure this review can only be a sketch – time restrictions will probably dictate how you tackle the NG. Regular visitors can take advantage of free admission to just drop in from time to time, savouring individual wings, rooms or even paintings. Those with limited time in the capital may likewise want to target particular areas of the collection – easily arranged thanks to the Gallery's nifty interactive multimedia system. Head for the ArtStart rooms on Levels 0 and 1 to print off a free personalised or a themed tour – find out who's behaving badly on the 'Drunkenness and Debauchery' tour or get the kids to track some beautifully painted Creepy Crawlies. Audio Guides are available by donation and feature a highlights tour of 30 masterpieces, but can also spoonfeed you a complete tour with commentaries on individual rooms, paintings and artists as well as on subject matter and techniques. Live guided tours set off daily and are supported by an excellent programme of temporary exhibitions, films, short talks and lectures – ask for details at the desk on arrival or pick up a copy of the Gallery's 'What's On' guide.

Easy on the eye, the NG can be hard on the feet. Benches and squishy leather sofas offer some respite for weary art pilgrims but for hungry culture vultures the gallery has two in-house options. The ultra civilized 'National Dining Rooms' in the Sainsbury Wing has waitress service, seasonal menus using British produce and a mural by Paula Rego. The Gallery's recently improved East Wing facilities (accessed via the street level Getty Entrance on Trafalgar Square) include a large, bustling café for less formal food opportunities as well as a very decent Espresso bar with ArtStart computer terminals.

Thwarted artistic ambitions can be consoled in the gallery's shops where postcards, mugs and exclusive gifts inspired by the works in the collection are on sale. A print on demand service means that you can take home a reproduction of any painting in the collection from a neat A4 size, right up to a giant A0 mega poster. The well-ordered main shop in the Sainsbury Wing also stocks a comprehensive range of art books.

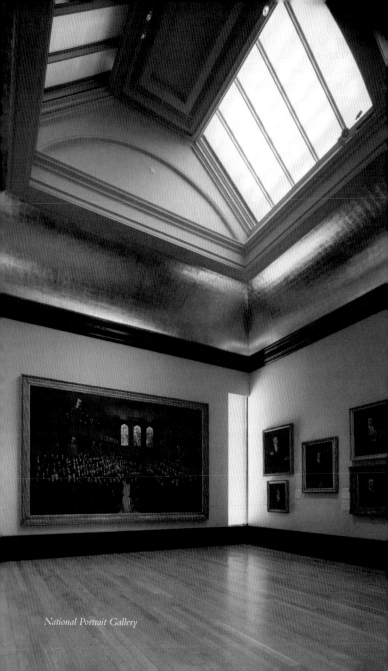

National Portrait Gallery

National Portrait Gallery

⊞ *St Martin's Place, WC2*
☎ *020 7306 0055 (access information only)*
☎ *020 7312 2463 (recorded information)*
🖉 *www.npg.org.uk*
🚆 *Charing Cross LU/Rail, Leicester Square LU*
🕐 *Daily 10.00-18.00, Thurs and Fri until 21.00*
💷 *Admission free (charge for some special exhibitions)*
👓 *Gift Shop & Bookshop*
🍽 *Café & Restaurant*
♿ *Wheelchair access*

Specialising in likenesses of famous British men and women through history, the NPG is perfect for people-watching. With a display of some 1,000 portraits in all media and more celebs than *Hello!*, here at least, it would be rude not to stare. The recent development programme means there's now even more to look at, with more exhibition space and better facilities – including not one but two places to have a coffee afterwards.

For a chronological view of Britain's finest, take the fast-track escalator to the second floor where the collection kicks off with the Plantagenet and Tudor monarchs. Beautifully displayed in an understated gallery (all deep-grey walls and fibreoptic lighting) the works here include Holbein's cartoon for his portrait of a bullish Henry VIII. Wall labels explain the niceties of his family tree, dramatised, if not entirely accurately, by one William Shakespeare – whose portrait by John Taylor was the first to be acquired by the Gallery. As you work your way downstairs, encounter a succession of monarchs, mistresses, men of letters and public figures and characters like the 18th-century Duchess of Queensberry, who 'still beautiful at 76, died of a surfeit of cherries'.

The Weldon Galleries on the second floor are home to the movers and shakers of Regency Britain – everyone from proto-feminist Mary Wollstonecraft to road surface pioneer John McAdam with a section devoted to 'Royalty, Celebrity and Scandal' thrown in for good measure. Founded in 1856, the gallery is a testament to the achievements and preoccupations of the 19th century and, unsurprisingly, most of the first floor is dedicated to Queen Victoria's great and good. The 'Statesmen's Gallery' is filled with the busts and portraits of stern, bewhiskered dignitaries. Empire builders (a jaunty Lord Baden-Powell among them), artists and scientists populate the anterooms. Writers get a look in too: a tousle-haired Lord Tennyson and a trio of Brontës.

The Early 20th Century galleries are prefaced by Sir James Guthrie's enormous *Some Statesmen of the Great War* out of which a centrally placed Winston Churchill stares knowingly. The 1918-1960 holdings are suspended in a series of glass screens and include personalities such as Lord Reith and Alexander Fleming although the arts are still represented by the likes of L.S. Lowry, Kingsley Amis and a curiously Mrs Tiggywinkle-like Beatrix Potter among others.

The Balcony Gallery looks at Britain 1960-1990 and offers a heady mix of pop culture and politics. On the ground floor, the Britain since 1990 rooms underline how the nature of fame has changed. Stand-up comedians, fashion designers, sports 'personalities' and models join the usual suspects from British public life pleading 'I'm a Celebrity, Get Me in Here!'. The Emmanuel Kaye Gallery attempts to redress the gallery's perceived bias towards the arts, with portraits of worthies from the worlds of science and technology.

The collection provides a gloriously voyeuristic tour through history, documenting changing attitudes and fashions more vividly than any history book. In an almost perverse reversal of the usual art gallery ethos, the celebrity of the subject holds sway over artistic merit – although that said there are works by big names like Kneller, Gainsborough and David Hockney. Although photography was cold-shouldered by the gallery until the 1960s it now features much more heavily in the more contemporary displays with works by photographers such as Johnny Shand Kydd and Tom Miller.

Visitors in search of a particular face in the crowd should investigate the 'Portrait Explorer' in the new IT gallery where touchscreens offer access to high-resolution images of the gallery's entire Primary Collection as well as parts of its Archive Collections. Users can also listen to interviews with artists and sitters, as well as print out a personalised tour of 12 works of art. For those with larger ambitions the gallery's Audio Guide (£2) provides commentaries on over 300 famous portraits.

Late night openings on Thursdays and Fridays have proved a popular innovation at the NPG – lectures, films and tours are scheduled for Thursday evenings while Friday nights take a musical theme. Information on these events and the temporary exhibition programme can be obtained from the Information Desk.

Down in the basement, the glass-roofed Portrait Café does a good line in coffee, tea and light snacks while up on third floor the Portrait Restaurant serves a more sophisticated menu at higher prices and offers stunning views of Trafalgar Square, Whitehall and the London Eye thrown in for free. The NPG's bookshop stocks titles ranging from biography to costume and those on a gift buying mission will find an eclectic selection in the shop.

The Photographers' Gallery

- 🖼 *5 and 8 Great Newport Street, WC2*
- ☎ *020 7831 1772*
- ✐ *www.photonet.org.uk*
- 🚇 *Leicester Square LU*
- 🕐 *Mon-Sat 11.00-18.00 (Thurs until 20.00), Sun 12.00-18.00*
- 🎟 *Admission free*
- 📖 *Bookshop*
- ☕ *Café*
- ♿ *Wheelchair access (ground floor only)*

The first independent gallery in Britain to be devoted to photography, the Photographers' Gallery runs an invigorating exhibition programme, showcasing new talent as well as holding retrospectives of established names. Its Print Sales Gallery offers vintage, modern and contemporary prints for sale, while an extensive selection of photography publications can be found in the bookshop. Having been on Great Newport Street since its inception in 1971, the gallery is due to move into smart new, architect-designed, premises with bigger and better facilities on Ramillies Street, Soho in 2011.

Queen's Gallery

- 🖼 *Buckingham Palace, SW1*
- ☎ *020 7766 7301*
- ✐ *www.royalcollection.org.uk*
- 🚇 *Green Park LU, St James's Park LU, Victoria LU/Rail*
- 🕐 *Daily (during exhibitions) 10.00-17.30 (last entry 16.30)*
- 🎟 *£8.50 (adults), £7.50 (concs), £4.25 (under 17s), free (under 5s)*
- 📖 *Shop*
- ♿ *Wheelchair access*

Even the Queen's Gallery wasn't immune from the refurb fever which swept through the city's museums at the turn of the millennium. The £20 million expansion of the Gallery's premises at Buckingham Palace has created an imposing new Doric portico, lofty double height entrance hall and staircase, and new – although highly traditional looking – galleries. The changes have been described as the most significant addition to Buck House in well over a century.

The gallery hosts a programme of changing exhibitions, showcasing different aspect of the extensive holdings of the Royal Collection. Held in trust by The Queen for her successors and the nation, the Royal Collection has largely been formed since the Restoration in 1660 and includes high calibre works of art in every medium from paintings and works on paper to ceramics, jewellery and textiles.

As you might expect, security is tight at the gallery, and airport style checks are in operation but the staff are courteous, friendly and helpful. The Gallery's shop sells scholarly publications about aspects of the collection as well as an assortment of right royal knick-knacks – from limited edition crockery, such as the official Diamond Wedding commemorative service, to cuddly toys.

Royal Academy of Arts

- 🏛 *Burlington House, Piccadilly, W1*
- ☏ *020 7300 8000*
- ☏ *020 7300 5760/5761 (recorded information)*
- ✎ *www.royalacademy.org.uk*
- 🚌 *Green Park LU, Piccadilly Circus LU, bus 9, 14, 19, 22, 38*
- 🕐 *Daily 10.00-18.00 (Fri until 22.00)*
- 🎟 *Admission free (to the John Madesjki Fine Rooms); Admission charge for exhibitions (varies according to exhibition)*
- ✎ *Shop*
- 🍽 *Café & Restaurant*
- ♿ *Wheelchair access*

Perhaps George III wasn't so mad – after all he did found this august institution (the oldest fine arts academy in Britain) in 1768. Today the Royal Academy is known for organising crowd-pleasing blockbuster exhibitions like 'Monet in the 20th Century', 'Cranach' and 'From Russia'. Punters flock to the RA's annual Summer Exhibition which, with over 1,000 exhibits, is the world's largest open art exhibition. Offering a mind-bogglingly diffuse vision of contemporary British art, the show attracts as much critical disdain as it does popular acclaim. The RA's popular 'Friends' scheme rewards members with free entry to exhibitions, a separate 'Friends' room and a glossy mag amongst other perks.

A statue of Sir Joshua Reynolds, the Academy's first president, greets visitors as they enter the courtyard of Burlington House. Works by Academicians, past and present, can be seen free of charge in the John Madejski Fine Rooms. This suite of elegant 18th-century rooms, which reopened following restoration in March 2004 with displays from the RA's permanent collection including works by Turner, Constable and Hockney. The RA's café and restaurant offer good light meals and the chance to see the chattering classes in action – but like the exhibitions and indeed the ladies' loos, they can get crowded. Piccadilly and surrounding area offers a range of alternatives on all counts if the queues are too daunting.

The Saatchi Gallery

⌧ Duke of York's HQ, King's Road, SW3

☎ 020 7823 2363

✍ www.saatchigallery.com

🚌 Sloane Square LU

🕐 Daily 10.00-18.00

🌐 Admission free

👓 Bookshop

☕ Café

♿ Disabled access

Housed in elegantly renovated ex-army premises, the latest incarnation of the Saatchi Gallery opened in October 2008. With 70,000 square feet of white-walled and wooden-floored gallery space there's plenty of room for Charles Saatchi to show off his famous and ever-developing contemporary art collection in a series of snappily titled temporary exhibitions. Controversial Brit-Art may be what the Saatchi is best known for in the popular imagination but the collection is truly international in scope – the inaugural exhibition was an ebullient introduction to the hottest names in Chinese art, while future shows will look at the latest in Indian, German, Middle Eastern and American art.

While the extensive main suite of galleries is given over to major 'survey' shows, up on Level 2 the Project Room showcases the work of a single artist within the collection, such as Aleksandra Mir's *Newsroom* series. On the same level, the Gallery Room, is given over to displays hosted by contemporary art auctioneers Phillips de Pury, the Saatchi Gallery's corporate partner. Their inaugural show was of new work by big-hitter Julian Schnabel. For all the conspicuous consumption on display, the gallery has a surprisingly egalitarian stance with free entry for all and an extensive virtual online gallery. The site offers, amongst other things, a commission-free sales service complete with a 'Showdown' where visitors vote weekly for their favourite online work, which are then exhibited at the Gallery.

Tate Britain

🖼 *Millbank, SW1*

☎ *020 7887 8888*

✎ *www.tate.org.uk*

🚌 *Pimlico LU*

🕐 *Daily 10.00-17.50 (until 22.00 first Friday of the month)*

💷 *Admission free (admission charges apply for major loan exhibitions)*

🛍 *Shops*

☕ *Café & Restaurant*

♿ *Disabled access (via the Manton Entrance)*

What was once simply known as 'the Tate' has been rationalised and rebranded for the 21st century as Tate Britain and Tate Modern. With its collection of modern international art happily installed downstream at Bankside, the Millbank branch of the Tate empire can concentrate on being the national gallery of British art – as founder Henry Tate intended back in the 19th-century. It's got plenty of material to work with too – the permanent collection of native art spans some 600 years from the Renaissance to the present day and features works by the lynchpins of British art including Hogarth, Gainsborough, Stubbs, Turner, Constable, the Blakes (William and Peter), Bacon and Moore.

And thanks to its Centenary Project, Tate Britain has more space in which to show off the goodies. Four new galleries, five refurbished galleries on the main floor and six new temporary exhibition rooms (the Linbury Galleries) on the lower floor, help to make this the largest display of British art in the world. The building work has also resulted in a crisp, rather antiseptic, new entrance and lobby (with shop and coffee bar) on Atterbury Street – although Tate die hards will probably still want to head for the high ground of the old Millbank entrance overlooking the Thames to meet friends.

In contrast to the thematic approach adopted over at Tate Modern, Tate Britain has plumped for a broadly chronological presentation, straightforwardly entitled 'Collections 1500-2008'. This 500 year period has been divided into two sequences: 1500-1900 (in the galleries on the west side of the building), and 1900 to the present (in the eastern galleries). Displays are changed regularly – a reshuffling process that rewards the frequent visitor but which means that the description which follows can only be a general overview. The display begins with the English Renaissance and ends with more contemporary fare by the likes of Sarah Lucas and Rebecca Warren but it's not merely a tunnel vision cruise through British art down the centuries. Themes such as 'Nature and Landscape', 'Court and Commerce', 'Objects and Materials' and 'The Grand Manner' are neatly embedded within the

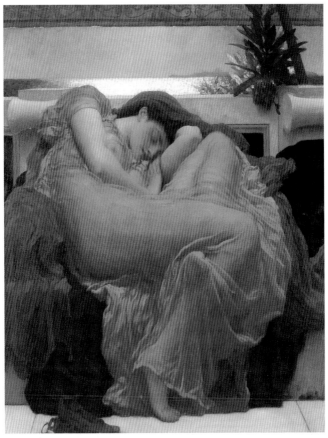

Frederick Lord Leighton, Flaming June 1895, Tate Britain

main chronological scheme and help vary the pace while showcasing gems such as Joseph Wright's portrait of the superbly languid Brooke Boothby and Gwen John's unsettling portrait of her brother's lover and muse, Dorelia.

Other rooms concentrate on the work of individual artists or small groups of artists – home grown talent in the shape of the Independent Group, Robyn Denny, Victor Passmore and Francis Bacon. Loans from high calibre private and public collections are juxtaposed with works from the Tate's collections giving regular visitors a chance to see familiar works in a slighter different context. Visitors will also notice an increase in sculpture and work in other media such as pottery and photography.

A vibrant programme of temporary exhibitions complements the permanent collection and these are staged in the new Linbury Galleries on the lower floor (level 1) and in the north-east corner of the main floor (level 2). The Camden Town Group was the subject of a recent show and, making the point that new art isn't just the preserve of Tate Modern, the gallery staged a retrospective of ex-pat painter Peter Doig. Tate Britain also hosts the now reliably controversial Turner Prize, awarded annually to a British artist under 50.

With all the hype surrounding the Turner prize it's easy to overlook the work of its namesake, JMW Turner, whose bequest to the nation is housed in the Clore Gallery, a purpose built suite of galleries adjoining the main building. Although at the time of writing the Turner displays are somewhat truncated while the major oil paintings tour the United States there are still several rooms showcasing his work. The selection in the 'Turner Gallery' aims to give a flavour of the collection with works like the artist's self portrait of c.1799, classical compositions like *Dido and Aeneas* and dramatic Romantic subjects like *The Fall of an Avalanche in the Grisons*. Turner's haunting, proto-Impressionistic oil sketches occupy two rooms, exploring subjects such as Venice and coastal scenes. 'Colour and Line' is a long running interactive exhibition (until 2012) examining Turner's revolutionary approaches to the mediums of watercolour and graphic work.

If you've still got time on your hands, free daily guided tours focus on highlights from different area of the collection, or you could try to catch the 15 minute 'painting of the month' talks for a more in-depth discussion of just one key work of art. For those who prefer machines to people, multimedia guides can be hired for £3.50 which allow users to listen to interviews with the artists and to learn from the horse's mouth what inspires them – and what critics think of their work. Touch Tours and Raised Images are available for visually impaired visitors – ask at the information desk or telephone 020 7401 5113 for details. The Art Trolley gets rolled out every weekend with a range of trails and drawing activities for children aged 3-11 years. Well stocked with art books and increasingly funky Tate merchandise, the Tate Britain shop is a must for most visitors and features a whole room devoted to postcards. The subterranean café serves decent sandwiches, cakes and coffees, although at busy times it can feel uncomfortably cramped. Just across the corridor, the restaurant offers more gracious and spacious dining in an elegant room with murals by artist Rex Whistler.

Tate Modern

⬚ *Bankside, SE1*
☏ *0208 7887 8888*
✎ *www.tate.org.uk*
🚍 *Southwark LU*
🕐 *Sun-Thurs 10.00-18.00, Fri-Sat 10.00-22.00*
♨ *Admission free (charges for some special exhibitions or events)*
🛍 *Shop*
🍽 *Cafés and Restaurant*
♿ *Wheelchair access*

Tate Modern is architectural recycling at its most audacious. The behemoth that was Bankside Power Station was transformed for the new millennium by Swiss architects Hertzog and de Meuron into a state-of-the-art gallery for the 21st century. First-time visitors cannot fail to be impressed by the sheer scale of the operation – it's quite unlike any other gallery in London. Some 4.2 million bricks and 218 miles of cabling went into making it. To really revel in the power and the glory, avoid the small riverside doorway and go in by the west entrance where a huge ramp leads you down into the Turbine Hall. At some 500ft long and 115ft high, this is the centrepiece of the building and the setting for series of specially-commissioned sculptures. Size does matters here and its fascinating to see how contemporary artists tackle this vast space – Anish Kapoor's giant 'hearing trumpet', Olafur Eliasson's mesmeric *Weather Project* and Doris Salcedo's crack in the floor *Shoibboleth* have been some of the responses so far.

But it's not just an ace building – there's a pretty good art collection too. Now that the former Tate Gallery on Millbank has become Tate Britain (British art from 1500 to present, see entry on p. 208), Tate Modern is home to the national collection of international 20th century art as well as a venue for new art. Its permanent collection displays are thematic rather than strictly chronological and have recently been redisplayed around pivotal moments in 20th century art history. 'Material Gestures' can be found on level 3 along with 'Poetry and Dream', while level 5 houses 'Conceptual Models' (recent contemporary acquisitions), 'Idea and Object' and 'States of Flux'. Each themed 'suite' contains several galleries, some devoted to individual artists, or pairs of artists, others to movements like Pop Art or Expressionism or aspects such as Cubist Drawings. Some galleries compare the work of two different artists such as Lichtenstein and Boccioni, Bacon and Picasso.

Displays are changed regularly, making life interesting for the regular visitor but rather more difficult for the guidebook compiler.

galleries central

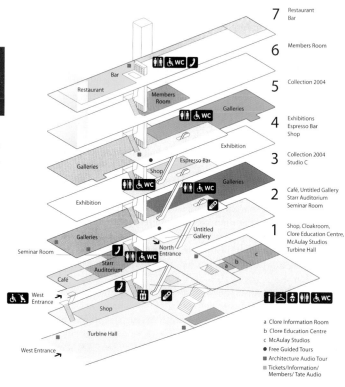

7 Restaurant
Bar

6 Members Room

5 Collection 2004

4 Exhibitions
Espresso Bar
Shop

3 Collection 2004
Studio C

2 Café, Untitled Gallery
Starr Auditorium
Seminar Room

1 Shop, Cloakroom,
Clore Education Centre,
McAulay Studios
Turbine Hall

Bar
Restaurant
Members Room
Galleries
Galleries
Exhibition
Espresso Bar
Shop
Galleries
Exhibition
Galleries
Untitled Gallery
North Entrance
Seminar Room
Starr Auditorium
Café
West Entrance
Shop
Turbine Hall
West Entrance

a Clore Information Room
b Clore Education Centre
c McAulay Studios
● Free Guided Tours
■ Architecture Audio Tour
■ Tickets/Information/
Members/ Tate Audio

Expect a challenging mix of big hitters like Picasso, Matisse, Leger, Beuys, Dubuffet, Giacometti, Pollock and Warhol as well as more recent stars such as Cornelia Parker and Langlands and Bell. Special exhibitions and displays are held in the galleries on level 4 and recent shows have included Louise Bourgeois and Cy Twombly. Each of the four themed 'suites' offers a complete visit in its own right and there are free daily guided tours of their highlights. Alternatively the Tate multimedia guide (£2) is a technologically advanced way of contextualising the collection – a mini-hand-held computer that offers interviews with artists, footage of them in action, commentaries on the works, music and interactive games. The guide also includes a children's tour. Free 'Tate Teaser' activity sheets for young visitors are available from the information desk while 'Start' is an educational resource offering a range of fun, drop-in activities. It's based on level 3 and is open at weekends (for times, consult the website). There's also a full programme of events aimed at adults such as film screenings and drop-in talks.

The astounding popularity of Tate Modern means that even its spacious galleries and concourses can still get crowded, with queues at its cafés and shops. Friday and Saturday late night openings are a good way of avoiding the hordes and have a pleasantly mellow atmosphere. If it all gets too frenetic the Rothko room on level 3 provides an ideal chill-out zone – its suite of maroon abstracts (originally destined for the Four Seasons Restaurant in New York) and subdued lighting are beautifully meditative, and there are plenty of benches for weary art lovers. Not all Tate Modern's rooms have such ample seating but portable viewing stools can be picked up from concourses and, given the distances you may find yourself covering, are a wise precaution.

Modern art can be thirsty, hungry work and Tate Modern has three options for those in need of refreshment. The restaurant in the glass lightbeam on level 7 offers table service and spectacular views of London, while the café on level 2 although minus the panorama, offers a good menu and reasonable coffee. Queues may be a problem at peak times but if it's just a coffee and a sandwich you're after then the Espresso bar on level 4 may do the job. Drinking fountains can be found on levels 1, 3, 4, and 5 and there is a picnic area for family use at weekends and during holidays.

Tate Modern's retail operation matches the scale of the rest of the building. The shop in the Turbine Hall includes a comprehensively stocked art bookshop with over 10,000 titles and an imaginative range of artist designed merchandise as well as the usual posters, prints and postcards.

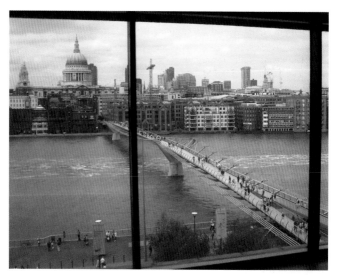

View from Tate Modern

For those planning a double dose of Tate, a fast boat service serves the two venues, capitalising on their riverside locations. Dashingly decorated by Damien Hirst, the boat runs every 40 minutes between Tate Britain and Tate Modern. Its journey time of 18 minutes includes a stop off at the London Eye. Tickets can be purchased at the respective Tates, on board or on-line.

Since its triumphant arrival onto London's cultural scene – on time and within budget – in May 2000, Tate Modern has proved to be the very model of a Millennium project. Over 25 million people have flocked to see it since it opened, *Time Out* readers voted it their favourite London building and it attracts around 5 million visitors annually. It is with some justification that Tate Modern can claim to be the most popular museum of modern art in the world but that doesn't mean that it's sitting back and taking it easy. A bold new building by Hertzog and de Meuron on the south side of the existing gallery was given planning permission in 2007 which, when it is completed in 2012, will provide additional gallery space for 21st century art as well as education and recreational facilities.

The Wallace Collection

⊞ *Hertford House, Manchester Square, W1*
☎ *020 7563 9500*
✎ *www.wallace-collection.org.uk*
🚌 *Baker Street LU, Bond Street LU, Oxford Circus LU*
🕐 *Daily 10.00-17.00*
🏷 *Admission free*
🛍 *Shop*
🍽 *Café (lunch booking advised, tel 020 7563 9505)*
♿ *Wheelchair access*

Bequeathed to the nation in 1897, the Wallace Collection is that rare creature, a seriously sexy museum. Housed in a sumptuous Italianate palazzo in a leafy Marylebone square, it's chock full of fine and decorative art works acquired in the 18th and 19th centuries by the aristocratic and scandalous Hertford family. Its 25 galleries are a cornucopia for connoisseurs, but the casual visitor will enjoy the Collection's ambience as much its artefacts: it has an old-fashioned aura of discreet luxury, with antique clocks ticking quietly in gracious rooms, and friendly, helpful room stewards.

Many famous paintings reside here – Frans Hals *The Laughing Cavalier*, Poussin's *A Dance to the Music of Time* and Fragonard's deliciously frothy *The Swing* among them. Hertford House is also home to top-notch old master paintings by Titian, Rubens, Murillo and Canaletto, and portraits by Gainsborough and Reynolds. Some of the subject matter is on the racy side – there's a wonderfully louche portrait of Nelson's squeeze Lady Hamilton, reclining on a leopardskin in a state of semi undress, as well as a clutch of risqué Dutch genre paintings like Jan Steyn's *The Lute Player*.

Clearly, the Hertford family had an appetite for the good things in life, and today a sumptuous refurbishment programme is bringing the gracious interiors of the Wallace back up to the mark. First time visitors, or lapsed regular ones, should prepare to have socks blown off by the lavish new interior schemes of the Oval Drawing Room and The Small Drawing Room. The former is a late Rococo masterpiece, decorated in pale blue moiré damask and featuring a suite of fleshy paintings by Boucher and the Comte d'Orsay's rolltop desk. Other recently completed rooms are the Large Drawing Room and the Study, the former a resplendently masculine space decked out in dark green silk against which the Dutch Old Master paintings and black and gold of the Boulle marquetry furniture sing out. In contrast the Study is an entirely feminine space with full-on coral colour scheme, decorated in the style of Marie Antoinette's boudoir and furnished with elegant

Riesener furniture once owned by the French queen. Also among the goodies in this room are two lavish Sèvres ice-cream coolers from the 'Catherine the Great' service – one of the most expensive ever produced in Europe. These pieces are just part of the Wallace's collection of Sèvres porcelain, the most complete museum collection of this type in the world.

On the ground floor, four galleries are given over to baronial-style displays of European and Oriental arms and armour, some of it incredibly elaborate. Exhibit A19, a pair of 16th-century chainmail trunks, puts a whole new perspective on macho underwear. Other displays feature gold boxes, Renaissance bronzes, medieval manuscripts and majolica pottery. A suite of galleries on the lower ground floor provide a venue for temporary exhibitions while the Ritblat Conservation Gallery explores some of the intricate processes that went into making Boulle marquetry furniture and 16th century armour.

Daily themed or collection tours help the visitor make the most of this diversity – given by Wallace Collection staff and other experts, these are free of charge and last about an hour (see website for times). Independent souls can opt for the audio guide, which offers a selected highlights tour as well as tours for the visually impaired and those with learning difficulties.

Visitor facilities here are in keeping with the high-end surroundings – the Marquessses of Hertford didn't slum it and neither will you. The airy courtyard of Hertford House, complete with glass roof, is now home to some blissfully spacious ladies' loos and a popular café/restaurant – lunch booking is advised. Alternatively, visitors may prefer to head for the cafés of nearby Marylebone High Street. The shop on the ground floor also has a suitably upmarket feel: its scholarly catalogues don't come cheap, but the guidebook to the collection is a good investment at under a tenner. As well as the usual posters and postcards, there's an imaginative range of gifts inspired by the collection including jewellery, colourful and kitsch 'Sèvres' tin picnic plates, and for kids a 'make your own cardboard Bascinet helmet' kit.

Right: Oval Drawing Room, The Wallace Collection

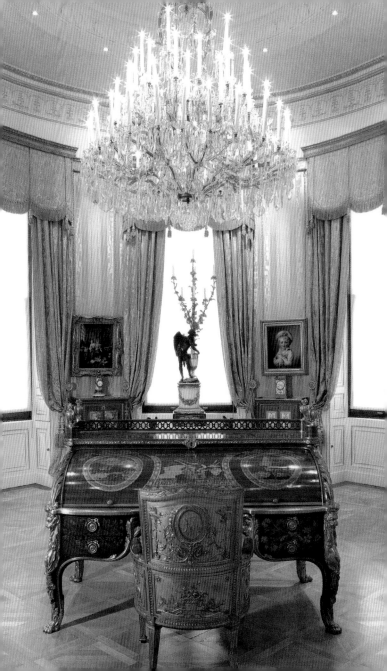

North

The Ben Uri Gallery –
The London Jewish Museum of Art

- 🖼 *108a Boundary Road, NW8*
- ☎ *020 7604 3991*
- ✍ *www.benuri.org.uk*
- 🚌 *Swiss Cottage LU or St John's Wood LU, bus 31, 139, 189*
- 🕐 *Mon-Thurs 10.00-17.00, Fri 1.00-15.00 (until 17.00 in summer), Sun 12.00-16.00 (closed Sat)*
- 💷 *Admission free*
- ♿ *Disabled access (ground floor only)*

The Ben Uri Art Society was founded in 1915 and is dedicated to promoting Jewish art as a fundamental part of Jewish heritage. Its permanent collection contains nearly 1,000 works by artists such as Lucien Pissarro, Jacob Epstein and R. B. Kitaj and is the world's largest holding of Anglo Jewish art. Treasures include David Bomberg's seminal *Ghetto Theatre* (1920), Mark Gertler's *Rabbi and Ribbitzin* and *Nude Standing* (1954) by Frank Auerbach.

After several years without a home of its own, the Society (rebranded as The Ben Uri Gallery) moved to its current premises in 2001, where it mounts a regular programme of exhibitions and events. The exhibitions usually (but not always) draw on works from the permanent collection and have included important retrospectives of Jewish artists like Ludwig and Else Meidner, Mark Gertler and William Roberts. The Ben Uri is co-organiser of the Jewish Artist of the Year competition, held biennially.

Camden Arts Centre

- 🖼 *Arkwright Road (corner of Finchley Road), NW3*
- ☎ *020 7472 5500*
- ✍ *www.camdenartscentre.org*
- 🚌 *Finchley Road LU, Hampstead LU, Finchley Road, Frognal Rail*
- 🕐 *Tues-Sun 10.00-18.00, Wed until 21.00*
- 💷 *Admission free*
- 📚 *Bookshop*
- ☕ *Café*
- ♿ *Wheelchair access*

A recent redevelopment (to the tune of £4.2 million) has breathed new life into this respected contemporary art venue. The swish new facilities include improved access, enhanced gallery space, on-site artists'

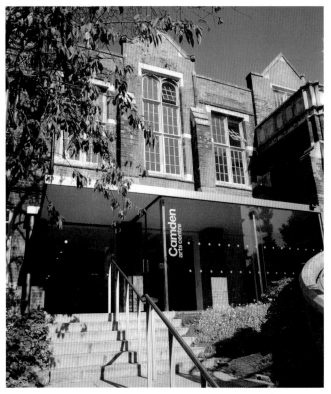

Camden Arts Centre

studios, a ceramic studio, and a rather fine café. What hasn't changed is the Centre's inspirational 'roll up your sleeves and get stuck in' approach to the visual arts with visitors being encouraged to get involved in the integrated programme of exhibitions, educational projects and courses, artist-led workshops, exhibition tours and talks. The centre maintains its policy of showing both established and emerging artists and recent exhibitions have showcased abstract artist Thomas Scheibitz and Swedish painter Karin Mamma Andersson. A rolling programme of artists' residencies is an added draw – residencies tend to last 6-8 weeks with regular 'open studio' slots allowing the public to see work in progress and talk to the artist. The foyer bookshop stocks an impressively up to the minute choice of art books, catalogues and periodicals as well as a range of limited edition and specially commissioned publications.

Centre for Recent Drawing

⌨ *2-4 Highbury Station Road, N1*

☎ *020 7871 7367*

✐ *www.c4rd.org.uk*

🚊 *Highbury and Islington LU/Rail*

🕐 *Wed-Fri 12.00-18.00*

♨ *Admission free*

The centre is run on a not-for-profit basis and its public exhibition space is dedicated to the often overlooked art of drawing. Regular exhibitions turn the spotlight on different drawing techniques and the centre also houses residencies for artists for whom drawing is at the core of their work.

Estorick Collection of Modern Italian Art

⌨ *Northampton Lodge, 39a Canonbury Square, N1*

☎ *020 7704 9522*

✐ *www.estorickcollection.com*

🚊 *Highbury and Islington LU/Rail*

🕐 *Wed-Sat 11.00-18.00, Sun 12.00-17.00*

♨ *£3.50 (adults), £2.50 (concessions), free (under 16s/students)*

🛍 *Shop*

☕ *Café*

♿ *Limited wheelchair access*

Works by Futurist artists Balla, Severini and Boccioni are at the heart of this superb private art collection, amassed by Eric and Salome Estorick after World War II. Opened in January 1998 and housed in a beautifully refurbished Georgian building, the collection has the distinction of being Britain's first museum devoted to modern Italian art. Works by Futurist artists such as Boccioni, Severini and Balla form the core of the collection but other major 20th-century Italian artists represented are metaphysical painter Giorgio de Chirico, Giorgio Morandi and master of the anorexic portrait, Amedeo Modigliani. Bronzes by Marino Marini and Giacomo Manzù are among the sculptures. Displays of the permanent collection change periodically for conservation reasons.

West

The Louise T Blouin Institute

⌂ *3 Olaf Street, W11*
☎ *020 7985 9600*
🖉 *www.ltbfoundation.org*
🚌 *Latimer Road LU, Shepherd's Bush LU, Holland Park LU*
🕐 *Tues 10.00-20.30, Wed-Sun 10.00-18.00*
♿ *Admission £9 (adults), £3 (children, concs)*
☕ *Café*
♿ *Wheelchair access*

Since opening in 2006, this sleek, white contemporary exhibition space has shown, among other things, lightworks by James Turrell and held a major retrospective of American architect Richard Meier. A programme of lectures and other events, such as music recitals, accompany the exhibitions.

Serpentine Gallery

⌂ *Kensington Gardens, W2*
☎ *020 7402 6075*
☎ *020 7298 1515 (recorded information)*
🖉 *www.serpentinegallery.org*
🚌 *Lancaster Gate LU, South Kensington LU, Knightsbridge LU*
🕐 *Daily 10.00-18.00*
♿ *Admission free*
📖 *Bookshop*
♿ *Wheelchair access*

Art and nature combine perfectly at this publicly-funded art gallery. Set in the pastoral 18th-century landscape of the Royal Park, and housed in a former 1930s tea pavilion, the Serpentine provides an informal, relaxed location for viewing exhibitions of modern and contemporary art. Often challenging and controversial, recent shows have profiled Derek Jarman and Maria Lassnig. The gallery's facilities were enhanced by a £4 million renovation a few years ago and its unique atmosphere and abundant natural light have been praised by artists and critics alike. Free gallery talks take place on selected Saturdays at 3pm.

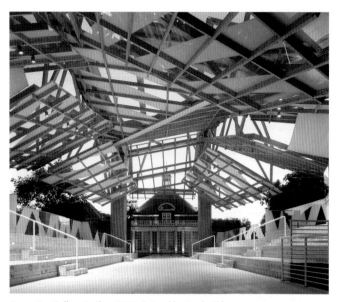

Serpentine Gallery Pavilion 2008, designed by Frank Gehry

The Anthony Shaw Collection

🖺 *11 Billing Place, SW10*

☎ *020 7353 3964*

✐ *www.anthonyshawcollection.org*

🕒 *Open by appointment only*

🚌 *Fulham Broadway LU*

🐾 *Admission Free*

An eclectic selection of British studio pottery from the 1970s to the present day assembled by couturier Anthony Shaw. Inspired by Kettle's Yard in Cambridge, the collection opened to the public in 2004 and is housed in Anthony's former parental home, a tiny mid 19th century house, complete with bohemian 50s décor. The cosy domestic setting is the antithesis of the froideur of 'white cube' galleries and Anthony is a friendly host, happy to talk about his collection. With over 50 top artists represented, such as Lucie Rie, Ewan Henderson, Mo Jupp and Clive Bowen, this is a great destination for pottery lovers. Displays change twice yearly and are often guest curated by people working in disciplines other than pottery.

South

Café Gallery

⊟ *By the lake, Southwark Park, SE16*

☎ *020 7237 1230*

✐ *www.cafegalleryprojects.org*

🚌 *Canada Water LU*

🕑 *Wed-Fri & Sun 11.00-16.00, Sat 12.00-16.00*

🅿 *Admission free*

♿ *Disabled access*

Tucked away in Southwark Park – one of London's oldest Metropolitan parks – this artist run enterprise has been described as 'the best kept art secret in Britain'. That perhaps shouldn't be a badge of honour for a public gallery that's been running for over 24 years but its exhibition programme of work by emerging artists is an invigorating one and the gallery has not one but two spaces to its name.

Dulwich Picture Gallery

⊟ *Gallery Road, SE21*

☎ *020 8693 5254*

✐ *www.dulwichpicturegallery.org.uk*

🚌 *North Dulwich Rail, West Dulwich Rail*

🕑 *Tues-Fri 10.00-17.00, Sat-Sun and Bank Holidays 11.00-17.00*

🅿 *£5 (adults), £4 (senior citizens), free (unemployed/disabled/students/ children), additional £4 charge for special exhibitions*

🛍 *Shop*

☕ *Café*

♿ *Wheelchair access*

Tucked away in a pleasant backwater of London, the DPG's small but perfectly-formed collection of Old Master paintings is a delight for art lovers. Arranged by school, the display has been described as a progression from the beer drinkers (Northern European artists) to the wine drinkers (the French, Spanish and Italian schools). A quick glance around the walls reveals a fair smattering of milk drinkers too – as in Rubens' voluptuous *Venus, Mars, Cupid* or Poussin's *The Nurture of Jupiter*.

Rembrandt's *Girl leaning on a window sill* is perhaps the gallery's most famous work and in days gone by was the one most copied by art students – an honour which today falls to Poussin, who is represented in the gallery by seven superlative paintings. The gallery is full of familiar faces and names – Murillo's *Flower Girl*, Joshua Reynold's bespectacled self-portrait, and Gainsborough's double portrait of beautiful chanteuses, the Linley sisters. Another famous beauty of her day, Lady Venetia Digby, appears here in a poignant deathbed portrait of her by Van Dyck. Guido Reni's *St Sebastian* has been restored to its original place of honour overlooking the gallery's central enfilade while, around the corner in the Italian Baroque gallery, Sebastiano Ricci's action-packed canvas *The Fall of the Rebel Angels* should be warning enough to keep viewers on the straight and narrow.

Concise, entertaining wall labels accompany the paintings and free tours are held on Saturdays and Sundays at 15.00. The gallery's distinctive building is as noteworthy as its contents – built by Sir John Soane (see p.72), it is England's oldest public gallery and was the inspiration behind Sir Giles Gilbert Scott's design for the classic red telephone box in the 1920s and many other art museums world-wide. Unlike your common or garden art gallery however, the DPG also includes a built-in mausoleum, where the mortal remains of the gallery's three founders are kept to this day.

The subject of a major millennial refurbishment, the gallery looks resplendent and also boasts a beautiful new Visitor Wing – a bronze and glass 'cloister' designed by Rick Mather. The elegant café housed here serves tasty light lunches, coffees and teas while over in the foyer of the main building, the shop stocks a good selection of books, cards and original gifts. A lively programme of loan exhibitions supplements the permanent collection – recent shows have included American art from the 1850s–1950s and vintage Chinese photographs.

Pump House Gallery

🏠 *Battersea Park, SW11 4NJ*

☎ *020 7350 0523*

🚇 *Sloane Square LU; Battersea Park or Queenstown Road Rail*

🕐 *Wed, Thurs, Sun and Bank Holidays 11.00-17.00 ;*
   Fri-Sat 11.00-16.00 (during exhibitions)

💷 *Admission free*

☕ *Café nearby in park*

Occupying a pretty lakeside setting in Battersea Park, this former Victorian waterpumping building now houses Wandsworth's only public art gallery. The gallery is dedicated to contemporary art and hosts six exhibitions a year of work by emerging and established artists, often featuring specially commissioned pieces, as well as touring exhibitions and locally curated projects.

South London Gallery

🖼 *65 Peckham Road, SE5*
☎ *020 7703 6120*
🖂 *www.southlondongallery.org*
🚌 *Elephant & Castle LU, then bus P3, 12 or 171; Oval LU, then bus 436, 36*
🕐 *Tues-Sun 12.00-18.00*
💷 *Admission free*
♿ *Wheelchair access*

Founded over a century ago to bring the best in contemporary art to the 'working people of South London', the South London Gallery continues to stage an exciting programme of new art exhibitions, off-site projects and live art events in parallel with an education programme working with local people. Its Baroque-style Victorian gallery space has recently hosted work by Eva Rothschild, Alfredo Jaar and Ryan Gander. The SLG will be opening additional exhibition and education space in the adjacent building in spring 2009, with a café being among the new facilities. The gallery's collection of Victorian and later British art, which includes work by Leighton, Millais and Spencer, is held in storage and may be viewed by appointment.

galleries south

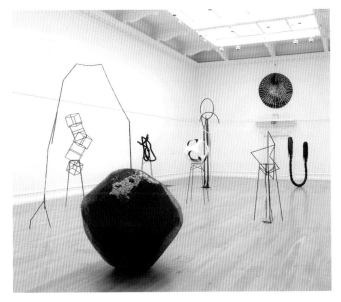

South London Gallery

225

East

Chisenhale Gallery

⊞ *64 Chisenhale Road, E3*
☎ *020 8981 4518*
⊘ *www.chisenhale.org.uk*
🚌 *Bethnal Green LU, Mile End LU*
🕐 *Wed-Sun 13.00-18.00*
♨ *Admission free*
♿ *Disabled access*

Located in a capacious former veneer works, Chisenhale runs as a non-profit making charity. It's a great place to see new work, specially commissioned by the gallery for the site, by artists at the start of their careers. Up to five new pieces are commissioned every year and recent shows have included Lucy Skaer's *The Siege* and paintings by Dan Perfect.

Matt's Gallery

⊞ *42-44 Copperfield Road, E3*
☎ *020 8983 1771*
⊘ *www.mattsgallery.org*
🚌 *Mile End LU*
🕐 *Wed-Sun 12.00-18.00 during exhibitions*
♨ *Admission free*
📚 *Bookshop*
♿ *Wheelchair Access*

Another gallery with charitable status and like the Chisenhale (above), all work exhibited here, be it painting, video installation or sculpture, is commissioned specially for the gallery space. Matt's also represents a number of artists – its 'stable' of well-respected contemporary artists includes Mike Nelson, Willie Doherty, Nathaniel Mellors and Lucy Gunning. The bookshop sells the gallery's own publications and there's a reading room and archive.

The Showroom

☎ 020 8983 4115

✍ www.theshowroom.org

This publicly-funded contemporary art gallery stages four exhibitions a year, with an emphasis on cross-disciplinary and collaborative shows. Artists are commissioned to make new work for the space and it's cutting-edge stuff – Showroom allumni include Jim Lambie, Sam Taylor-Wood and Eva Rothschild. At the time of going to press the Showroom is closed pending a move to bigger premises in West London – they will be reopening in May 2009 with a show by the film-making duo The Otolith Group.

Whitechapel Art Gallery

🗔 80-82 Whitechapel High Street, E1

☎ 020 7522 7888

✍ www.whitechapel.org

🚌 Aldgate East LU

🕓 Whitechapel Laboratory (during expansion works) open Wed-Sun 11.00-18.00, Thurs talks until 21.00, Fri music until 23.00

🎟 Admission free

📖 Bookshop

♿ Disabled access

Now one of Britain's leading venues for exhibitions of modern and contemporary art, the Whitechapel opened in 1901 with the aim of bringing major artworks to London's East End. It's certainly achieved that goal with distinction – Picasso's *Guernica* was shown here in 1939 and in the post-war peri od the Whitechapel showcased trailblazing artists such as Jackson Pollock, Joseph Beuys and David Hockney. More recently, artists as various as Cornelia Parker, Langlands & Bell, and Marcus Coates have featured here. At the time of going to press the Whitechapel is in the throes of an exciting multi-million pound development project which will see the gallery expanding next door into the former Passmore Edwards Library building. The new Whitechapel, which is due to open in 2009, will include a gallery for showing international art collections, a gallery for specially commissioned work, an archive gallery and an education/research room, as well as a new street facing café. In the meantime the Whitechapel has become the 'Whitechapel Laboratory' – a venue for exhibitions, live music, poetry, talks and film – accessed via a temporary entrance in Angel Alley.

Outskirts

Bethlem Gallery

⌧ *Bethlem Royal Hospital, Monks Orchard Road, Beckenham, Kent, BR3 3BX*

☎ *0203 228 4835*

✍ *www.bethlemgallery.com*

🚌 *Eden Park or East Croydon Rail then bus 119/194*

🕐 *Call before visiting as opening times vary*

💷 *Admission free*

This gallery shows contemporary work by artists with mental health problems. Part of the Bethlem Royal Hospital, the gallery holds four exhibitions a year as well as collaborating on shows with other organisations, such as the Museum of Croydon. The Bethlem Royal Hospital Archives & Museum (see p. 165) has been known to purchase works for their collection from the exhibitions and such is the popularity of the gallery's programme that there is always a waiting list of artists wanting to exhibit.

Marianne North Gallery

⌧ *Royal Botanic Gardens, Kew, TW9*

☎ *020 8332 5655 (information line)*

✍ *www.kew.org*

🚌 *Kew Gardens LU*

🕐 *Daily 9.30 onwards (phone or see website for closing time)*

💷 *Admission (includes entrance to Kew Gardens) £13 (adults), £12 concessions, free (under 17s)*

🛍 *Shops*

☕ *Cafés*

Marianne North was a Victorian artist who specialised in painting flowers with remarkable single-mindedness. An indefatigable traveller, she voyaged across the world to paint plants in their natural habitat, visiting Australia and New Zealand at the suggestion of Charles Darwin. Although she lacked any formal art training, Miss North was a fast worker and today some 832 of her distinctive oil paintings can be seen in the purpose-built gallery she gave to the Botanic Gardens. Now some 125 years old, the structure is showing its age and requires serious conservation. The gallery is currently closed until October 2009 for refurbishment and a fundraising project is underway – see website for details.

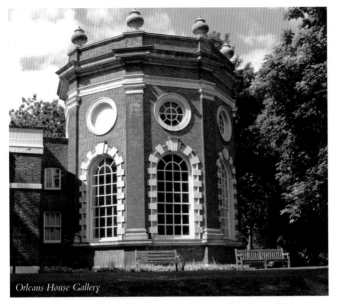

Orleans House Gallery

Orleans House Gallery and the Stables Gallery

🏠 *Riverside, Twickenham, TW1*

☎ *020 8831 6000*

🖱 *www.richmond.gov.uk*

🚌 *Richmond LU/Rail, St Margarets Rail, Twickenham Rail*

🕐 *Tue-Sat 13.00-17.30 (closes 16.30 Oct-Mar), Sun & Bank Hols 14.00-17.30*

💷 *Admission free*

🛍 *Small shop*

☕ *Café*

♿ *Wheelchair access (to ground floor and Octagon Room)*

A vibrant and varied programme of events means a new exhibition opens here every ten weeks or so. The work of local artists, designers and photographers, and of young curators is showcased in these two galleries, as well as items from the Borough of Richmond's Art Collection (18th-20th century art). Orleans House was once a royal residence, but if that doesn't cut any ice with the kids, the activity packs and half term and weekend workshops should do the trick. An injection of Lottery cash has paid for a much-needed upgrade of the Stables area – improved lighting and heating, the installation of a studio for an artist in residence and a café. If you run out of things to do on this side of the river, you can hop on a ferry to Ham House (see p.171) on the other bank.

229

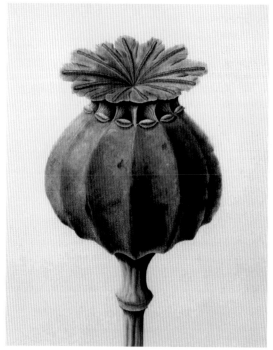

Brigid Edwards, Poppy Seed Head, 1999, Shirley Sherwood Gallery

The Riverside Gallery

⌨ *Old Town Hall, Whittaker Avenue, Richmond TW9*

☎ *020 8831 6000*

✍ *www.richmond.gov.uk/arts*

🚌 *Richmond LU/Rail*

🕐 *Mon, Wed, Thurs, Fri 10.00-18.00; Tues & Sat 10.00-17.00*

💷 *Admission Free*

♿ *Disabled Access*

Managed by Orleans House Gallery, the Riverside runs a year-round rolling programme of art exhibitions. Shows are usually of work by living artists and embrace a wide range of media from photography, painting, poetry and sculpture to installation art. The Old Town Hall also houses the Museum of Richmond (see p. 181) as well as the local studies collection, reference library and tourist information centre.

Shirley Sherwood Gallery

📖 *Royal Botanic Gardens, Kew, TW9*

☎ *020 8332 5655 (information line)*

🖂 *www.kew.org*

🚌 *Kew Gardens LU*

🕐 *Daily 9.30 onwards (phone or see website for closing time)*

💷 *Admission (includes entrance to Kew Gardens) £13 (adults),*
   £12 concessions, free (under 17s)

🛍 *Shops*

☕ *Cafés*

Kew holds one of the world's greatest collections of botanical art but until this gallery opened in 2008, had nowhere to display these often fragile works. Designed by architects Walters & Cohen and built next to the Marianne North Gallery (see above), this sleek, purpose built gallery finally allows the public the chance to see Kew's gems.

Stanley Picker Gallery

📖 *Faculty of Art, Design & Architecture, Kingston University,*
   Knights Park, Kingston upon Thames, KT1 2QJ

☎ *020 85478074*

🚌 *Kingston Rail then 10 minute walk*

🕐 *Tue-Fri 12.00-18.00, Sat 12.00-16.00, Mon by appointment*

💷 *Admission free*

Established in 1997, this gallery holds a rolling programme of events and exhibitions. The Fellowship Programme of the same name provides leading Fine Art and Design practitioners with the opportunity to develop an innovative project that is premiered at the Gallery.

The Toilet Gallery

📖 *151 Clarence Road, Kingston Upon Thames, KT1*

☎ *07881 832291*

🖂 *www.toiletgallery.org*

🚌 *Kingston Rail*

🕐 *Wed-Fri 13.00-18.00, Sat 10.00-18.00, Sun 12.00-17.00*

💷 *Admission free*

Located in a former 1950s ladies' toilet block, this is surely one of London's most unusual art venues. Rescued from grotty dereliction by Paul Stafford, the enterprising Director of Kingston University's Studies in Art & Design, the loos were transformed into a gallery space and opened by art luminaries Gilbert and George in 2003 (appropriately by cutting toilet roll ribbon). The gallery is now a focus for avant garde art exhibitions and events.

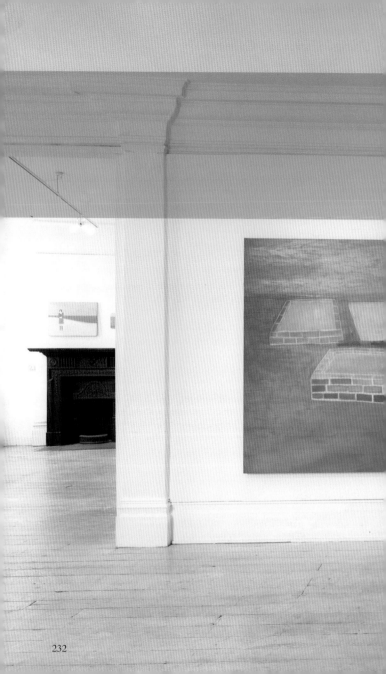

Commercial
Galleries

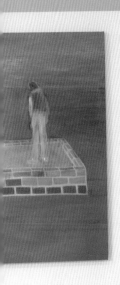

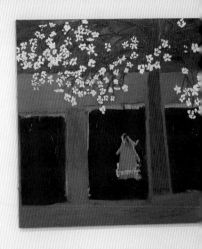

Commercial Art Galleries

A s befits one of the world's pre-eminent art capitals, London is positively brimming over with commercial galleries. In fact there are literally scores of these 'art shops', catering for all tastes and pockets but, given the vagaries of commerce, this introduction doesn't attempt to provide exhaustive listings. Rather, its selection aims to give some idea of the range of galleries in London and to act as a springboard for independent exploration.

Art lovers planning to do some serious gallery-going should look out for *Galleries*, a monthly magazine with gossipy art world editorial, reviews and a reasonably comprehensive listings of current shows. In a similar vein, the more specialised bi-monthly listings leaflet *New Exhibitions of Contemporary Art* gives the lowdown on where to sample the latest trends. Both publications come complete with maps and are available free of charge at participating galleries.

Once Cork Street was shorthand for the place to see the best in contemporary art but, although 'the street' is still home to some prestigious and long-established galleries, top-quality, cutting edge art emporia can now be found all over London. In the east of London, Hackney has reinvented itself as the city's artist quarter and is chock-a-block with galleries and studios, many of which are part of the 'Hidden Art' network (ring 020 7729 3800, or visit www.hiddenart.com for more details). Hoxton too has got in on the act while over at Bankside, Tate Modern has helped to transform Southwark into a new focal point for contemporary and modern art. Although Bond Street and St James's remain the heartland of the most exclusive Old Masters and modern art dealers, really dedicated gallery-goers now have to venture well beyond the cosseted confines of W1 to keep up to date. But the extra travelling is well worth the effort – London's gallery scene is diverse and vibrant.

For those short on time or energy, art fairs are a great way of cutting down the legwork. A variety of these shindigs are held throughout the year in the capital, conveniently uniting often far flung galleries under one roof. Some – like The London Original Print Fair – are more specialist than others but all are perfect for those intent on seeing (or indeed, buying) a lot of art in one hit. A listing of some of the most well known is included below.

Of course there's no denying that with their minimalist, white-walled interiors, telephone-number price tags and well-bred staff, some galleries can appear intimidating. Look beyond the classy accoutrements though and the bottom line is that galleries are essentially shops selling a commodity – and remember that no retailer ever made money by turning people away. There's no need to brazen it out, galleries are just as much a magnet for scruffy art students as they are for Gucci-clad collectors. (Incidentally, if you're not 'just looking' but in the market for a little something to put over the mantelpiece, do bear in mind that most galleries, no matter how plush, carry stock at a wide range of prices, and that it's always worth asking a dealer for their 'best price'). Look out for galleries that are part of the Arts Council backed 'Own Art' scheme – aimed at helping artists, galleries as well as consumers – this is a great package that offers up to £2,000 worth of interest free credit to customers at participating galleries (www.artscouncil.org.uk/ownart).

In the context of this guide though, what's equally pertinent is that commercial galleries can often be the place to see museum-quality art work. Many galleries put on a new exhibition every 4-6 weeks (a much faster turnaround than bureaucracy-bound museums), with particularly important shows being accompanied by glossy, sometimes scholarly catalogues, and attracting serious media coverage. As exhibitions at public art galleries increasingly come with a hefty entrance fee, perhaps it's not so far-fetched to see commercial galleries as fulfilling an egalitarian, even educational, role – after all, they're open to the public, are free of charge and generally less crowded than congested blockbuster shows at museums. Perhaps culture and capitalism aren't such strange bedfellows after all.

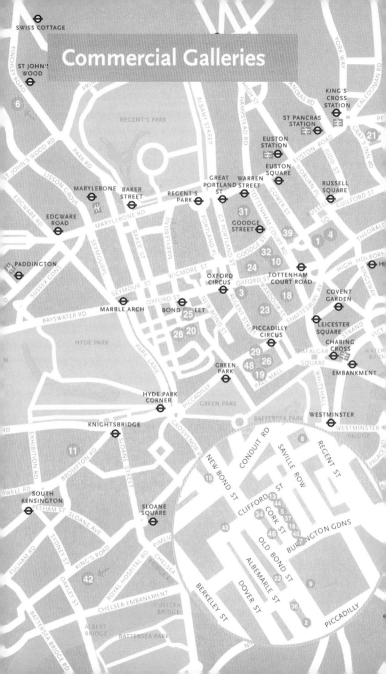

Commercial Galleries

SWISS COTTAGE

ST JOHN'S WOOD

FINCHLEY ROAD

KING'S CROSS STATION

6

ST PANCRAS STATION

YORK WAY

CALEDONIAN RD

REGENT'S PARK

ALBANY STREET

HAMPSTEAD RD

HIGH ST

EUSTON STATION

EUSTON ROAD

GRAY'S INN RD

21

ST JOHN'S WOOD RD

PRIN

PARK RD

EUSTON SQUARE

JUDD ST

WOBURN PL

RUSSELL SQUARE

EDGWARE ROAD

LISSON GROVE

MARYLEBONE

BAKER STREET

REGENT'S PARK

GREAT PORTLAND ST

WARREN STREET

COWER ST

GUILFORD ST

EDGWARE RD

MARYLEBONE RD

GT PORTLAND ST

TOTTENHAM COURT RD

31

THEOBAL

EDGWARE ROAD

SEYMOUR

BAKER ST

GOODGE STREET

39

4

PADDINGTON

SUSSEX GDNS

WIGMORE ST

PORTLAND PL

GOODGE ST

32

10

HIGH HOLBORN

H

SEYMOUR ST

OXFORD CIRCUS

24

COVENT GARDEN

KINGSWAY

MARBLE ARCH

OXFORD ST

BOND STREET

3

OXFORD ST

WARDOUR ST

TOTTENHAM COURT ROAD

18

BAYSWATER RD

25

23

SHAFTESBURY AVE

LEICESTER SQUARE

STRAND

HYDE PARK

28 20

PICCADILLY CIRCUS

CHARING CROSS

WATER BRID

PARK LANE

29

48 26

TRAFALGAR SQUARE

EMBANKMENT

GREEN PARK

19

PALL MALL

WHITEHALL

HYDE PARK CORNER

PICCADILLY

GREEN PARK

BATTERSEA PARK

WESTMINSTER

KNIGHTSBRIDGE

GROSVENOR

8

CONDUIT RD

SAVILLE ROW

REGENT ST

WESTMINSTER BRIDGE

PALACE

11

EXHIBITION RD

BROMPTON RD

SLOANE STREET

15

NEW BOND ST

CLIFFORD ST

13

44

CORK ST

5

37

SOUTH KENSINGTON

PELHAM ST

SLOANE AVE

34

18

40

BURLINGTON GDNS

TWELL RD

SLOANE SQUARE

43

46

OLD BOND ST

SYDNEY ST

OAKLEY ST

KING'S ROAD

42

ROYAL HOSPITAL RD

PIMLIC

CHELSEA

ALBEMARLE ST

22

DOVER ST

9

BERKELEY ST

36

2

PICCADILLY

CHELSEA EMBANKMENT

CHELSEA BRIDGE

ALBERT BRIDGE

BATTERSEA BRIDGE RD

BATTERSEA PARK

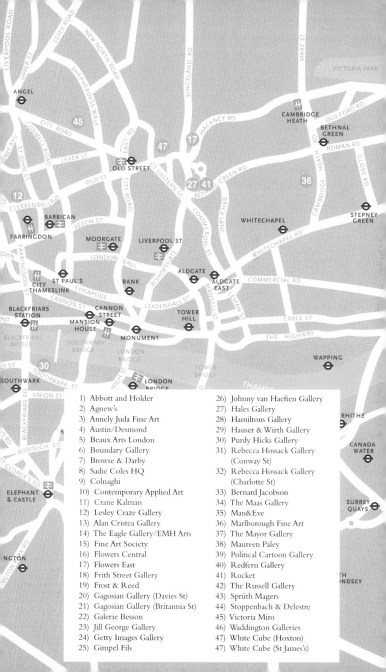

ANGEL

LIVERPOOL ROAD

ESSEX ROAD

UPPER ST

NEW NORTH ROAD

SHEPHERDESS WALK

CITY ROAD

GOSWELL ROAD

CORSHAM ST

LEVER ST

EAST RD

FERRY AVE

ST JOHN'S

CLERKENWELL RD

BARBICAN

BEECH ST

MOORGATE

LONDON WALL

FARRINGDON

FARRINGDON RD

ST PAUL'S

CITY
THAMESLINK

CHEAPSIDE

BANK

BLACKFRIARS
STATION

CANNON ST

MANSION
HOUSE

CANNON
STREET

MONUMENT

BLACKFRIARS
BRIDGE

SOUTHWARK
BRIDGE

SOUTHWARK

UNION ST

BLACKFRIARS RD

BOROUGH RD

ST GEORGE'S RD

ELEPHANT
& CASTLE

KENNINGTON

NEW NORTH ROAD

KINGSLAND RD

HACKNEY RD

OLD STREET

GREAT EASTERN ST

OLD ST

BETHNAL GREEN RD

COMMERCIAL ST

BRICK LANE

LIVERPOOL ST

BISHOPSGATE

ALDGATE

ALDGATE
EAST

WHITECHAPEL RD

COMMERCIAL RD

LEADENHALL ST

MANSELL ST

LEMAN ST

CABLE ST

THE HIGHWAY

TOWER
HILL

TOWER
BRIDGE

LONDON
BRIDGE

HIGH ST

MARE ST

CAMBRIDGE
HEATH

OLD FORD RD

BETHNAL
GREEN

ROMAN RD

CAMBRIDGE HEATH

GLOBE RD

STEPNEY
GREEN

WHITECHAPEL

WHITECHAPEL RD

WAPPING

VICTORIA PARK

ROTHERHITHE

CANADA
WATER

SURREY
QUAYS

BERMONDSEY

THAMES

45 12 47 17 27 41 36 30

1) Abbott and Holder
2) Agnew's
3) Annely Juda Fine Art
4) Austin/Desmond
5) Beaux Arts London
6) Boundary Gallery
7) Browse & Darby
8) Sadie Coles HQ
9) Colnaghi
10) Contemporary Applied Art
11) Crane Kalman
12) Lesley Craze Gallery
13) Alan Cristea Gallery
14) The Eagle Gallery/EMH Arts
15) Fine Art Society
16) Flowers Central
17) Flowers East
18) Frith Street Gallery
19) Frost & Reed
20) Gagosian Gallery (Davies St)
21) Gagosian Gallery (Britannia St)
22) Galerie Besson
23) Jill George Gallery
24) Getty Images Gallery
25) Gimpel Fils

26) Johnny van Haeften Gallery
27) Hales Gallery
28) Hamiltons Gallery
29) Hauser & Wirth Gallery
30) Purdy Hicks Gallery
31) Rebecca Hossack Gallery
    (Conway St)
32) Rebecca Hossack Gallery
    (Charlotte St)
33) Bernard Jacobson
34) The Maas Gallery
35) Man&Eve
36) Marlborough Fine Art
37) The Mayor Gallery
38) Maureen Paley
39) Political Cartoon Gallery
40) Redfern Gallery
41) Rocket
42) The Russell Gallery
43) Sprüth Magers
44) Stoppenbach & Delestre
45) Victoria Miro
46) Waddington Galleries
47) White Cube (Hoxton)
47) White Cube (St James's)

Commercial Gallery Listing:

Abbott and Holder

30 Museum Street, WC1
020 7637 3981
www.abbottandholder.co.uk
Mon-Sat 09.30-18.00 (Thurs until 19.00)

A browser's (and buyer's) paradise. Abbott and Holder was founded in 1936 and deals in reasonably priced English watercolours, drawings and oils from the 18th-20th centuries. Ranged over three floors, the displays nearly always include a temporary exhibition on the first floor.

Agnew's

43 Old Bond Street, W1
020 7290 9250
www.agnewsgallery.com
Mon-Fri 09.30-17.30, Sat by appointment only

The gallery is known for its stock of Old Masters, but it also deals in English paintings, drawings and watercolours as well as 20th century and contemporary British work.

Annely Juda Fine Art

23 Dering Street, W1
020 7629 7578
www.annelyjudafineart.co.uk
Mon-Fri 10.00-18.00, Sat 11.00-17.00

Top-notch contemporary and modern art.

Austin/Desmond

Pied Bull Yard, 68-69 Great Russell Street, Bloomsbury, WC1
020 7242 4443
www.austindesmond.com
Mon-Fri 10.30-17.30, Sat 11-14.30

Modern British paintings, ceramics and sculptures.

Beaux Arts London

22 Cork Street, W1
020 7437 5799
www.beauxartslondon.co.uk
Mon-Fri 10-17.30, Sat 10-13.30

Best-known for showing Modern British names like Frink and Hepworth, this gallery increasingly shows young, upcoming British artists.

Boundary Gallery

98 Boundary Road, NW8
020 7624 1126
www.boundarygallery.com
Wed-Sat 11.00-18.00 and by appointment

This gallery deals in Modern British and contemporary art, specialising in colourists and works by Anglo-Jewish artists.

Browse & Darby

19 Cork Street, W1
020 7734 7984
www.browseanddarby.co.uk
Mon-Fri 10.00-17.30, Sat 11.00-14.00

Late 19th-century and early 20th-century English and French art, as well as contemporary paintings and sculpture.

Sadie Coles HQ

35 Heddon Street, W1
020 7434 2227
www.sadiecoles.com
Tues-Sat 10.00-18.00

This gallery shows work by emerging and established contemporary artists from around the world.
And
69 South Audley Street, W1K 2QZ
020 7493 8611
Tues-Sat 11.00-18.00

Colnaghi

15 Old Bond Street, W1
020 7491 7408
www.colnaghi.co.uk
Mon-Fri 10.00-18.00

Old Master paintings and drawings. Founded in 1760, the gallery is one of the oldest galleries in Europe and something of an Old Master itself.

Contemporary Applied Art

2 Percy Street, W1
020 7436 2344
www.caa.org.uk
Mon-Sat 10.00-18.00

This well-respected artists' organisation celebrated its 60th anniversary in 2008. The gallery holds changing exhibitions upstairs, with a selection of members' work on show downstairs. Offering covetable jewellery, textiles, ceramics, furniture, metal and wood work.

Crane Kalman

- *178 Brompton Road, SW3*
- *020 7584 7566*
- *www.cranekalman.com*
- *Mon-Fri 10.00-18.00, Sat 10.00-16.00*

Handily located on the Knightsbridge shopping drag, this gallery is a specialist in post-war Modern British, international and contemporary art. Artists include Bomberg, Hans Hofmann and Winifred Nicholson.

Lesley Craze Gallery

- *33-35A Clerkenwell Green, EC1*
- *020 7608 0393*
- *www.lesleycrazegallery.co.uk*
- *Tues-Sat 10.00-17.30 (until 21.00 first Thurs in the month), Mondays in November & December*

Delectable contemporary jewellery, metalsmithing and textiles from an international stable of makers.

commercial galleries

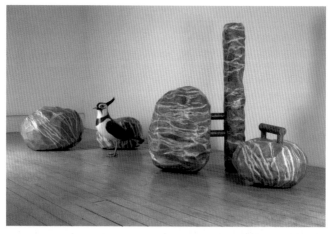

Denise De Cordova, Brontes and the Gogottes 2007, Eagle Gallery/EMH Arts

Alan Cristea Gallery

 31 & 34 Cork Street, W1
 020 7439 1866
 www.alancristea.com
 Mon-Fri 10.00-17.30, Sat 10.00-13.00

This gallery specialises in prints by an international range of artists.

The Eagle Gallery/EMH Arts

 159 Farringdon Road, EC1
 020 7833 2674
 www.emmahilleagle.com
 Wed-Fri 11.00-18.00, Sat 11.00-16.00

Mainly conceptual and abstract art on show here, although the gallery also publishes limited edition artists' books.

Fine Art Society

 148 New Bond Street, W1
 020 7629 5116
 www.faslondon.com
 Mon-Fri 9.30-17.30, Sat 10.00-13.00

If you're trawling up Bond Street having done the rounds of Cork Street, keep some time and energy in reserve for this superb gallery – or, indeed, make it first on your list. Always a pleasure to visit, the FAS stocks a carefully edited selection of British art and design from the 17th century to the present day. The Society's new gallery was completed in 2005 to show work by contemporary artists such as Keith Coventry and Jason Martin.

Flowers Central

 21 Cork Street, W1
 020 7439 7766
 www.flowerseast.com
 Mon-Fri 10.00-18.00, Sat 10.00-14.00

And

Flowers East

 82 Kingsland Road, E2
 020 7920 7777
 www.flowerseast.com
 Tues-Sat 10.00-18.00

Flowers East and Central offer contemporary art with a strong graphics element. Gallery artists include Peter Howson, Nicola Hicks and George Blacklock. They also represent work by upcoming artists.

241

Frith Street Gallery

17-18 Golden Square, W1

www.frithstreetgallery.com

Tue-Fri 10.00-18.00, Sat 11.00-17.00

Established in 1989, this gallery moved from its original Frith Street premises in 2007. The gallery represents a stable of 22 contemporary British and international artists.

Frost & Reed

2-4 King Street, St James's, W1

020 7839 4645

www.frostandreed.com

Mon-Fri 10.00-18.00

Established in 1808, this gallery deals in 19th and 20th century art featuring big names like Giacommetti, Chagall, and Dufy. They recently opened a contemporary gallery within its King Street premises, showing works by artists such as Marcel Dyf and Karen Gunderson.

Gagosian Gallery

17-19 Davies Street, W1

020 7493 3020

www.gagosian.com

Mon-fri 10.00-18.00, (Sats during exhibitions)

Post-war and contemporary international art.

And

6-24 Britannia Street, WC1X

020 7841 9960

www.gagosian.com

Tues-Sat 10.00-18.00

This vast branch of the Gagosian empire opened in May 2004, becoming at a stroke Europe's largest commercial art gallery space. Formerly municipal garages in the eternally up-and-coming King's Cross, the premises is host to high profile, large scale shows.

Galerie Besson

15 Royal Arcade, 28 Old Bond Street, W1

020 7491 1706

www.galeriebesson.co.uk

Mon-Fri 10.00-17.30

Ceramics gallery showing works by 20th-century masters like Lucie Rie, and Bernard Leach, as well as contemporary names like Jim Malone and Elizabeth Fritsch.

Jill George Gallery

38 Lexington Street, W1

020 7439 7319

www.jillgeorgegallery.co.uk

Mon-Fri 10.00-18.00 (Thurs until 20.00), Sat 11.00-17.00

Contemporary British paintings, drawings, watercolours and prints. Exhibitions change every 5 weeks.

Getty Images Gallery

46 Eastcastle Street, W1

020 7291 5380

www.gettyimagesgallery.com

Mon-Fri 10.00-18.30, Sat 12.00-18.00

Life through a lens at London's largest independent photographic gallery. Regularly changing exhibitions with prints available to buy in a huge variety of formats and framing options.

Gimpel Fils

30 Davies Street, W1

020 7493 2488

www.gimpelfils.com

Mon-Fri 10.00-17.30, Sat 11.00-16.00

Long-established gallery showing modern and contemporary art.

Johnny van Haeften Gallery

13 Duke Street, St James's, SW1

020 7930 3062

www.johnnyvanhaeften.com

Mon-Fri 10.00-18.00

Specialists in 17th and 18th century Dutch and Fleming Old Master paintings.

Hales Gallery

Tea Building, 7 Bethnal Green Road, E1

020 7033 1938

www.halesgallery.com

Wed-Sat 11.00-18.00

Hales Gallery shows contemporary art by young British and International artists. Among the 14 artists on its books are Bob & Roberta Smith, Tomoko Takahashi and Trevor Appleson.

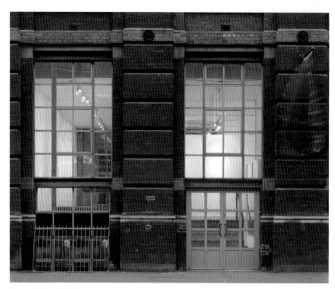

Purdy Hicks Gallery

Hamiltons Gallery

- 13 Carlos Place, W1
- 020 7499 9494
- www.hamiltonsgallery.com
- Tues-Fri 10.00-18.00, Sat 11.00-16.00

Modern and contemporary photography, includes work by Herb Ritts and Alison Jackson.

Hauser & Wirth Gallery

- 196a Piccadilly W1
- 020 7287 2300
- www.hauserwirth.com
- Tues-Sat 10.00-18.00

Housed in a magnificent Lutyens building (formerly a bank), this London branch of Swiss gallery Hauser & Wirth opened in 2003. Their stable of contemporary artists includes some impressive names – Louise Bourgeois and Paul McCarthy to name but two – and the gallery also owns the estate of Eva Hesse.

Purdy Hicks Gallery

   65 Hopton Street, Bankside, SE1
   020 7401 9229
   www.purdyhicks.com
   Mon-Fri 10.00-18.00, Sat 11.00-18.00

Estelle Thompson and Arturo di Stefano are among the 14 contemporary artists represented by this Southwark-based gallery.

Rebecca Hossack Gallery

   2a Conway Street, W1
   020 7436 4899
   www.r-h-g.co.uk
   Mon-Sat 10.00-18.00

Specialists in Aboriginal and non-western art as well as contemporary art. Arranged over 3 storeys the gallery's Conway Street exhibition space also includes a garden, which is sometimes used to display sculpture.
And

   28 Charlotte Street, W1T 2NA
   020 7255 2828

Smaller premises than above but also with changing programme of exhibitions.

Bernard Jacobson

   6 Cork Street, W1
   020 7734 3431
   www.jacobsongallery.com
   Mon-Fri 10.00-18.00, Sat 11.00-13.00

Contemporary and Modern, with a particular focus on British and American art.

The Maas Gallery

   15a Clifford Street, W1
   020 7734 2302
   www.maasgallery.com
   Mon-Fri 10.00-17.30

Victorian and Pre-Raphaelite art. 'Antiques Roadshow' viewers will recognise proprietor Rupert Maas as one of the art experts on the programme.

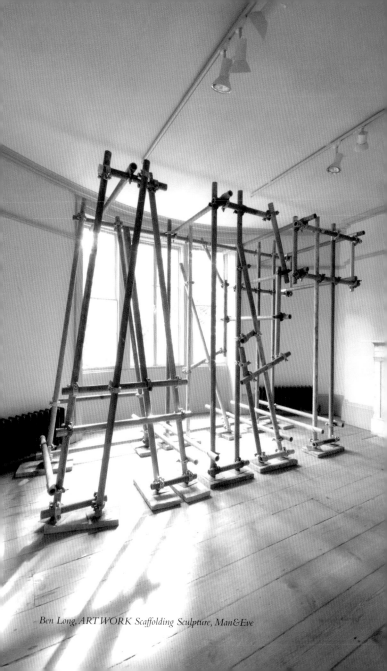

Ben Long, ARTWORK Scaffolding Sculpture, Man&Eve

Man&Eve

1311 Kennington Park Road, SE11
020 7582 7861
www.manandeve.co.uk
Wed-Sat 12.00-18.00 during exhibitions; other times by appointment

This gallery opened in 2006 and its stable of interesting emerging artists includes the likes of Ben Long, Joe Duggan, Esther Teichmann and Henrietta Simpson. New kid on the block it may be but this establishment has already attracted the attention of style bible *Wallpaper* magazine, which rates it as 'one of our favourite young London galleries'.

Marlborough Fine Art

6 Albemarle Street, W1
020 7629 5161
www.marlboroughfineart.com
Mon-Fri 10.00-17.30, Sat 10.00-12.30

Another big name on the contemporary art scene. Marlborough's impressive stable includes artists such as Francis Bacon, Lucien Freud and Paula Rego. The gallery also sells graphics by modern masters like Picasso.

The Mayor Gallery

22a Cork Street, W1
020 7734 3558
www.mayorgallery.com
Mon-Fri 10.00-17.30, Sat 10.00-13.00 (except August)

The first gallery to open on Cork Street way back in 1925, the Mayor Gallery specialises in Dada and Surrealist art, as well as showing Pop art and works by British artists.

Maureen Paley

21 Herald Street, E2
020 7729 4112
www.maureenpaley.com
Wed-Sun 11.00-18.00, and by appointment

Contemporary art – and how. The gallery represents about 15 artists including Paul Noble, Gillian Wearing, Wolfgang Tillmans and Rebecca Warren.

Political Cartoon Gallery

32 Store Street, WC1E
020 7580 1114
www.politicalcartoon.co.uk
Mon-Fri 9.30-17.30, Sat 11.30-17.30

Political cartoons from the satirists of the 19th, 20th and 21st centuries, including household names such as 'Giles', 'Marc' and 'Fougasse'. Recent exhibitions have showcased Palestinian cartoonist Naji Al-Ali and the work of Sir David Low.

Redfern Gallery

20 Cork Street, W1
020 7734 1732
www.redfern-gallery.com
Mon-Fri 11.00-17.30, Sat 11.00-14.00

Contemporary and modern paintings, sculpture, drawings and prints.

Rocket

Tea Building, 56 Shoreditch High Street, E1
020 7729 7594
www.rocketgallery.com
Tues-Sat 11.00-18.00, Sat 12.00-18.00

Rocket deals with international artists, specialising in abstract and minimalist art, as well as exhibiting work by photographers such as Martin Parr.

The Russell Gallery

12 Lower Richmond Road, SW15
020 8780 5228
www.russell-gallery.com
Tues-Sat 10.00-17.30

This Putney based gallery opened in 2003 and shows mainly figurative British art by the likes of Julian Bailey, Mary Fedden and Christopher Hall. The gallery is also promotes young up-and-coming artists.

Sprüth Magers

7A Grafton Street, W1
020 7408 1613
www.spruthmagerslee.com
Tues-Sat 10.00-18.00

This gallery shows international contemporary work and represents big names such as Dan Flavin and Nan Goldin.

commercial galleries

Stoppenbach & Delestre

25 Cork Street, W1
020 7734 3534
www.artfrancais.com
Mon-Fri 10.00-17.30, Sat 10.00-13.00

French 19th and 20th-century art, including works by the Barbizon school, can be found at this gallery.

Victoria Miro

16 Wharf Road, N1
020 7336 8109
www.victoria-miro.com
Tues-Sat 10.00-18.00

Not one but four Turner Prize nominees are represented by the gallery: Ian Hamilton Finlay, Peter Doig, Isaac Julien and Phil Collins, as well as two winners Chris Ofili and Grayson Perry.

Waddington Galleries

11 Cork Street, W1
020 7851 2200
www.waddington-galleries.com
Mon-Fri 10.00-18.00, Sat 11.00-13.30

Established in the 1960s, Waddington's is still swinging and a regular haunt for collectors and scruffy art students alike. Expect to see interesting hangs of blue chip modern art and work by classy contemporary artists such as Patrick Caulfield, Barry Flanagan and Ian Davenport.

White Cube

48 Hoxton Square, N1
020 7930 5373
www.whitecube.com
Tues-Sat 10.00-18.00

And

25-26 Mason's Yard (off Duke Street), St James's, SW1
020 7930 5373
Tues-Sat 10.00-18.00

So cutting-edge it hurts, White Cube is the ne plus ultra of galleries dealing in contemporary art. The sleek purpose built new gallery in Mason's Yard opened in 2006 and houses two gallery spaces while the Hoxton gallery is based in a chic converted 1920s industrial building. Perhaps most famous for representing Damien Hirst, White Cube also exhibits a range of European and British artists.

Exhibition & Heritage Venues

Age Exchange Reminiscence Centre

- 🏠 11 Blackheath Village, SE3
- ☎ 020 8318 9105
- ✉ administrator@age-exchange.org.uk
- ✉ www.age-exchange.org.uk
- 🚆 Blackheath Rail
- 🕐 Mon-Fri 10.00-17.00, Sat 10.00-16.00
- 💷 Admission free (charge for groups)
- ☕ Café

This voluntary organisation arranges inter-generation activities and projects, based around the reminiscences of older people. The organisation also runs a small museum and shop.

Asia House

- 🏠 63 New Cavendish Street, W1G 7LP
- ☎ 020 7307 5454
- ✉ enquires@asiahouse.co.uk
- 🚆 Oxford Circus LU, Regents Park LU, Portland Street LU
- 🕐 Mon-Fri 09.00-19.00, Sat 10.00-18.00 (during exhibitions only); Gallery open Mon-Sat 10.00-18.00
- 💷 Admission free
- ☕ Café

Based in an elegant neo-Classical 18th-century townhouse, Asia House is a pan-Asian organisation promoting appreciation and understanding of Asian countries, their arts, religions and economies. Its state of the art gallery is used for exhibitions of historical and contemporary visual arts, crafts and photography.

BFI Southbank

- 🏠 Belvedere Road, SE1
- ☎ 02 7928 3232
- ✉ www.bfi.org.uk
- 🚆 Waterloo Rail/LU, Charing Cross Rail/LU, Embankment LU
- 💷 Gallery free
- 🛍 Shop
- ☕ Café

Film buffs love to 'bag' unusual movies in the much the same way that climbers 'bag' mountains – and this is one of the key places in London to do just that. A heady programme of classic and contemporary films, special film seasons, festivals and events make this a must for film fans. There's also a purpose built gallery for free entry 'moving image art' exhibitions as well as a Mediatheque offering on-demand access to hours of digital film.

Brunei Gallery

🖾 *School of Oriental & African Studies,*
   University of London, Thornhaugh Street, WC1
☎ *020 7898 4915 / 020 7898 4046 (recorded information)*
🖉 *www.soas.ac.uk/gallery*
🚇 *Russell Square LU*
🕐 *Tues-Sat 10.30-17.00*
🎟 *Admission free*
📖 *Bookshop*
🍽 *Café*

A gallery dedicated to showing works from Asia and Africa, historic and contemporary. The Japanese-inspired roof garden is also open to the public (same opening hours at the gallery). Dedicated to forgiveness, the garden opened in 2001 and offers a place for quiet contemplation as well as being a venue for theatrical and musical events, and tea ceremonies.

Canada House Gallery

🖾 *Trafalgar Square, SW1Y*
☎ *020 7258 6600*
🕐 *Mon-Fri 10.00-18.00*
🚇 *Charing Cross Rail/LU, Leicester Square LU*
🎟 *Admission free*
♿ *Disabled access*

Canada House hosts regular exhibitions of Canadian art with an emphasis on the contemporary.

Discover Greenwich

🖾 *Pepys Building, Old Royal Naval College, SE10*
☎ *0800 389 3341 (freephone)*
☎ *020 8269 4791 (other enquiries)*
🖉 *www.greenwichfoundation.org.uk*
🚇 *Cutty Sark DLR, Greenwich Rail/DLR*
🕐 *Daily 10.00-17.00*
🎟 *Admission free*
📖 *Shop*
♿ *Wheelchair Access*
🍽 *Café*

Packed with history and sensational classical architecture, Maritime Greenwich has rightly been designated a World Heritage Site. As well as being the location of London's oldest Royal Park and top attractions such as the Royal Observatory, the Cutty Sark, and the National Maritime Museum, Greenwich is also home to the Old Royal Naval College, designed by Christopher Wren. The Painted Hall and Chapel can be viewed daily 10.00-17.00 and are well worth a peek, en route up to the RO and NMM. Probably the finest dining hall in the West, Wren's Painted Hall contains paintings by James Thornhill, including a vast ceiling decoration, a 19-year labour of love for which he was paid by the yard and finally knighted.

The visitor centre is a good starting point for first time visitors to Greenwich but at present is closed for a multi-million pound redevelopment. Scheduled to re-open in early 2010 'Discover Greenwich' will include a permanent exhibition about the history of Greenwich, from its early days as one of Henry VIII's many royal palaces to its development as a hub of naval activity, providing a home to the Royal Hospital for Seamen and later the Royal Naval College. The facilities will not only feature a Tourist Information Centre, but also a 'learning suite' as well as all the usual places for you to spend your money – a shop, café, bar and brasserie.

The Hellenic Centre

- 16-18 Paddington Street, W1
- 020 7487 5060
- www.helleniccentre.org
- Baker Street & Bond Street LU
- Mon-Sun 10.00-19.00
- Admission free
- Shop

The hellenic Centre hosts one major exhibition a year – such as 'Icons through the Centuries' – and occasional smaller shows on a Greek theme.

The Mall Galleries

- Carlton House Terrace, The Mall, SW1
- 020 7930 6844
- info@mallgalleries.org.uk
- www.mallgalleries.org.uk
- Charing Cross LU/Rail, Piccadilly Circus LU
- Daily 10.00-17.00 (during exhibitions)
- £2.50 (adults), £1.50 (concessions), free (children)
- Bookshop
- Café

The Mall Galleries is run by the Federation of British Artists, an umbrella organisation which represents the work of nine art societies. Exhibitions change regularly so it's advisable to phone in advance before visiting.

Royal College of Art Gallery

- *Kensington Gore, SW7*
- *020 7590 4444*
- *Daily 10.00-18.00 (during exhibitions)*
- *High Street Kensington LU*
- *Admission free*

The Royal College stages its degree show between May and July, but also plays host to other exhibitions featuring the work of its post-graduate students and external shows organised by selected partners. Lectures by leading figures from the worlds of art and design are another draw.

Somerset House

- *Strand, London, WC2*
- *020 7845 4600*
- *www.somerset-house.org.uk*
- *Charing Cross LU/Rail, Covent Garden LU, Holborn LU, Temple LU (except Sun)*
- *Mon-Sat 10.00-18.00, Sun and Bank Holidays 12.00-18.00*
- *Admission free*
- *Wheelchair access*
- *Shop*
- *Café & Restaurant*

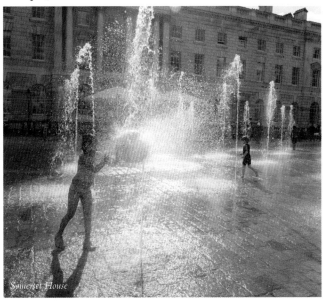

Somerset House

This magisterial 18th-century complex was the work of Sir William Chambers, architect to King George III. Built on the site of the Renaissance palace belonging to Lord Protector Somerset, the present Somerset House was designed as what amounted to an early government office block, housing public offices for the Surveyor General and 'the Register of Births, Marriages and Deaths' (also known as Hatched, Matched and Dispatched). Chambers' rather austere Palladian creation was also the original home of the Royal Academy (see p. 206) so it was entirely fitting the Courtauld Gallery (see p. 192) moved here from Portman Square in 1990.

A major refurbishment and restoration was undertaken and today a fountain now plays in the expansive central courtyard where civil servants once parked their cars. On summer evenings the courtyard plays host to open air music concerts and film screening, in winter it transforms into an ice rink. The space inhabited until recently by the Gilbert Collection has now been replaced by the new Embankment Galleries which will host a distinctive programme of curator led exhibitions covering architecture, art, design, fashion, and photography. Thankfully the Gilbert Collection has not been lost to London visitors – this dazzling array of gold, silver objets d'arts and micro-mosaics will transfer to the V&A in 2009.

Thames Barrier Visitor Centre

Unity Way, Woolwich, SE18

020 8305 4188

www.environment-agency.gov.uk

Charlton Rail (then bus 177 or 180), North Greenwich LU (then bus 472 or 161)

Daily 10.30-16.30 (April-Sept), 11.00-15.30 (Oct-March)

£2 (adults), £1.50 (OAPs), £1 (children)

Café

The Visitor Centre gives you a great view of the barrier and includes a display board exhibition, working model of the barrier and an 8 minute video documenting its construction.

Archives & Libraries

This listing is not intended to be exhaustive – London's archives and libraries merit a guide in their own right. In addition, many of the museums and galleries listed in this book also have their own research libraries and archives and more information about these can usually be found on the relevant institution's website.

African and Asian Visual Artists Archive

▢ *Diversity Art Forum, Learning Resources Centre, University of East London, Docklands Campus, Royal Albert Way, E16*

☎ *020 8223 7676*

✎ *www.aavaa.org.uk*

🕐 *Mon & Wed 09.00-18.00, Tues 10.00-20.00, Thurs 09.00-15.00*

An archive of material on visual artists and crafts people of African and Asian origin working in Britain.

Ashmole Archive

▢ *Dept of Classics, King's College London, Strand, WC2*

✎ *geoffrey.waywell@kcl.ac.uk*

The Ashmole is a photographic archive of ancient Greek sculpture, which can be viewed by appointment only.

Black Cultural Archives

▢ *1 Othello Close, SE11 4RE*

☎ *020 7582 8516*

✎ *www.bcaheritage.org.uk*

🕐 *Archive currently closed to receive visitors*

The Black Cultural Archive is a community based heritage organisation and archive which collects, preserves and celebrates the history and culture of black people in Britain. The archive's collection is currently closed to visitors while a major cataloguing project takes place. Work is also underway to establish a black Heritage Centre and purpose built archive in Brixton which will open in 2011.

British Airways Archive and Museum Collection

▢ *Building 387 (E121), PO Box 10, Heathrow Airport, Hounslow, Middlesex, TW6 2JA*

☎ *0208 513 7508*

✎ *www.bamuseum.com*

🕐 *Wed, Thurs, Fri 10.00-14.00 by appointment only*

An extensive document archive recording the formation, development and operations of British Airways and its predecessor companies. Memorabilia and artefacts are joined by over 130 uniforms from the 1930s to the present day, along with a large collection of aircraft models and pictures. An important collection of thousands of photographs is also available as well as probably the most complete set of aviation posters in the UK.

RIBA British Architectural Library

🖃 *66 Portland Place, W1B*
☎ *020 7580 5533*
🖎 *www.architecture.com*
🕐 *Tues 10-20.00, Wed-Fri 10-17.00, Sat 10-13.30*

The UK's largest archives relating to architecture and architectural history, and one of the finest in the world. Free public access to the library was introduced in January 2008. See also the RIBA Architecture Study Rooms at the V&A (p. 261).

British Library

🖃 *96 Euston Road, NW1*
☎ *020 7412 7332*
🖎 *www.bl.uk*

The British Library Galleries are already mentioned in this book, but the library offers many other services and events including lectures and concerts, a bookshop and educational services. Public tours of the building take place every Monday, Wednesday, Friday and Saturday. Oh and by the way, it also has just about the largest collection of books in the world.

British Olympic Library

🖃 *1 Wandsworth Plain, SW18*
☎ *020 8871 2677*
🖎 *www.olympics.org.uk*

This library contains everything to do with the Olympics and British Olympians including general information about the Games and official reports and handbooks from each of the Olympics and Winter Olympics. Phone in advance for an appointment before visiting.

BT Archives

🖃 *Third Floor, Holborn Telephone Exchange,*
   268-270 High Holborn, WC1V 7EE
☎ *Historical enquiries 020 7440 4220*
🖎 *www.bt.com/archives*
🕐 *Tues & Thurs 10.00-16.00 by appointment only*

BT Archives preserves the historical information of British Telecommunications plc and its predecessors from the early part of the 19th century up

appendix

to the present day. The archive contains telephone directories dating back to 1880, historical records, as well as the historic photographic, video and film collections of BT and Post Office Telecommunications.

City of Westminster Archives Centre

⌨ *10 St Ann's Street, SW1P 2DE*

☎ *020 7641 5180*

🖉 *www.westminster.gov.uk*

🕐 *Tues-Thurs 10.00-19.00, Fri & Sat 10.00-17.00*

The archives contain varied collections relating to the history of Westminster and include the business records for companies such as Liberty, Jaeger and Lobbs as well as theatre programmes, maps and local government records from 1460.

Courtauld Institute of Art Libraries

⌨ *Somerset House, Strand, WC2R*

☎ *020 7848 2701 (Library) / 020 7848 2745 (Witt & Conway Libraries)*

🖉 *www.courtauld.ac.uk*

🕐 *Witt & Conway Libraries open Mon-Fri 10.00-18.00 (except Easter & Christmas holidays) by reader's card only; Book Library by appointment*

London's pre-eminent centre for the study of history of art has three libraries. The book library is aimed squarely at academics and contains a major collection of art books, periodical and exhibition catalogues, while the Witt Library contains some two million reproductions of works by over 70,000 artists, organised alphabetically within national schools. The Conway Library performs a similar service for architecture and sculpture, with over one million images, photographs and cuttings.

Crafts Council Research Library

⌨ *44a Pentonville Road, Islington, N1*

☎ *020 7806 2502*

🖉 *www.craftscouncil.org.uk*

🕐 *Wed & Thurs 10.00-13.00 or 14.00-17.00 by appointment*

A free to browse library containing books, journals and videos relating to craft technique and practice, funding directories, as well as exhibition catalogues and Crafts Council research reports.

The Women's Library

⌨ *London Metropolitan University, Old Castle Street, E1*

☎ *020 7320 2222*

🖉 *www.thewomenslibrary.ac.uk*

🕐 *Reading Room open Tues-Fri 9.30-17.00 (Thurs until 20.00), Sat 10.00-16.00; Exhibitions open Mon-Fri 9.30-17.30 (Thurs until 20.00), Sat 10.00-16.00*

This archive of women's history and reference material is the oldest and most extensive women's resource in Europe, established in 1926. Thanks to a Lottery grant the Library moved to its current, well-appointed premises in 2002. Its facilities include a reading room and an exhibition hall which hosts high quality changing exhibitions on often challenging themes.

Hammersmith and Fulham Archives & Local History Centre

⌨ *The Lilla Huset , 191 Talgarth Road, W6 8BJ*

☎ *020 8741 5159 or 020 8753 3850*

✎ *www.lbhf.gov.uk*

🕐 *Mon & Thurs 09.30-4.30, Tues 09.30-19.45, Sat 9.30-16.30 (2nd Sat in month only)*

Appointments are not necessary, but if you know what material you would like to use, phone ahead and the staff here will have it waiting for your arrival!

Lambeth Palace Library

⌨ *Lambeth Palace Road, SE1*

☎ *020 7898 1400*

✎ *www.lambethpalacelibrary.org*

🕐 *Mon-Fri 10.00-17.00*

This library, founded in 1610 by Archbishop Bancroft, is one of the oldest public libraries in Britain. It is the principal library and record office for the history of the Church of England.

London Metropolitan Archives

⌨ *40 Northampton Road, EC1*

☎ *020 7332 3820*

✎ *www.cityoflondon.gov.uk*

🕐 *Mon, Wed and Fri 09.30-16.45; Tues and Thurs 09.30-19.30; open alternate Saturdays 09.30-16.45*

A treasure trove for anyone researching anything about London or Londoners. As country record office for Greater London, the LMA holds authority records for bodies such as the GLC and LCC, records for over 900 London parishes, business records, family papers and hospital archives (including letters from Florence Nightingale).

Marx Memorial Library

⌨ *37a Clerkenwell Green, EC1*

☎ *020 7253 1485*

✎ *www.marx-memorial-library.org*

🕐 *Mon 13.00-18.00, Tues and Thurs 13.00-18.00, Wed 13.00-20.00, Sat by appointment*

Books, pamphlets and periodicals covering all aspects of Marxism, the 'science' of Socialism and the history of working class movements. The library also contains an archive on the Spanish Civil War.

London Archaeological Archive & Research Centre

⌖ *Mortimer Wheeler House, 46 Eagle Wharf Road, N1*

☎ *020 7566 9317*

🖉 *www.museumoflondon.org.uk*

🕐 *Mon-Fri 10.00-16.00, first and third Sat of the month 10.00-16.00*
   (researchers only, by appointment)

♿ *Wheelchair access*

The LAARC holds information on over 5,000 London sites and archaeological projects from the past 100 years, including records and finds from archaeological digs. This Museum of London venue is also home to the museum's social and working history collections.

National Art Library

⌖ *V & A Museum, Cromwell Road, SW7*

☎ *020 7942 2400*

🖉 *www.vam.ac.uk*

🕐 *Tue-Sat 10.00-17.30 (Fri until 18.30)*

A major public reference library on the fine and decorative arts. Entry by reader's ticket.

National Portrait Gallery

⌖ *Heinz Archive and Library, Orange Street, WC2H*

☎ *020 7321 6617*

🖉 *www.npg.org.uk*

🕐 *By appointment Tues-Fri 10.00-17.00*

This archive contains drawings, prints and photographs of British portraits dating from 1400 to the present day.

National Sound Archive

⌖ *(part of The British Library), 96 Euston Road, NW1*

☎ *020 7412 76767*

🖉 *sound-archive@bl.uk*

🖉 *www.bl.uk/nsa*

🕐 *Listening Service: by appointment*

One of the largest sound archives in the world with over 3 million sound recordings. The extensive collection covers music (classical, popular, world and folk), drama and literature, oral history, dialects and accents, and wildlife sounds. Open to the public but readers using the Readers' Room must apply for a pass.

appendix

The National Archives

- 🖳 *Kew, Surrey, TW9*
- ☎ *020 8876 3444*
- ✎ *www.nationalarchives.gov.uk*
- 🕐 *Mon & Fri 09.00-17.00, Tues & Thurs 09.00-19.00,*
  Wed 10.00-17.00, Sat 09.30-17.00
- 📚 *Bookshop*
- 🍴 *Restaurant & Café/Bar*

What used to be the Public Record Office has amalgamated with the Historical Manuscripts Commission to form the National Archives. Based in an impressive waterside building in Kew, this is the UK government's official archive and holds 900 years of official records, from the Domesday book to the latest government paper. Records are normally made available to the public when they have been archived for 30 years and can be accessed by anyone over the age of 14 on production of proof of address and identity (for UK/Eire citizens) or passport (for citizens of other countries).

For those researching family history, Kew is now also home to the archive of the Family Records Centre. This is the repository for census returns from 1841-1891, non-conformist records and records of the Prerogative Court of Canterbury, wills and administrations, as well as records of birth, deaths and marriages, dating back to 1837.

Regular exhibitions drawing on material in the National Archives are also held here – recent offerings have included a look at 'Britain during the Cold War' and 'The History of Alcohol'.

If you can't make it to Kew, the DocumentsOnline service (www.nationalarchives.gov.uk/documentsonline) provides online access to over a million digital images of documents held in the National Archives.

The Puppet Centre Trust

- 🖳 *BAC, Lavender Hill, SW11*
- ☎ *020 7228 5335 (enquiries)*
- ✎ *www.puppetcentre.org.uk*
- 🚍 *Clapham Junction Rail*
- 🕐 *Library open by appointment only*
- ♿ *Wheelchair access*

The Puppet Centre Trust is the national development agency for the art form of puppetry. The centre houses a collection of over 4,000 books, journals, videos, DVDs and photographs on puppetry and related art forms.

RIBA Architecture Study Rooms

⌂ *V&A Museum, South Kensington, SW7*

☎ *020 7942 2043 or 020 7307 3708*

✎ *www.vam.ac.uk*

🕐 *Tues-Sat 10.00-17.00*

A partnership between the V&A and the RIBA allowing access to the RIBA's outstanding collection of architectural drawings and manuscripts in the RIBA Architecture Study Rooms, housed alongside the V&A's Prints & Drawings Study Room. The collections comprise the RIBA's collection of drawings and archive and the V&A's collection of drawings, photographs and prints. An appointment system operates for the RIBA material.

The Royal Mail Archive

⌂ *Freeling House, Phoenix Place, WC1X*

☎ *020 7239 2570*

✎ *www.postalheritage.org.uk*

🕐 *Mon-Fri 10.00-17.00 (Thurs until 19.00), selected Saturdays 10.00-17.00*

The archive, tucked away near Mount Pleasant sorting office, contains records of the Post Office and Royal Mail from 1636 to the present. It's a great place to find out more about the history of the postal service – the archive of staff records are a useful resource for family history researchers while the collection of British stamps runs from the Penny Black onwards. A small exhibition area holds regularly changing philatelic displays.

The Salvation Army Heritage Centre

⌂ *House 14, William Booth College, Denmark Hill, SE5*

☎ *020 7737 3327*

✎ *www.salvationarmy.org.uk/heritage*

🕐 *Tues, Wed & Thurs 09.30-15.30 by appointment*

The Heritage Centre includes a reference library and archive and is open to researchers by appointment. Among the treasures in the archive are the papers of Sally Am founders William and Catherine Booth, plus a host of SA publications and records from UK local centres. The museum remains closed while new premises are sought.

Science Museum Library

⌂ *Imperial College Road, SW7*

☎ *020 7942 4242*

✎ *www.sciencemuseum.org.uk*

🕐 *Mon-Fri 10.00-17.00*

A national reference library for the history of science and technology.

The V&A Archives

⌨ *Blyth House, 23 Blyth Road, W14*
🕐 *Archive of Art and Design: 020 7602 0281 ext. 209*
🕐 *Beatrix Potter Collections: 020 7602 0281 ext. 212*
🕐 *V&A Archive: 020 7602 5886*
✎ *www.vam.ac.uk/resources*
🕐 *Tues-Fri 10.00-16.30 by appointment*

The V&A Archives contain 3 different archives. The Art and Design archive offers rich picking for art researchers. This archive's holdings reflects the V&A's own collections but has a particular emphasis on 20th and 21st century designers. The archives of key players such as Eileen Grey, Lucienne and Robin Day and Eduardo Paolozzi are just some of the treasures. The Beatrix Potter Collections hold important material relating to the famous writer/illustrator and include drawings, watercolours and original literary manuscripts. The V&As own institutional archives are another significant resource for researchers and include details of the history of museum itself and the provenance of its millions of objects.

The Wiener Library

⌨ *4 Devonshire Street, W1*
☎ *020 7636 7247*
✎ *www.wienerlibrary.co.uk*
🕐 *Mon-Fri 10.00-17.30*

The Wiener Library is one of the world's most extensive archives on the Holocaust and Nazi era. Formed in 1933 by Dr Alfred Wiener, the Library's unique collection of over one million items includes published and unpublished works, press cuttings, photographs and eyewitness testimony. The Library aims to provide a resource to oppose anti-Semitism and other forms of prejudice and intolerance. The library will be moving from its current location in 2009 and is seeking funding to secure a new permanent location – see website for details.

appendix

Useful Addresses

Arts Council England, London

2 Pear Tree Court, London, EC1R 0DS
Tel: 0845 300 6200
enquiries@artscouncil.org.uk
www.artscouncil.org.uk
The national development agency for the arts.

Artsline

C/o 21 Pine Court, Wood Lodge Gardens, Bromley BR1 2WA
Tel: 020 7388 2227
admin@artsline.org.uk
www.artsline.org.uk
A campaigning disability access charity that provides details of access at arts venues. Artsline has an online website of approved accessible arts and entertainment venues and the website has recently undergone a transformation into an interactive online database. The friendly telephone advice service however continues for those who prefer to speak to a 'real person'.

Campaign for Drawing

7 Gentleman's Row, Enfield, EN2 6PT
Tel: 020 8351 1719
info@campaignfordrawing.org
www.campaignfordrawing.org
The Campaign for Drawing's aim is to encourage everyone to draw. Its annual drawing fest, The Big Draw, proves that drawing can be a public activity. Every October, 1,000 venues across Britain, from large national institutions to village halls, join in to offer many thousands of people of all ages the chance to discover that drawing is enjoyable, liberating and at everyone's fingertips.

Campaign for Museums

Grosvenor Gardens House,
35-37 Grosvenor Gardens, SW1W
Tel: 020 7233 9796
www.campaignformuseums.org.uk
www.mgm.org.uk
The Campaign's major activity is running the annual Museums and Galleries month, a UK wide celebration of museums and galleries.

Contemporary Art Society

11-15 Emerald Street, WC1N
Tel: 020 7831 1243
cas@contempart.org.uk
www.contempart.org.uk
A national non-profit agency that supports contemporary artists through the promotion of collecting and commissioning by individuals, and public and private bodies across the UK. The Society offers a programme of tours and events for its members and gives advice to companies and individuals who want to start their own collections.

ENGAGE (The National Association for Gallery Education)

Suite AG, City Cloisters, 196 Old Street, EC1V 9FR
Tel: 020 7490 4690
info@engage.org
www.engage.org
A membership organisation for gallery, art and educational professionals which promotes access to, enjoyment and understanding of the visual arts through education.

English Heritage

PO Box 569, Swindon, SN2 2YP
Tel: 0870 333 1181
customers@english-heritage.org.uk
www.english-heritage.org.uk

English Heritage manages historic houses and sites throughout the country, over 400 of which are open to the public (with free entry for EH members). If you want to find out more, phone and ask for an information pack.

The Museums, Libraries & Archives Council (MLA)

Victoria House, Southampton Row, WC1B 4EA
Tel: 020 7273 1444
info@mla.gov.uk
www.mla.gov.uk

The government agency for museums, galleries, libraries and archives, launched in 2000 as the strategic body for this sector.

Museums Association

24 Calvin Street, E1 6NW
Tel: 020 7426 6910
www.museumsassociation.org

The MA represents the people and institutions that make up Britain's museums and galleries. Its publication, *Museums Journal*, is a must read for those working in the sector and for those hoping to do so.

The National Art Collections Fund

Millais House, 7 Cromwell Place, SW7
Tel: 020 7225 4800
info@artfund.org
www.artfund.org

Becoming a member of the NACF gives free entry to over 200 museums and galleries as well as discounts on special exhibitions, access to special events and behind the scenes tours as well as an excellent free magazine. Your money contributes funds for the purchase of works of art for Britain's museums and galleries.

The National Trust

Central Office: Heelis, Kemble Drive, Swindon, SN2 2NA
Tel: 01793 817400
Tel: 0844 800 1895 (membership enquiries)
enquiries@thenationaltrust.org.uk
www.nationaltrust.org.uk

Founded in 1895 this independent heritage charity today protects some 350 gardens and houses, over 550 miles of coastline and 600,000 acres of countryside across England, Wales and Northern Ireland. Membership ensures free entry to all their sites.

VisitBritain

Head Office, Thames Tower, Black's Road, W6
Tel: 020 8846 9000
www.visitbritain.com

Britain's national tourism agency.

London Degree Shows

Degree and foundation shows are held by art colleges and universities in London during the summer months from May to August. They are a great opportunity to view the latest in art and craft, and if you attend on the opening day you can mingle with trendy art students, view their creations, drink cheap wine and maybe spot a potential art investment. Contact details for the various London art institutions are listed below. For current information about degree shows throughout the country, see the website set up by the Candid Arts Trust (candidarts.com).

Byam Shaw School of Art
- 2 Elthorne Road, Archway, N19
- 020 7514 2350
- www.csm.arts.ac.uk

The degree show is normally held in June/July. For further information phone the above number.

Camberwell College of Arts
- Peckham Road, SE5
- Wilsons Road, SE5
- 020 7514 6301
- www.camberwell.arts.ac.uk

The degree and foundation shows are held during June, the MA shows in July at Peckham Road. Contact the above number for details.

Central Saint Martin's College of Art and Design
- Southampton Row, WC1B
- 107-109 Charing Cross Rd, WC2H
- 020 7514 7022
- www.csm.arts.ac.uk

Central Saint Martin's puts on both undergraduate and post graduate shows in June. The disciplines covered include fine art, scenography and theatre, textile and fashion design, ceramics and graphic design.

Chelsea College of Art & Design
- Chelsea College of Art & Design, 16 John Islip St, SW1P 4JU
- 020 7514 7751
- enquiries@chelsea.arts.ac.uk
- www.chelsea.arts.ac.uk

The foundation, MA and design shows usually take place between May and September with the popular MA Fine Art show being hosted in June/July, depending on term dates.

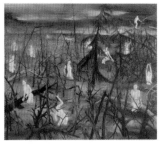

Chelsea College of Art & Design

Goldsmiths College

⌨ *New Cross, SE14*
☎ *020 7717 2210*
✉ *art@gold.ac.uk*
✎ *www.goldsmiths.ac.uk*

Fine art, creative curating and textiles are the things to see here. Undergraduate shows are held in June, postgraduate shows in July although the exact dates vary from year to year – contact the above number for more information.

Kingston University

⌨ *Faculty of Art, Design & Architecture, Knights Park, Kingston, KT1 2QJ*
☎ *020 8547 8867*
✎ *www.kingston.ac.uk/design*

The university's degree show includes the work of fashion designers, photographers, graphic artists, architecture and landscape design students, product designers, and students of fine art. Shows tend to take place in mid June. The faculty is also home to the Stanley Picker Gallery (see p. 231), an exhibition space that holds a rolling programme of lectures and exhibitions. The University also runs the Dorich House Museum (see p. 167) and the avant-garde Toilet Gallery (see p. 231).

London College of Fashion

⌨ *20 John Princes Street, W1G 0BJ*
☎ *020 7514 7400*
✎ *www.fashion.arts.ac.uk*

Most of the degree catwalk shows are in June and are by invitation only, but please enquire on the above number for related exhibitions of students' work. The College includes the Cordwainers College (182 Mare Street, E8) who also hold their shows in June and July.

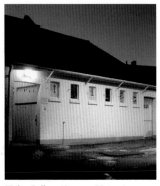

Toilet Gallery, Kingston University

London College of Communication

⌨ *Elephant & Castle, SE1 6SB*
☎ *020 7514 6500*
✎ *www.lcc.arts.ac.uk*

This college, formerly known as the London College of Printing, has degree and foundation shows from mid May to the end of July. The disciplines covered include Graphic Design, Typography, Photography, Photojournalism as well as film and video making.

London Metropolitan University

⌨ *133 Whitechapel High Street, E1*
☎ *020 7423 0000*
✎ *www.londonmet.ac.uk*

This university – the result of a merger between London Guildhall and North London – hosts its degree show in June. The disciplines include fine art, design, restoration and jewellery making.

Middlesex University

⌨ *Cat Hill Campus, Barnet, Herts, EN4*
☎ *020 8411 5000*
✎ *www.mdx.ac.uk*

Middlesex University's School of Art holds its degree show in June and displays work from many disciplines from printed textiles to jewellery design to fine art.

Royal College of Art
- Kensington Gore, SW7
- The Sculpture School, 15-25 Howie St, Battersea, SW11
- 020 7590 4498 (show hotline)
- www.rca.ac.uk

The Royal College hosts its degree shows on two sites between May and July. The disciplines covered include fine and applied arts, design, architecture and graphics, fashion & textiles which are all held at the Kensington Gore address, while sculpture is exhibited at the Howie Street site.

The Slade School of Art
- University College London, Gower Street, WC1E
- 020 7679 2313
- www.ucl.ac.uk/slade

The Slade School holds undergraduate and post graduate shows in May and June. The disciplines covered include fine art, sculpture, photography and fine art media (photography, film and video and print).

University of East London
- 4-6 University Way, E16
- (All Campuses) 020 8223 3000
- www.uel.ac.uk

The UEL holds its degree shows between June and July. Subjects include fine art, graphic design, textile design, fashion, digital arts and photography.

University of the Arts London
- www.arts.ac.uk

This new university launched in 2004 and is the only one dedicated to the arts in the UK and the biggest of its kind in Europe. Its collegiate structure brings together five London art and design institutions, namely Chelsea College of Art, Camberwell College of Art, London College of Communication, London College of Fashion and Central St Martin's (see separate listings for details).

Wimbledon College of Art
- Main Building, Merton Hall Rd, SW19 3QA
- 020 7514 9641
- www.wimbledon.ac.uk

This school holds its undergraduate degree show in June and its postgraduate show in July. Disciplines include sculpture, printmaking, fine art and theatre design. The foundation course show is held at the Palmerston Road site in June.

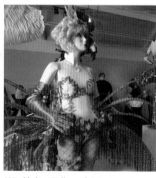

Wimbledon College of Art

London Art Fairs

January

The London Art Fair
Business Design Centre, Islington, N1
www.londonartfair.co.uk
This busy art fair celebrated its 20th anniversary in 2008 and brings together over 100 galleries, showcasing the brightest and best in modern British and international contemporary art.

Collect
www.craftscouncil.org.uk/collect
International art fair for museum-quality contemporary applied art – that's glass, jewellery, metalwork, textiles, woodwork and furniture to you and me. Formerly held at the V&A, but future venue(s) are yet to be confirmed at time of writing.

February

20/21 International Art Fair
Royal College of Art, Kensington Gore, SW7
www.20-21intartfair.com
Launched in 2007, this fair shows modern and contemporary art from around the world but with a strong UK content.

March/October

The Affordable Art Fair
Battersea Park, SW11
www.affordableartfair.com
Popular biannual art fair aimed at first time art buyers and showing contemporary art with pricetags from £30 to £3,000.

April

The London Original Print Fair
Royal Academy of Arts, Burlington Gardens, W1
www.londonprintfair.com
This well-established event at the RA brings together nearly 50 dealers, between them showing the gamut of graphic work from early printmakers to contemporary practitioners like Bridget Riley and David Hockney.

June

The Grosvenor House Art and Antiques Fair
Grosvenor House, Park Lane, W1
www.grosvenor-antiquesfair.co.uk
Every year 90 or so international art and antiques dealers set up shop at this posh Mayfair hotel for one of the most prestigious events in the art world calendar. With millions of pounds worth of tip-top stock, dating from the mists of time to the present day, this event is a must for connoisseurs with serious money to spend.

September

20/21 British Art Fair
Royal College of Art, Kensington Gore, SW7
www.britishartfair.co.uk
Celebrating its 20th anniversary in 2008, this fair is the only one exclusively devoted to British art from 1900 to the present. Fifty or so leading dealers wheel out the big names of this century and last, but this is also a place to spot overlooked and up and coming artists too.

September/October

The Goldsmiths Fair
Goldsmiths' Hall, junction of Foster Lane/Gresham Street, EC2
www.thegoldsmiths.co.uk
A magnet for magpies and jewellery lovers, this fair showcases a glittering selection of work by top jewellery designer-makers. It's a great opportunity to meet the makers themselves, find out more about their work and perhaps even purchase or commission a piece. The sumptuous surroundings of the historic Goldsmith's Hall are a bonus.

October

Origin
Somerset House, Strand, WC2
www.craftscouncil.org.uk/origin
This lively decorative and applied arts fair replaced the much-loved Chelsea Crafts Fair in 2006. Housed in a purpose built pavilion in the stately courtyard of Somerset House, the fair is a major selling event for top designer-makers from the UK and abroad and offers visitors the chance not only to see and buy beautiful work but to meet the creative talent behind it.

Frieze Art Fair
Regent's Park, NW1
www.friezeartfair.com
This international contemporary art fair has gone from strength to strength since its launch in 2003, attracting visitors and column inches in numbers. Organised by the publishers of frieze art magazine, it brings together around 150 hand-picked galleries from around the world and places them in the sylvan setting of Regent's Park. A dynamic programme of artists' projects, events and talks accompanies the event.

Zoo
Royal Academy of Arts, Burlington Gardens, W1
www.zooartfair.com
A non-profit fair bringing together a heady art-world cocktail of galleries, project spaces, artist collectives, curatorial groups and publications. Set up in 2004, the fair has grown in size and influence, becoming another venue for punters eager to spot the next big thing.

Art London
Royal Hospital, Chelsea, SW3
www.artlondon.net
An invigorating mix of work by established artists and young unknowns, shown in an outsized marquee in the grounds of the Royal Hospital.

January/April/October

The Decorative Art and Antiques Fair
Battersea Park, SW11
www.decorativefair.com
Thrice yearly art fair, held in a marquee in Battersea Park, and dedicated to 'antiques for interiors' and 20th century design.

General Index

index

Subject Index

index

index

index

Image Credits

p.4 The Great Court © British Museum, p.6 Shackleton's crows nest © All Hallows by the Tower Undercroft, p.9 Banqueting House © Historic Royal Palaces, p.15 Frieze from the Parthenon © British Museum, p.16 Benin Mask © British Museum, p.19 © British Optical Association Museum & Library, p.21 © Imperial War Museum, p.23 © Cartoon Museum, p.26 © Design Museum, p.29 Fashion and Textile Museum © Michael Cockerham, p.31 © Foundling Museum, p.33 © Benjamin Franklin House, p.34 © Library and Museum of Freemasonry, p.38 © Handel House Museum, p.43 Crystal Gallery in the Hunterian Museum © The Royal College of Surgeons of England, p.45 © Imperial War Museum, p.49 © Dr Johnson's House, p.55 © London Transport Museum, p.58 © Museum of London, p.63 © Old Operating Theatre Museum & Herb Garret, p.64 © Petrie Museum of Egyptian Archaeology, p.69 Shakespeare's Globe © Pawel Libera, p.73 © Sir John Soane's Museum, p.76 Tower of London © Historic Royal Palaces/Stephen Pond, p.79 Chinese ivory diagnostic doll © Wellcome Library, p.81 © Dean and Chapter of Westminster, p.85 Fenton House © NTPL/Nadia Mackenzie, p.86 © The Freud Museum, p.90 © Keats House, p.93 © Royal Air Force Museum, p.97 © NTPL/Dennis Gilbert, p.105 © Museum of Brands, p.109 © National History Museum, p.110 © National History Museum, p.113 © National History Museum, p.117 © Science Museum, p.118 © Science Museum, p.121 John Madejski Garden © Morley von Sternberg, p.122 Coronation Herald's boots © The Moscow Kremlin Museums, p.125 © Richard Waite, p.126 © William Morris Society, p.131 Eltham Palace © English Heritage Photo Library, p.136 © Horniman Museum & Gardens, p.139 © National Maritime Museum, p.142 Queen's House © National Maritime Museum, p.145 Royal Observatory Greenwich © National Maritime Museum, p.147 © Wimbledon Lawn Tennis Museum, p.149 © Dennis Severs House, p.151 Geffrye Museum © Chris Ridley, p.153 © Museum of London Docklands, p.156 © Museum of London Docklands, p.159 © Ragged School Museum, p.161 © V&A Museum of Childhood, p.162 © V&A Museum of Childhood, The Maze © Bethlem Art and History Collections, p.168 Down House © English Heritage Photo Library, p.170 © Audrey Walker/Embroiderers' Guild, p.172 Hampton Court Palace © Historic Royal Palaces, p.175 Kew Palace © Historic Royal Palaces, p.179 Museum No.1 © RBG Kew, p.180 © Museum of Croydon, p.183 Osterley Park © NTPL/Rupert Truman, p.184 Queen Charlotte's Cottage © Historic Royal Palaces, p.188 National Portrait Gallery © Colin Streater, p.190 © Andrew Kershman, p.193 Renoir © Samuel Courtauld Trust/The Courtauld Gallery, p.196 © Sheila Burnett, p.199 Vincent van Gogh © The National Gallery, p.202 © Colin Streater/National Portrait Gallery, p.209 © Frederick Lord Leighton/Collection Museo de Arte de Ponce, p.214 View from Tate © Alexander Hug, p.217 © Wallace Collection, p.219 © Katherine Green, p.222 Serpentine Gallery © 2008 Gehry Partners LLP, p.225 © Andy Keate, p.229 © Orleans House Gallery, p.230 Poppy Seed Head © RBG Kew/Brigid Edwards, p.232 © Tom Hammick/Eagle Gallery, p.240 © Denise De Cordova/Eagle Gallery, p.244 © Purdy Hicks, p.246 © Ben Long/Man&Eve, p.253 © Gideon Mendel, p.265 © Chelsea College of Art & Design, p.266 © Toilet Gallery, p.267 © Wimbledon College of Art, p.282 © Dulwich Picture Gallery

Order our other Metro Titles

The following titles are also available from Metro Publications. Please send your order along with a cheque made payable to Metro Publications Ltd to the address below. Postage and packaging is free, please allow 14 days for delivery.

Alternatively call our customer order line on 020 8533 7777 (Visa/Mastercard/Switch), Open Mon-Fri 9am-6pm

metropublications ltd
PO Box 6336, London, N1 6PY
www.metropublications.com / info@metropublications.com

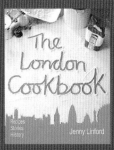

The London Cookbook
by Jenny Linford
£14.99

Tuck into an evocative taste of London! A celebration of the capital's food culture, 'The London Cookbook' is an appetising mixture of recipes, reminiscences, history and photography.

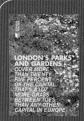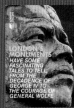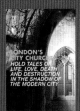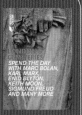

LONDON'S PARKS AND GARDENS COVER MORE THAN TWENTY FIVE PERCENT OF THE CAPITAL, THAT'S A LOT MORE GRASS BETWEEN TOES THAN ANY OTHER CAPITAL IN EUROPE

LONDON'S MONUMENTS HAVE SOME FASCINATING TALES TO TELL, FROM THE DECADENCE OF GEORGE IV TO THE COURAGE OF GENERAL WOLFE

LONDON'S CITY CHURCHES HOLD TALES OF LIFE, LOVE, DEATH AND DESTRUCTION IN THE SHADOW OF THE MODERN CITY

SPEND THE DAY WITH MARC BOLAN, KARL MARX, ENID BLYTON, KEITH MOON, SIGMUND FREUD AND MANY MORE

'Explore London' with our new range of pocket guides:

London's Parks and Gardens, Nana Ocran, £6.99
London's Monuments, Andrew Kershman, £7.99
London's City Churches, Stephen Millar, £6.99
London's Cemeteries, Darren Beach, £6.99

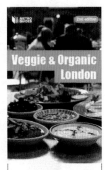

Veggie & Organic London
by Russell Rose
£7.99

London Architecture
by Marianne Butler
£8.99

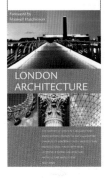

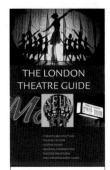

London Theatre Guide
by Richard Andrews
£8.99

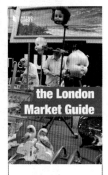

London Market Guide
by Andrew Kershman
£7.99

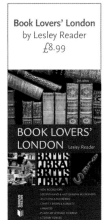

Book Lovers' London
by Lesley Reader
£8.99

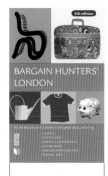

Bargain Hunters' London
by Andrew Kershman
£7.99

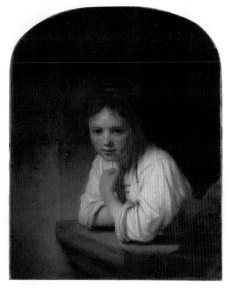

Dulwich Picture Gallery